PENGUIN BOOKS

WRITERS AT WORK

WRITERS AT WORK

The *Paris Review* Interviews

SELECTED BY KAY DICK

PENGUIN BOOKS

Penguin Books Ltd, Harmondsworth,
Middlesex, England
Penguin Books Australia Ltd, Ringwood,
Victoria, Australia

These interviews, first published in the *Paris Review*, were
published in Great Britain by Secker & Warburg, 1958, 1963, 1968
Published in Penguin Books 1972

Made and printed in Great Britain by
Richard Clay (The Chaucer Press) Ltd,
Bungay, Suffolk
Set in Linotype Georgian

CONTENTS

E. M. FORSTER

'That is not all "Arctic Summer" – there is almost half as much of it again – but that's all I want to read, because now it goes off, or at least I think so, and I do not want my voice to go out into the air while my heart is sinking. It will be more interesting to consider what the problems before me were, and why I was unlikely to solve them. I should like to do this, though it may involve us a little in fiction-technicalities . . .'

So said E. M. Forster, addressing an audience at the Aldeburgh Festival of 1951. He had been reading part of an unfinished novel called "Arctic Summer". At the end of the reading, he went on to explain why he had not finished the novel, which led him to mention what he called 'fiction-technicalities'.

Following up on Mr Forster's Aldeburgh remarks, we have tried to record his views on such matters as he gave them in an interview at King's College, Cambridge, on the evening of June 20th, 1952.

A spacious and high-ceilinged room, furnished in the Edwardian taste. One's attention is caught by a massive carved wooden mantelpiece of elaborate structure holding blue china in its niches. Large gilt-framed portrait-drawings on the walls (his Thornton ancestors and others), a 'Turner' by his great-uncle, and some modern pictures. Books of all sorts, handsome and otherwise, in English and French; armchairs decked in little shawls; a piano, a solitaire-board, and the box of a Zoe-trope; profusion of opened letters; slippers neatly arranged in a waste-paper basket.

In reading what follows the reader must imagine Mr Forster's manner, which though of extreme amenity is a firm one: precise, yet none the less elusive, administering a series of tiny surprises. He makes a perpetual slight displacement of the expected emphasis. His habit was to *answer our questions by brief statements, followed by decorative asides, often of great interest, but very difficult to reproduce.*

INTERVIEWERS: To begin with, may we ask you again, why did you never finish 'Arctic Summer'?

FORSTER: I have really answered this question in the foreword I wrote for the reading. The crucial passage was this:

'... whether these problems are solved or not, there remains a still graver one. What is going to happen? I had got my antithesis between the civilized man, who hopes for an Arctic Summer in which there is time to get things done, and the heroic man. But I had not settled what is going to happen, and that is why the novel remains a fragment. The novelist should, I think, always settle when he starts what is going to happen, what his major event is to be. He may alter this event as he approaches it, indeed he probably will, indeed he probably had better, or the novel becomes tied up and tight. But the sense of a solid mass ahead, a mountain round or over or through which [*he interposed*, 'in this case it would be *through*'] the story must somehow go, is most valuable and, for the novels I've tried to write, essential.'

INTERVIEWERS: How much is involved in this 'solid mass'? Does it mean that all the important steps in the plot must also be present in the original conception?

FORSTER: Certainly not all the steps. But there must be something, some major object towards which one is to approach. When I began *A Passage to India* I knew that something important happened in the Malabar Caves, and that it would have a central place in the novel – but I didn't know what it would be.

INTERVIEWERS: But if you didn't know what was going to happen to the characters in either instance, why was the case of *A Passage to India* so different from that of 'Arctic Summer'? ... In both cases you had your antithesis.

FORSTER: The atmosphere of 'Arctic Summer' did not approach the density of what I had in *A Passage to India*.

Let me see how to explain. The Malabar Caves represented an area in which concentration can take place. A cavity. (*We noticed that he always spoke of the caves quite literally – as for instance when he interrupted himself earlier to say that the characters had to pass* 'through' *them*.) They were something to focus everything up: they were to engender an event like an egg. What I had in 'Arctic Summer' was thinner, a background and colour only.

INTERVIEWERS: You spoke of antitheses in your novels. Do you regard these as essential to any novel you might write?

FORSTER: Let me think. ... There was one in *Howards End*. Perhaps a rather subtler one in *The Longest Journey*.

INTERVIEWERS: Would you agree that all your novels not only deal with some dilemma but are intended to be both true and useful in regard to it – so that if you felt a certain dilemma was too extreme, its incompatibles too impossible to reconcile, you wouldn't write about it?

FORSTER: True and lovable would be my antithesis. I don't think useful comes into it. I'm not sure that I would be put off simply because a dilemma that I wanted to treat was insoluble; at least, I don't think I should be.

INTERVIEWERS: While we are on the subject of planning novels, has a novel ever taken an unexpected direction?

FORSTER: Of course, that wonderful thing, a character running away with you – which happens to everyone – that's happened to me, I'm afraid.

INTERVIEWERS: Can you describe any technical problem that especially bothered you in one of the published novels?

FORSTER: I had trouble with the junction of Rickie and Stephen. [The hero of *The Longest Journey* and his half-brother.] How to make them intimate, I mean. I fumbled about a good deal. It is all right once they are together. ... I didn't know how to get Helen to Howards End. That part is all contrived. There are too many letters. And again, it is all right once she is there. But ends always give me trouble.

INTERVIEWERS: Why is that?

FORSTER: It is partly what I was talking about a moment

ago. Characters run away with you, and so won't fit on to what is coming.

INTERVIEWERS: Another question of detail. What was the exact function of the long description of the Hindu festival in *A Passage to India*?

FORSTER: It was architecturally necessary. I needed a lump, or a Hindu temple if you like – a mountain standing up. It is well placed; and it gathers up some strings. But there ought to be more after it. The lump sticks out a little too much.

INTERVIEWERS: To leave technical questions for a moment, have you ever described any type of situation of which you have had no personal knowledge?

FORSTER: The home-life of Leonard and Jacky in *Howards End* is one case. I knew nothing about that. I believe I brought it off.

INTERVIEWERS: How far removed in time do you have to be from an experience to describe it?

FORSTER: Place is more important than time in this matter. Let me tell you a little more about *A Passage to India*. I had a great deal of difficulty with the novel, and thought I would never finish it. I began it in 1912, and then came the war. I took it with me when I returned to India in 1921, but found what I had written wasn't India at all. It was like sticking a photograph on a picture. However, I couldn't *write* it when I was in India. When I got away, I could get on with it.

INTERVIEWER: Some critics have objected to your way of handling incidents of violence. Do you agree with their objections?

FORSTER: I think I solved the problem satisfactorily in *Where Angels Fear to Tread*. In other cases, I don't know. The scene in the Malabar Caves is a good substitute for violence. Which were the incidents you didn't like?

INTERVIEWERS: I have always been worried by the suddenness of Gerald's death in *The Longest Journey*.* Why did you treat it in that way?

* The famous fifth chapter in *The Longest Journey* begins 'Gerald died that afternoon'.

FORSTER: It had to be passed by. But perhaps it was passed by in the wrong way.

INTERVIEWERS: I have also never felt comfortable about Leonard Bast's seduction of Helen in *Howards End*. It is such a sudden affair. It seems as though we are not told enough about it for it to be convincing. One might say that it came off allegorically but not realistically.

FORSTER: I think you might be right. I did it like that out of a wish to have surprises. It has to be a surprise for Margaret, and this was best done by making it a surprise for the reader too. Too much may have been sacrificed to this.

INTERVIEWERS: A more general question. Would you admit to there being any symbolism in your novels? Lionel Trilling rather seems to imply that there is, in his books on you – symbolism, that is, as distinct from allegory or parable. 'Mrs Moore,' he says, 'will act with a bad temper to Adela, but her actions will somehow have a good echo; and her children will be her further echo. . . .'

FORSTER: No, I didn't think of that. But mightn't there be some of it elsewhere? Can you try me with some more examples?

INTERVIEWERS: The tree at Howards End? [A wych-elm, frequently referred to in the novel.]

FORSTER: Yes, that was symbolical; it was the genius of the house.

INTERVIEWERS: What was the significance of Mrs Wilcox's influence on the other characters after her death?

FORSTER: I was interested in the imaginative effect of someone alive, but in a different way from other characters – living in other lives.

INTERVIEWERS: Were you influenced by Samuel Butler in this? I mean by his theories of vicarious immortality?

FORSTER: No. (*Pause.*) I think I have a more poetical mind than Butler's.

INTERVIEWERS: Now can we ask you a few questions about the immediate business of writing? Do you keep a notebook?

FORSTER: No, I should feel it improper.

INTERVIEWERS: But you would refer to diaries and letters?

FORSTER: Yes, that's different.

INTERVIEWERS: When you go, say, to the circus, would you ever feel, 'how nice it would be to put that in a novel'?

FORSTER: No, I should feel it improper. I never say 'that might be useful'. I don't think it is right for an author to do so. (*He spoke firmly.*) However I have been inspired on the spot. 'The Story of a Panic' is the simplest example; 'The Road from Colonus' is another. Sense of a place also inspired me to write a short story called 'The Rock', but the inspiration was poor in quality, and the editors wouldn't take the story. But I have talked about this in the introduction to my short stories.

INTERVIEWERS: Do you pre-figure a shape to your novels?

FORSTER: No, I am too unvisual to do so. (*We found this surprising in view of his explanation of the Hindu festival scene above.*)

INTERVIEWERS: Does this come out in any other way?

FORSTER: I find it difficult to recognize people when I meet them, though I remember about them. I remember their voices.

INTERVIEWERS: Do you have any Wagnerian leitmotiv system to help you keep so many themes going at the same time?

FORSTER: Yes, in a way, and I'm certainly interested in music and musical methods. Though I shouldn't call it a system.

INTERVIEWERS: Do you write every day, or only under inspiration?

FORSTER: The latter. But the act of writing inspires me. It is a nice feeling ... (*indulgently*). Of course, I had a very literary childhood. I was the author of a number of works between the ages of six and ten. There were 'Ear-rings through the Keyhole' and 'Scuffles in a Wardrobe'.

INTERVIEWERS: Which of your novels came first to your mind?

FORSTER: Half of *A Room with a View*. I got that far, and then there must have been a hitch.

INTERVIEWERS: Did you ever attempt a novel of an entirely different sort from the ones you have published?

FORSTER: For some time I had the idea of an historical novel. The setting was to have been a Renaissance one. Reading *Thaïs* (by Anatole France) finally decided me to try it. But nothing came of it in the end.

INTERVIEWERS: How do you name your characters?

FORSTER: I usually find the name at the start, but not always. Rickie's brother had several names (*He showed us some early manuscript portions of* The Longest Journey *in which Stephen Wonham appeared as Siegfried; also an omitted chapter, which he described as 'extremely romantic'.*) Wonham is a country name and so is Quested. (*We looked at an early draft of* A Passage to India *in which to his surprise the heroine was found going under the name of Edith. This was later changed to Janet, before becoming Adela.*) Herriton I made up. Munt was the name of my first governess in the house in Hertfordshire. There really was a family called Howard who once owned the real Howards End. *Where Angels Fear to Tread* should have been called 'Monteriano', but the publisher thought this wouldn't sell. It was Dent [Professor E. J. Dent] who gave me the present title.

INTERVIEWERS: How much do you admit to modelling your characters on real people?

FORSTER: We all like to pretend we don't use real people, but one does actually. I used some of my family. Miss Bartlett was my Aunt Emily – they all read the book but they none of them saw it. Uncle Willie turned into Mrs Failing. He was a bluff and simple character (*correcting himself*) – bluff without being simple. Miss Lavish was actually a Miss Spender. Mrs Honeychurch was my grandmother. The three Miss Dickinsons condensed into two Miss Schlegels. Philip Herriton I modelled on Professor Dent. He knew this, and took an interest in his own progress. I have used several tourists.

INTERVIEWERS: Do all your characters have real life models?

FORSTER: In no book have I got down more than the people I like, the person I think I am, and the people who irritate me. This puts me among the large body of authors who are not really novelists, and have to get on as best they can with these three categories. We have not the power of observing the variety of life and describing it dispassionately. There are a few who have done this. Tolstoi was one, wasn't he?

INTERVIEWERS: Can you say anything about the process of turning a real person into a fictional one?

FORSTER: A useful trick is to look back upon such a person with half-closed eyes, fully describing certain characteristics. I am left with about two-thirds of a human being and can get to work. A likeness isn't aimed at and couldn't be obtained, because a man's only himself amidst the particular circumstances of his life and not amid other circumstances. So that to refer back to Dent when Philip was in difficulties with Gino, or to ask one and one-half Miss Dickinsons how Helen should comport herself with an illegitimate baby would have ruined the atmosphere and the book. When all goes well, the original material soon disappears, and a character who belongs to the book and nowhere else emerges.

INTERVIEWERS: Do any of your characters represent yourself at all?

FORSTER: Rickie more than any. Also Philip. And Cecil [in *A Room with a View*] has got something of Philip in him.

INTERVIEWERS: What degree of reality do your characters have for you after you have finished writing about them?

FORSTER: Very variable. There are some I like thinking about. Rickie and Stephen, and Margaret Schlegel – they are characters whose fortunes I have been interested to follow. It doesn't matter if they died in the novel or not.

INTERVIEWERS: We have got a few more questions

about your work as a whole. First, to what degree is each novel an entirely fresh experiment?

FORSTER: To quite a large extent. But I wonder if experiment is the word?

INTERVIEWERS: Is there a hidden pattern behind the whole of an author's work, what Henry James called 'a figure in the carpet'? (*He looked dubious.*) Well, do you like having secrets from the reader?

FORSTER (*brightening*): Ah now, that's a different question.... I was pleased when Peter Burra* noticed that the wasp upon which Godbole meditates during the festival in *A Passage to India* had already appeared earlier in the novel.

INTERVIEWERS: Had the wasps any esoteric meaning?

FORSTER: Only in the sense that there is something esoteric in India about all animals. I was just putting it in; and afterwards I saw it was something that might return non-logically in the story later.

INTERVIEWERS: How far aware are you of your own technical cleverness in general?

FORSTER: We keep coming back to that. People will not realize how little conscious one is of these things; how one flounders about. They want us to be so much better informed than we are. If critics could only have a course on writers' *not* thinking things out – a course of lectures ... (*He smiled*).

INTERVIEWERS: You have said elsewhere that the authors you have learned most from were Jane Austen and Proust. What did you learn from Jane Austen technically?

FORSTER: I learned the possibilities of domestic humour. I was more ambitious than she was, of course; I tried to hitch it on to other things.

INTERVIEWERS: And from Proust?

FORSTER: I learned ways of looking at character from him. The modern sub-conscious way. He gave me as much of the modern way as I could take. I couldn't reach Freud or Jung myself; it had to be filtered to me.

* Burra was the author of the preface to the 'Everyman' Edition of *A Passage to India*.

INTERVIEWERS: Did any other novelists influence you technically? What about Meredith?

FORSTER: I admired him – *The Egoist* and the better constructed bits of the other novels; but then that's not the same as his influencing me. I don't know if he did that. He did things I couldn't do. What I admired was the sense of one thing opening into another. You go into a room with him, and then that opens into another room, and that into a further one.

INTERVIEWERS: What led you to make the remark quoted by Lionel Trilling, that the older you got the less it seemed to you to matter that an artist should 'develop'?

FORSTER: I am more interested in achievement than in advance on it and decline from it. And I am more interested in works than in authors. The paternal wish of critics to show how a writer dropped off or picked up as he went along seems to me misplaced. I am only interested in myself as a producer. What was it Mahler said? – 'anyone will sufficiently understand me who will trace my development through my nine symphonies'. This seems odd to me; I couldn't imagine myself making such a remark; it seems too uncasual. Other authors find themselves much more an object of study. I am conceited, but not interested in myself in this particular way. Of course I like reading my own work, and often do it. I go gently over the bits that I think are bad.

INTERVIEWERS: But you think highly of your own work?

FORSTER: That was implicit, yes. My regret is that I haven't written a bit more – that the body, the corpus, isn't bigger. I think I am different from other writers; they profess much more worry (I don't know if it is genuine). I have always found writing pleasant, and don't understand what people mean by 'throes of creation'. I've enjoyed it, but believe that in some ways it is good. Whether it will last, I have no idea.

P. N. Furbank
F. J. H. Haskell

WILLIAM FAULKNER

This conversation took place in New York City early in 1956.

INTERVIEWER: Mr Faulkner, you were saying a while ago that you don't like interviews.

FAULKNER: The reason I don't like interviews is that I seem to react violently to personal questions. If the questions are about the work, I try to answer them. When they are about me, I may answer or I may not, but even if I do, if the same question is asked tomorrow, the answer may be different.

INTERVIEWER: How about yourself as a writer?

FAULKNER: If I had not existed, someone else would have written me, Hemingway, Doestoevski, all of us. Proof of that is that there are about three candidates for the authorship of Shakespeare's plays. But what is important is *Hamlet* and *Midsummer Night's Dream*, not who wrote them, but that somebody did. The artist is of no importance. Only what he creates is important, since there is nothing new to be said. Shakespeare, Balzac, Homer have all written about the same things, and if they had lived one thousand or two thousand years longer, the publishers wouldn't have needed anyone since.

INTERVIEWER: But even if there seems nothing more to be said, isn't perhaps the individuality of the writer important?

FAULKNER: Very important to himself. Everybody else should be too busy with the work to care about the individuality.

INTERVIEWER: And your contemporaries?

FAULKNER: All of us failed to match our dream of perfection. So I rate us on the basis of our splendid failure to do the impossible. In my opinion, if I could write all my work again, I am convinced that I would do it better, which is the healthiest condition for an artist. That's why he keeps on working, trying again; he believes each time that this time he will do it, bring it off. Of course he won't, which is why this condition is healthy. Once he did it, once he matched the work to the image, the dream, nothing would remain but to cut his throat, jump off the other side of that pinnacle of perfection into suicide. I'm a failed poet. Maybe every novelist wants to write poetry first, finds he can't, and then tries the short story, which is the most demanding form after poetry. And, failing at that, only then does he take up novel writing.

INTERVIEWER: Is there any possible formula to follow in order to be a good novelist?

FAULKNER: Ninety-nine per cent talent ... 99 per cent discipline ... 99 per cent work. He must never be satisfied with what he does. It never is as good as it can be done. Always dream and shoot higher than you know you can do. Don't bother just to be better than your contemporaries or predecessors. Try to be better than yourself. An artist is a creature driven by demons. He don't know why they choose him and he's usually too busy to wonder why. He is completely amoral in that he will rob, borrow, beg, or steal from anybody and everybody to get the work done.

INTERVIEWER: Do you mean the writer should be completely ruthless?

FAULKNER: The writer's only responsibility is to his art. He will be completely ruthless if he is a good one. He has a dream. It anguishes him so much he must get rid of it. He has no peace until then. Everything goes by the board: honour, pride, decency, security, happiness, all, to get the book written. If a writer has to rob his mother, he will not hesitate; the 'Ode on a Grecian Urn' is worth any number of old ladies.

INTERVIEWER: Then could the *lack* of security, happiness, honour, be an important factor in the artist's creativity?

FAULKNER: No. They are important only to his peace and contentment, and art has no concern with peace and contentment.

INTERVIEWER: Then what would be the best environment for a writer?

FAULKNER: Art is not concerned with environment either; it doesn't care where it is. If you mean me, the best job that was ever offered to me was to become a landlord in a brothel. In my opinion it's the perfect milieu for an artist to work in. It gives him perfect economic freedom; he's free of fear and hunger; he has a roof over his head and nothing whatever to do except keep a few simple accounts and to go once every month and pay off the local police. The place is quiet during the morning hours, which is the best time of the day to work. There's enough social life in the evening, if he wishes to participate, to keep him from being bored; it gives him a certain standing in his society; he has nothing to do because the madam keeps the books; all the inmates of the house are females and would defer to him and call him 'sir'. All the bootleggers in the neighbourhood would call him 'sir'. And he could call the police by their first names.

So the only environment the artist needs is whatever peace, whatever solitude, and whatever pleasure he can get at not too high a cost. All the wrong environment will do is run his blood-pressure up; he will spend more time being frustrated or outraged. My own experience has been that the tools I need for my trade are paper, tobacco, food, and a little whisky.

INTERVIEWER: Bourbon, you mean?

FAULKNER: No, I ain't that particular. Between scotch and nothing, I'll take scotch.

INTERVIEWER: You mentioned economic freedom. Does the writer need it?

FAULKNER: No. The writer doesn't need economic freedom. All he needs is a pencil and some paper. I've never known anything good in writing to come from having accepted any free gift of money. The good writer never applies to a foundation. He's too busy writing something. If he isn't first rate he fools himself by saying he hasn't got time or economic freedom. Good art can come out of thieves, bootleggers, or horse swipes. People really are afraid to find out just how much hardship and poverty they can stand. They are afraid to find out how tough they are. Nothing can destroy the good writer. The only thing that can alter the good writer is death. Good ones don't have time to bother with success or getting rich. Success is feminine and like a woman; if you cringe before her, she will override you. So the way to treat her is to show her the back of your hand. Then maybe she will do the crawling.

INTERVIEWER: Can working for the movies hurt your own writing?

FAULKNER: Nothing can injure a man's writing if he's a first-rate writer. If a man is not a first-rate writer, there's not anything can help it much. The problem does not apply if he is not first rate, because he has already sold his soul for a swimming-pool.

INTERVIEWER: Does a writer compromise in writing for the movies?

FAULKNER: Always, because a moving picture is by its nature a collaboration, and any collaboration is compromise because that is what the word means – to give and to take.

INTERVIEWER: Which actors do you like to work with most?

FAULKNER: Humphrey Bogart is the one I've worked with best. He and I worked together in *To Have and Have Not* and *The Big Sleep*.

INTERVIEWER: Would you like to make another movie?

FAULKNER: Yes, I would like to make one of George Orwell's *1984*. I have an idea for an ending which would prove the thesis I'm always hammering at: that man is indestructible because of his simple will to freedom.

INTERVIEWER: How do you get the best results working for the movies?

FAULKNER: The moving-picture work of my own which seemed best to me was done by the actors and the writer throwing the script away and inventing the scene in actual rehearsal just before the camera turned. If I didn't take, or feel I was capable of taking, motion-picture work seriously, out of simple honesty to motion pictures and myself too, I would not have tried. But I know now that I will never be a good motion-picture writer; so that work will never have the urgency for me which my own medium has.

INTERVIEWER: Would you comment on that legendary Hollywood experience you were involved in?

FAULKNER: I had just completed a contract at MGM and was about to return home. The director I had worked with said, 'If you would like another job here, just let me know and I will speak to the studio about a new contract.' I thanked him and came home. About six months later I wired my director friend that I would like another job. Shortly after that I received a letter from my Hollywood agent enclosing my first week's paycheque. I was surprised because I had expected first to get an official notice or recall and a contract from the studio. I thought to myself the contract is delayed and will arrive in the next mail. Instead, a week later I got another letter from the agent, enclosing my second week's paycheque. That began in November 1932 and continued until May 1933. Then I received a telegram from the studio. It said: *William Faulkner, Oxford, Miss. Where are you? MGM Studio.*

I wrote out a telegram: *MGM Studio, Culver City, California, William Faulkner.*

The young lady operator said, 'Where is the message, Mr Faulkner?' I said, 'That's it.' She said, 'The rule book says that I can't send it without a message, you have to say something.' So we went through her samples and selected – I forget which one – one of the canned anniversary greeting messages. I sent that. Next was a long-distance telephone call from the studio directing me to get on the first aeroplane, go to New Orleans, and report to Director Browning. I could have got on a train in Oxford and been in New Orleans eight hours later. But I obeyed the studio and went to Memphis, where an aeroplane did occasionally go to New Orleans. Three days later one did.

I arrived at Mr Browning's hotel about six p.m. and reported to him. A party was going on. He told me to get a good night's sleep and be ready for an early start in the morning. I asked him about the story. He said, 'Oh, yes.

Go to room so and so. That's the continuity writer. He'll tell you what the story is.'

I went to the room as directed. The continuity writer was sitting in there alone. I told him who I was and asked him about the story. He said, 'When you have written the dialogue I'll let you see the story.' I went back to Browning's room and told him what had happened. 'Go back,' he said, 'and tell that so and so – Never mind, you get a good night's sleep so we can get an early start in the morning.'

So the next morning in a very smart rented launch all of us except the continuity writer sailed down to Grand Isle, about a hundred miles away, where the picture was to be shot, reaching there just in time to eat lunch and have time to run the hundred miles back to New Orleans before dark.

That went on for three weeks. Now and then I would worry a little about the story, but Browning always said, 'Stop worrying. Get a good night's sleep so we can get an early start tomorrow morning.'

One evening on our return I had barely entered my room when the telephone rang. It was Browning. He told me to come to his room at once. I did so. He had a telegram. It said: *Faulkner is fired. MGM Studio.* 'Don't worry,' Browning said. 'I'll call that so and so up this minute and not only make him put you back on the payroll but send you a written apology.' There was a knock on the door. It was a page with another telegram. This one said: *Browning is fired. MGM Studio.* So I came back home. I presume Browning went somewhere too. I imagine that continuity writer is still sitting in a room somewhere with his weekly salary cheque clutched tightly in his hand. They never did finish the film. But they did build a shrimp village – a long platform on piles in the water with sheds built on it something like a wharf. The studio could have bought dozens of them for forty or fifty dollars apiece. Instead, they built one of their own, a false one. That is, a platform with a single wall on it, so that when you opened the door and stepped through it, you stepped right on off to the ocean itself. As they built it, on the first day, the

Cajun fisherman paddled up in his narrow tricky pirogue made out of a hollow log. He would sit in it all day long in the broiling sun watching the strange white folk building this strange imitation platform. The next day he was back in the pirogue with his whole family, his wife nursing the baby, the other children, and the mother-in-law, all to sit all that day in the broiling sun to watch this foolish and incomprehensible activity. I was in New Orleans two or three years later and heard that the Cajun people were still coming in for miles to look at that imitation shrimp platform which a lot of white people had rushed in and built and then abandoned.

INTERVIEWER: You say that the writer must compromise in working for the motion pictures. How about his writing? Is he under any obligation to his reader?

FAULKNER: His obligation is to get the work done the best he can do it; whatever obligation he has left over after that he can spend any way he likes. I myself am too busy to care about the public. I have no time to wonder who is reading me. I don't care about John Doe's opinion on my or anyone else's work. Mine is the standard which has to be met, which is when the work makes me feel the way I do when I read *La Tentation de Saint Antoine*, or the Old Testament. They make me feel good. So does watching a bird make me feel good. You know that if I were reincarnated, I'd want to come back a buzzard. Nothing hates him or envies him or wants him or needs him. He is never bothered or in danger and he can eat anything.

INTERVIEWER: What technique do you use to arrive at your standard?

FAULKNER: Let the writer take up surgery or bricklaying if he is interested in technique. There is no mechanical way to get the writing done, no short cut. The young writer would be a fool to follow a theory. Teach yourself by your own mistakes; people learn only by error. The good artist believes that nobody is good enough to give him advice. He has supreme vanity. No matter how much he admires the old writer, he wants to beat him.

INTERVIEWER: Then would you deny the validity of technique?

FAULKNER: By no means. Sometimes technique charges in and takes command of the dream before the writer himself can get his hands on it. That is *tour de force* and the finished work is simply a matter of fitting bricks neatly together, since the writer knows probably every single word right to the end before he puts the first one down. This happened with *As I lay Dying*. It was not easy. No honest work is. It was simple in that all the material was already at hand. It took me just about six weeks in the spare time from a twelve-hour-a-day job at manual labour. I simply imagined a group of people and subjected them to the simple universal natural catastrophes, which are flood and fire, with a simple natural motive to give direction to their progress. But then, when technique does not intervene, in another sense writing is easier too. Because with me there is always a point in the book where the characters themselves rise up and take charge and finish the job – say somewhere about page 275. Of course I don't know what would happen if I finished the book on page 274. The quality an artist must have is objectivity in judging his work, plus the honesty and courage not to kid himself about it. Since none of my work has met my own standards, I must judge it on the basis of that one which caused me the most grief and anguish, as the mother loves the child who became the thief or murderer more than the one who became the priest.

INTERVIEWER: What work is that?

FAULKNER: *The Sound and the Fury.* I wrote it five separate times, trying to tell the story, to rid myself of the dream which would continue to anguish me until I did. It's a tragedy of two lost women: Caddy and her daughter. Dilsey is one of my own favourite characters, because she is brave, courageous, generous, gentle, and honest. She's much more brave and honest and generous than me.

INTERVIEWER: How did *The Sound and the Fury* begin?

FAULKNER: It began with a mental picture. I didn't

realize at the time it was symbolical. The picture was of the muddy seat of a little girl's drawers in a pear-tree, where she could see through a window where her grandmother's funeral was taking place and report what was happening to her brothers on the ground below. By the time I explained who they were and what they were doing and how her pants got muddy, I realized it would be impossible to get all of it into a short story and that it would have to be a book. And then I realized the symbolism of the soiled pants, and that image was replaced by the one of the fatherless and motherless girl climbing down the rainpipe to escape from the only home she had, where she had never been offered love or affection or understanding.

I had already begun to tell the story through the eyes of the idiot child, since I felt that it would be more effective as told by someone capable only of knowing what happened, but not why. I saw that I had not told the story that time. I tried to tell it again, the same story through the eyes of another brother. That was still not it. I told it for the third time through the eyes of the third brother. That was still not it. I tried to gather the pieces together and fill in the gaps by making myself the spokesman. It was still not complete, not until fifteen years after the book was published, when I wrote as an appendix to another book the final effort to get the story told and off my mind, so that I myself could have some peace from it. It's the book I feel tenderest towards. I couldn't leave it alone, and I never could tell it right, though I tried hard and would like to try again, though I'd probably fail again.

INTERVIEWER: What emotion does Benjy arouse in you?

FAULKNER: The only emotion I can have for Benjy is grief and pity for all mankind. You can't feel anything for Benjy because he doesn't feel anything. The only thing I can feel about him personally is concern as to whether he is believable as I created him. He was a prologue, like the gravedigger in the Elizabethan dramas. He serves his purpose and is gone. Benjy is incapable of good and evil because he had no knowledge of good and evil.

INTERVIEWER: Could Benjy feel love?

FAULKNER: Benjy wasn't rational enough even to be selfish. He was an animal. He recognized tenderness and love though he could not have named them, and it was the threat to tenderness and love that caused him to bellow when he felt the change in Caddy. He no longer had Caddy; being an idiot he was not even aware that Caddy was missing. He knew only that something was wrong, which left a vacuum in which he grieved. He tried to fill that vacuum. The only thing he had was one of Caddy's discarded slippers. The slipper was his tenderness and love which he could not have named, but he knew only that it was missing. He was dirty because he couldn't co-ordinate and because dirt meant nothing to him. He could no more distinguish between dirt and cleanliness than between good and evil. The slipper gave him comfort even though he no longer remembered the person to whom it had once belonged, any more than he could remember why he grieved. If Caddy had reappeared he probably would not have known her.

INTERVIEWER: Does the narcissus given to Benjy have some significance?

FAULKNER: The narcissus was given to Benjy to distract his attention. It was simply a flower which happened to be handy that fifth of April. It was not deliberate.

INTERVIEWER: Are there any artistic advantages in casting the novel in the form of an allegory, as the Christian allegory you used in *A Fable*?

FAULKNER: Same advantage the carpenter finds in building square corners in order to build a square house. In *A Fable* the Christian allegory was the right allegory to use in that particular story, like an oblong square corner is the right corner with which to build an oblong rectangular house.

INTERVIEWER: Does that mean an artist can use Christianity simply as just another tool, as a carpenter would borrow a hammer?

FAULKNER: The carpenter we are speaking of never lacks that hammer. No one is without Christianity, if we agree on what we mean by the word. It is every individual's individual code of behaviour by means of which he makes himself a better human being than his nature wants to be, if he followed his nature only. Whatever its symbol – cross or crescent or whatever – that symbol is man's reminder of his duty inside the human race. Its various allegories are the charts against which he measures himself and learns to know what he is. It cannot teach man to be good as the textbook teaches him mathematics. It shows him how to discover himself, evolve for himself a moral code and standard within his capacities and aspirations, by giving him a matchless example of suffering and sacrifice and the promise of hope. Writers have always drawn, and always will draw, upon the allegories of moral consciousness, for the reason that the allegories are matchless – the three men in *Moby Dick*, who represent the trinity of conscience: knowing nothing, knowing but not caring, knowing and caring. The same trinity is represented in *A Fable* by the young Jewish pilot officer, who said, 'This is terrible. I refuse to accept it, even if I must refuse life to do so'; the old French Quartermaster General, who said, 'This is terrible, but we can weep and bear it'; and the English battalion runner, who said, 'This is terrible, I'm going to do something about it.'

INTERVIEWER: Are the two unrelated themes in *The Wild Palms* brought together in one book for any symbolic purpose? Is it as certain critics intimate a kind of aesthetic counterpoint, or is it merely haphazard?

FAULKNER: No, no. That was one story – the story of Charlotte Rittenmeyer and Harry Wilbourne, who sacrificed everything for love, and then lost that. I did not know it would be two separate stories until after I had started the book. When I reached the end of what is now the first section of *The Wild Palms*, I realized suddenly that something was missing, it needed emphasis, something to lift it like counterpoint in music. So I wrote on the 'Old Man' story until 'The Wild Palms' story rose back to pitch. Then I stopped the 'Old Man' story at what is now its first section, and took up 'The Wild Palms' story until it began again to sag. Then I raised it to pitch again with another section of its antithesis, which is the story of a man who got his love and spent the rest of the book fleeing from it, even to the extent of voluntarily going back to jail where he would be safe. They are only two stories by chance, perhaps necessity. The story is that of Charlotte and Wilbourne.

INTERVIEWER: How much of your writing is based on personal experience?

FAULKNER: I can't say. I never counted up. Because 'how much' is not important. A writer needs three things, experience, observation, and imagination, any two of which, at times any one of which, can supply the lack of the others. With me a story usually begins with a single idea or memory or mental picture. The writing of the story is simply a matter of working up to that moment, to explain why it happened or what it caused to follow. A writer is trying to create believable people in credible moving situations in the most moving way he can. Obviously he must use as one of his tools the environment which he knows. I would say that music is the easiest means in which to express, since it came first in man's experience and history. But since words are my talent, I must try to express clumsily in words what the pure music would have done better. That is, music would express better and simpler, but I prefer to use words, as I prefer to read rather than listen. I prefer silence to sound, and the image produced by words occurs in silence. That is, the thunder and the music of the prose take place in silence.

INTERVIEWER: Some people say they can't understand your writing, even after they read it two or three times. What approach would you suggest for them?

FAULKNER: Read it four times.

INTERVIEWER: You mentioned experience, observation, and imagination as being important for the writer. Would you include inspiration?

FAULKNER: I don't know anything about inspiration, because I don't know what inspiration is – I've heard about it, but I never saw it.

INTERVIEWER: As a writer you are said to be obsessed with violence.

FAULKNER: That's like saying the carpenter is obsessed with his hammer. Violence is simply one of the carpenter's tools. The writer can no more build with one tool than the carpenter can.

INTERVIEWER: Can you say how you started as a writer?

FAULKNER: I was living in New Orleans, doing whatever kind of work was necessary to earn a little money now and then. I met Sherwood Anderson. We would walk about the city in the afternoon and talk to people. In the evenings we would meet again and sit over a bottle or two while he talked and I listened. In the forenoon I would never see him. He was secluded, working. The next day we would repeat. I decided that if that was the life of a writer, then becoming a writer was the thing for me. So I began to write my first book. At once I found that writing was fun. I even forgot that I hadn't seen Mr Anderson for three weeks until he walked in my door, the first time he ever came to see me, and said, 'What's wrong? Are you mad at me?' I told him I was writing a book. He said, 'My God,' and walked out. When I finished the book – it was *Soldier's Pay* – I met Mrs Anderson on the street. She asked how the book was going, and I said I'd finished it. She said, 'Sherwood says that he will make a trade with you. If he doesn't have to read your manuscript he will tell his publisher to accept it.' I said, 'Done', and that's how I became a writer.

INTERVIEWER: What were the kinds of work you were doing to earn that 'little money now and then'?

FAULKNER: Whatever came up. I could do a little of almost anything – run boats, paint houses, fly airplanes. I never needed much money because living was cheap in New Orleans then, and all I wanted was a place to sleep, a little food, tobacco, and whisky. There were many things I could do for two or three days and earn enough money to live on for the rest of the month. By temperament I'm a vagabond and a tramp. I don't want money badly enough to work for it. In my opinion it's a shame that there is so much work in the world. One of the saddest things is that the only thing a man can do for eight hours a day, day after day, is work. You can't eat eight hours a day nor

drink for eight hours a day nor make love for eight hours –
all you can do for eight hours is work. Which is the reason
why man makes himself and everybody else so miserable
and unhappy.

INTERVIEWER: You must feel indebted to Sherwood
Anderson, but how do you regard him as a writer?

FAULKNER: He was the father of my generation of
American writers and the tradition of American writing
which our successors will carry on. He has never received
his proper evaluation. Dreiser is his older brother and
Mark Twain the father of them both.

INTERVIEWER: What about the European writers of
that period?

FAULKNER: The two great men in my time were Mann
and Joyce. You should approach Joyce's *Ulysses* as the il-
literate Baptist preacher approaches the Old Testament:
with faith.

INTERVIEWER: How did you get your background in
the Bible?

FAULKNER: My Great-Grandfather Murry was a kind
and gentle man, to us children anyway. That is, although he
was a Scot, he was (to us) neither especially pious nor stern
either: he was simply a man of inflexible principles. One
of them was, everybody, children on up through all adults
present, had to have a verse from the Bible ready and glib
at tongue-tip when we gathered at the table for breakfast
each morning; if you didn't have your scripture verse
ready, you didn't have any breakfast; you would be excused
long enough to leave the room and swot one up (there was
a maiden aunt, a kind of sergeant-major for this duty, who
retired with the culprit and gave him a brisk breezing
which carried him over the jump next time).

It had to be an authentic, correct verse. While we were
little, it could be the same one, once you had it down good,
morning after morning, until you got a little older and bigger, when one morning (by this time you would be pretty
glib at it, galloping through without even listening to yourself since you were already five or ten minutes ahead, already among the ham and steak and fried chicken and

grits and sweet potatoes and two or three kinds of hot bread) you would suddenly find his eyes on you – very blue, very kind and gentle, and even now not stern so much as inflexible; and next morning you had a new verse. In a way, that was when you discovered that your childhood was over; you had outgrown it and entered the world.

INTERVIEWER: Do you read your contemporaries?

FAULKNER: No, the books I read are the ones I knew and loved when I was a young man and to which I return as you do to old friends: the Old Testament, Dickens, Conrad, Cervantes – *Don Quixote*. I read that every year, as some do the Bible. Flaubert, Balzac – he created an intact world of his own, a bloodstream running through twenty books – Dostoevski, Tolstoi, Shakespeare. I read Melville occasionally, and of the poets Marlowe, Campion, Jonson, Herrick, Donne, Keats, and Shelley. I still read Housman. I've read these books so often that I don't always begin at page one and read on to the end. I just read one scene, or about one character, just as you'd meet and talk to a friend for a few minutes.

INTERVIEWER: And Freud?

FAULKNER: Everybody talked about Freud when I lived in New Orleans, but I have never read him. Neither did Shakespeare. I doubt if Melville did either, and I'm sure Moby Dick didn't.

INTERVIEWER: Do you ever read mystery stories?

FAULKNER: I read Simenon because he reminds me something of Chekhov.

INTERVIEWER: What about your favourite characters?

FAULKNER: My favourite characters are Sarah Gamp – a cruel, ruthless woman, a drunkard, opportunist, unreliable, most of her character was bad, but at least it was character; Mrs Harris, Falstaff, Prince Hal, Don Quixote, and Sancho of course. Lady Macbeth I always admire. And Bottom, Ophelia, and Mercutio – both he and Mrs Gamp coped with life, didn't ask any favours, never whined. Huck Finn, of course, and Jim. Tom Sawyer I never liked much – an awful prig. And then I like Sut Lovingood, from a book written by George Harris about 1840 or '50 in the

Tennessee mountains. He had no illusions about himself, did the best he could; at certain times he was a coward and knew it and wasn't ashamed; he never blamed his misfortunes on anyone and never cursed God for them.

INTERVIEWER: Would you comment on the future of the novel?

FAULKNER: I imagine as long as people will continue to read novels, people will continue to write them, or vice versa; unless of course the pictorial magazines and comic strips finally atrophy man's capacity to read, and literature really is on its way back to the picture writing in the Neanderthal cave.

INTERVIEWER: And how about the function of the critics?

FAULKNER: The artist doesn't have time to listen to the critics. The ones who want to be writers read the reviews, the ones who want to write don't have the time to read reviews. The critic too is trying to say 'Kilroy was here.' His function is not directed towards the artist himself. The artist is a cut above the critic, for the artist is writing something which will move the critic. The critic is writing something which will move everybody but the artist.

INTERVIEWER: So you never feel the need to discuss your work with anyone?

FAULKNER: No, I am too busy writing it. It has got to please me and if it does I don't need to talk about it. If it doesn't please me, talking about it won't improve it, since the only thing to improve it is to work on it some more. I am not a literary man but only a writer. I don't get any pleasure from talking shop.

INTERVIEWER: Critics claim that blood relationships are central in your novels.

FAULKNER: That is an opinion and, as I have said, I don't read critics. I doubt that a man trying to write about people is any more interested in blood relationships than in the shape of their noses, unless they are necessary to help the story move. If the writer concentrates on what he does need to be interested in, which is the truth and the human heart, he won't have much time left for anything else, such

as ideas and facts like the shape of noses or blood relationships, since in my opinion ideas and facts have very little
connection with truth.

INTERVIEWER: Critics also suggest that your characters
never consciously choose between good and evil.

FAULKNER: Life is not interested in good and evil. Don
Quixote was constantly choosing between good and evil,
but then he was choosing in his dream state. He was mad.
He entered reality only when he was so busy trying to cope
with people that he had no time to distinguish between
good and evil. Since people exist only in life, they must devote their time simply to being alive. Life is motion, and
motion is concerned with what makes man move – which is
ambition, power, pleasure. What time a man can devote to
morality, he must take by force from the motion of which
he is a part. He is compelled to make choices between good
and evil sooner or later, because moral conscience demands
that from him in order that he can live with himself tomorrow. His moral conscience is the curse he had to accept
from the gods in order to gain from them the right to
dream.

INTERVIEWER: Could you explain more what you mean
by motion in relation to the artist?

FAULKNER: The aim of every artist is to arrest motion,
which is life, by artificial means and hold it fixed so that a
hundred years later, when a stranger looks at it, it moves
again since it is life. Since man is mortal, the only immortality possible for him is to leave something behind him
that is immortal since it will always move. This is the
artist's way of scribbling 'Kilroy was here' on the wall of
the final and irrevocable oblivion through which he must
someday pass.

INTERVIEWER: It has been said by Malcolm Cowley
that your characters carry a sense of submission to their
fate.

FAULKNER: That is his opinion. I would say that some of
them do and some of them don't, like everybody else's
characters. I would say that Lena Grove in *Light in August*
coped pretty well with hers. It didn't really matter to her in

her destiny whether her man was Lucas Birch or not. It was her destiny to have a husband and children and she knew it, and so she went out and attended to it without asking help from anyone. She was the captain of her soul. One of the calmest, sanest speeches I ever heard was when she said to Byron Bunch at the very instant of repulsing his final desperate and despairing attempt at rape, 'Ain't you ashamed? You might have woke the baby.' She was never for one moment confused, frightened, alarmed. She did not even know that she didn't need pity. Her last speech for example: 'Here I ain't been travelling but a month, and I'm already in Tennessee. My, my, a body does get around.'

The Bundren family in *As I Lay Dying* pretty well coped with theirs. The father having lost his wife would naturally need another one, so he got one. At one blow he not only replaced the family cook, he acquired a gramophone to give them all pleasure while they were resting. The pregnant daughter failed this time to undo her condition, but she was not discouraged. She intended to try again, and even if they all failed right up to the last, it wasn't anything but just another baby.

INTERVIEWER: And Mr Cowley says you find it hard to create characters between the ages of twenty and forty who are sympathetic.

FAULKNER: People between twenty and forty are not sympathetic. The child has the capacity to do but it can't know. It only knows when it is no longer able to do – after forty. Between twenty and forty the will of the child to do gets stronger, more dangerous, but it has not begun to learn to know yet. Since his capacity to do is forced into channels of evil through environment and pressures, man is strong before he is moral. The world's anguish is caused by people between twenty and forty. The people around my home who have caused all the interracial tension – the Milams and the Bryants (in the Emmet Till murder) and the gangs of Negroes who grab a white woman and rape her in revenge, the Hitlers, Napoleons, Lenins – all these people are symbols of human suffering and anguish, all of them between twenty and forty.

INTERVIEWER: You gave a statement to the papers at the time of the Emmet Till killing. Have you anything to add to it here?

FAULKNER: No, only to repeat what I said before: that if we Americans are to survive it will have to be because we choose and elect and defend to be first of all Americans; to present to the world one homogenous and unbroken front, whether of white Americans or black ones or purple or blue or green. Maybe the purpose of this sorry and tragic error committed in my native Mississippi by two white adults on an afflicted Negro child is to prove to us whether or not we deserve to survive. Because if we in America have reached that point in our desperate culture when we must murder children, no matter for what reason or what colour, we don't deserve to survive, and probably won't.

INTERVIEWER: What happened to you between *Soldier's Pay* and *Sartoris* – that is what caused you to begin the Yoknapatawpha saga?

FAULKNER: With *Soldier's Pay* I found out writing was fun. But I found out afterwards that not only each book had to have a design but the whole output or sum of an artist's work had to have a design. With *Soldier's Pay* and *Mosquitoes* I wrote for the sake of writing because it was fun. Beginning with *Sartoris* I discovered that my own little postage stamp of native soil was worth writing about and that I would never live long enough to exhaust it and that by sublimating the actual into the apocryphal I would have complete liberty to use whatever talent I might have to its absolute top. It opened up a gold mine of other people, so I created a cosmos of my own. I can move these people around like God, not only in space but in time too. The fact that I have moved my characters around in time successfully, at least in my own estimation, proves to me my own theory that time is a fluid condition which has no existence except in the momentary avatars of individual people. There is no such thing as *was* – only *is*. If *was* existed, there would be no grief or sorrow. I like to think of the world I created as being a kind of keystone in the universe; that small as that keystone is, if it were ever taken away the universe itself would collapse. My last book will be the Doomsday Book, the Golden Book, of Yoknapatawpha County. Then I shall break the pencil and I'll have to stop.

Jean Stein

GEORGES SIMENON

Mr Simenon's study in his rambling white house on the edge of Lakeville, Connecticut, after lunch on a January day of bright sun. The room reflects its owner: cheerful, efficient, hospitable, controlled. On its walls are books of law and medicine, two fields in which he has made himself an expert; the telephone directories from many parts of the world to which he turns in naming his characters; the map of a town where he has just set his forty-ninth Maigret novel; and the calendar on which he has X-ed out in heavy crayon the days spent writing the Maigret – one day to a chapter – and the three days spent revising it, a labour which he has generously interrupted for this interview.

In the adjoining office, having seen that everything is arranged comfortably for her husband and the interviewer, Mme Simenon returns her attention to the business affairs of a writer whose novels appear six a year and whose contracts for books, adaptations, and translations are in more than twenty languages.

With great courtesy and in a rich voice which gives to his statements nuances of meaning much beyond the ordinary range, Mr Simenon continues a discussion begun in the dining-room.

SIMENON: Just one piece of general advice from a writer has been very useful to me. It was from Colette. I was writing short stories for *Le Matin*, and Colette was literary editor at that time. I remember I gave her two short stories and she returned them and I tried again and tried again. Finally she said, 'Look, it is too literary, always too literary.' So I followed her advice. It's what I do when I write, the main job when I rewrite.

INTERVIEWER: What do you mean by 'too literary'? What do you cut out, certain kinds of words?

SIMENON: Adjectives, adverbs, and every word which is

there just to make an effect. Every sentence which is there just for the sentence. You know, you have a beautiful sentence – cut it. Every time I find such a thing in one of my novels it is to be cut.

INTERVIEWER: Is that the nature of most of your revision?

SIMENON: Almost all of it.

INTERVIEWER: It's not revising the plot pattern?

SIMENON: Oh, I never touch anything of that kind. Sometimes I've changed the names while writing: a woman will be Helen in the first chapter and Charlotte in the second, you know; so in revising I straighten this out. And then, cut, cut, cut.

INTERVIEWER: Is there anything else you can say to beginning writers?

SIMENON: Writing is considered a profession, and I don't think it is a profession. I think that everyone who does not *need* to be a writer, who thinks he can do something else, ought to do something else. Writing is not a profession but a vocation of unhappiness. I don't think an artist can ever be happy.

INTERVIEWER: Why?

SIMENON: Because, first, I think that if a man has the urge to be an artist, it is because he needs to find himself. Every writer tries to find himself through his characters, through all his writing.

INTERVIEWER: He is writing for himself?

SIMENON: Yes. Certainly.

INTERVIEWER: Are you conscious there will be readers of the novel?

SIMENON: I know that there are many men who have more or less the same problems I have, with more or less intensity, and who will be happy to read the book to find the answer – if the answer can possibly be found.

INTERVIEWER: Even when the author can't find the answer do the readers profit because the author is meaningfully fumbling for it?

SIMENON: That's it. Certainly. I don't remember whether I have ever spoken to you about the feeling I have had for several years. Because society today is without a very strong religion, without a firm hierarchy of social classes, and people are afraid of the big organization in which they are just a little part, for them reading certain novels is a little like looking through the keyhole to learn what the neighbour is doing and thinking – does he have the same inferiority complex, the same vices, the same temptations? This is what they are looking for in the work of art. I think many more people today are insecure and are in a search for themselves.

There are now so few literary works of the kind Anatole France wrote, for example, you know – very quiet and elegant and reassuring. On the contrary, what people today want are the most complex books, trying to go into every corner of human nature. Do you understand what I mean?

INTERVIEWER: I think so. You mean this is not just because today we think we know more about psychology but because more readers need this kind of fiction?

SIMENON: Yes. An ordinary man fifty years ago – there are many problems today which he did not know. Fifty years ago he had the answers. He doesn't have them any more.

INTERVIEWER: A year or so ago you and I heard a critic ask that the novel today return to the kind of novel written in the nineteenth century.

SIMENON: It is impossible, completely impossible, I think. (*Pausing*): Because we live in a time when writers do not always have barriers around them, they can try to present characters by the most complete, the most full expression. You may show love in a very nice story, the first ten months of two lovers, as in the literature of a long time ago. Then you have a second kind of story: they begin to be bored; that was the literature of the end of the last century. And then, if you are free to go further, the man is fifty and tries to have another life, the woman gets jealous, and you have children mixed in it; that is the third story. We are the third story now. We don't stop when they marry, we don't stop when they begin to be bored, we go to the end.

INTERVIEWER: In this connection, I often hear people ask about the violence in modern fiction. I'm all for it, but I'd like to ask why you write of it.

SIMENON: We are accustomed to see people driven to their limit.

INTERVIEWER: And violence is associated with this?

SIMENON: More or less. (*Pausing*): We no longer think of a man from the point of view of some philosophers; for a long time man was always observed from the point of view that there was a God and that man was the king of creation. We don't think any more that man is the king of creation. We see man almost face to face. Some readers still would like to read very reassuring novels, novels which give them a comforting view of humanity. It can't be done.

INTERVIEWER: Then if the readers interest you, it is because they want a novel to probe their troubles? Your role is to look into yourself and –

SIMENON: That's it. But it's not only a question of the artist's looking into himself but also of his looking into others with the experience he has of himself. He writes with sympathy because he feels that the other man is like him.

INTERVIEWER: If there were no readers you would still write?

SIMENON: Certainly. When I began to write I didn't have the idea my books would sell. More exactly, when I began to write I did commercial pieces – stories for magazines and things of that kind – to earn my living, but I didn't call it writing. But for myself, every evening, I did some writing without any idea that it would ever be published.

INTERVIEWER: You probably have had as much experience as anybody in the world in doing what you have just called commercial writing. What is the difference between it and non-commercial?

SIMENON: I call 'commercial' every work, not only in literature but in music and painting and sculpture – any art – which is done for such-and-such a public or for a certain kind of publication or for a particular collection. Of course, in commercial writing there are different grades. You may have things which are very cheap and some very good. The books of the month, for example, are commercial writing; but some of them are almost perfectly done, almost works of art. Not completely, but almost. And the same with certain magazine pieces; some of them are wonderful. But very seldom can they be works of art, because a work of art can't be done for the purpose of pleasing a certain group of readers.

INTERVIEWER: How does this change the work? As the author you know whether or not you tailored a novel for a market, but, looking at your work from the outside only, what difference would the reader see?

SIMENON: The big difference would be in the concessions. In writing for any commercial purpose you have always to make concessions.

INTERVIEWER: To the idea that life is orderly and sweet, for example?

SIMENON: And the view of morals. Maybe that is the most important. You can't write anything commercial without accepting some code. There is always a code — like the code in Hollywood, and in television and radio. For example, there is now a very good programme on television, it is probably the best for plays. The first two acts are always first-class. You have the impression of something completely new and strong, and then, at the end the concession comes. Not always a happy end, but something comes to arrange everything from the point of view of a morality or philosophy — you know. All the characters who were beautifully done, change completely in the last ten minutes.

INTERVIEWER: In your non-commercial novels you feel no need to make concessions of any sort?

SIMENON: I never do that, never, never, never. Otherwise I wouldn't write. It's too painful to do if it's not to go to the end.

INTERVIEWER: You have shown me the manila envelopes you use in starting novels. Before you actually begin writing, how much have you been working consciously on the plan of that particular novel?

SIMENON: As you suggest, we have to distinguish here between consciously and unconsciously. Unconsciously I probably have two or three, not novels, not ideas about novels, but themes in my mind. I never even think that they might serve for a novel; more exactly, they are the things about which I worry. Two days before I start writing a novel I consciously take up one of those ideas. But even before I consciously take it up I first find some atmosphere. Today there is a little sunshine here. I might remember such and such a spring, maybe in some small Italian town, or some place in the French provinces or in Arizona, I don't know, and then, little by little, a small world will come into my mind, with a few characters. Those characters will be taken partly from people I have known and partly from pure imagination – you know it's a complex of both. And then the idea I had before will come and stick around them. They will have the same problem I have in my mind myself. And the problem – with those people – will give me the novel.

INTERVIEWER: This is a couple of days before?

SIMENON: Yes, a couple of days. Because as soon as I have the beginning I can't bear it very long; so the next day I take my envelope, take my telephone book for names, and take my town map – you know, to see exactly where things happen. And two days later I begin writing. And the beginning will be always the same; it is almost a geometrical problem; I have such a man, such a woman, in such surroundings. What can happen to them to oblige them to go to their limit? That's the question. It will be sometimes a very simple incident, anything which will change their lives. Then I write my novel chapter by chapter.

INTERVIEWER: What has gone on the planning envelope? Not an outline of the action?

SIMENON: No, no. I know nothing about the events when I begin the novel. On the envelope I put only the names of the characters, their ages, their families. I know nothing whatever about the events that will occur later. Otherwise it would not be interesting to me.

INTERVIEWER: When do the incidents begin to form?

SIMENON: On the eve of the first day I know what will happen in the first chapter. Then, day after day, chapter after chapter, I find what comes later. After I have started a novel I write a chapter each day without ever missing a day. Because it is a strain, I have to keep pace with the novel. If, for example, I am ill for forty-eight hours, I have to throw away the previous chapters. And I never return to that novel.

INTERVIEWER: When you did commercial fiction, was your method at all similar?

SIMENON: No. Not at all. When I did a commercial novel I didn't think about that novel except in the hours of writing it. But when I am doing a novel now I don't see anybody, I don't speak to anybody, I don't take a phone call – I live just like a monk. All the day I am one of my characters. I feel what he feels.

INTERVIEWER: You are the same character all the way through the writing of that novel?

SIMENON: Always, because most of my novels show what happens around one character. The other characters are always seen by him. So it is in this character's skin I have to be. And it's almost unbearable after five or six days. This is one of the reasons my novels are so short; after eleven days I can't – it's impossible. I have to – It's physical. I am too tired.

INTERVIEWER: I should think so. Especially if you drive the main character to his limit.

SIMENON: Yes. Yes.

INTERVIEWER: And you are playing this role with him, you are –

SIMENON: Yes, and it's awful. That is why, before I start a novel – this may sound foolish here, but it is the truth – generally a few days before the start of a novel I look to see that I don't have any appointments for eleven days. Then I call the doctor. He takes my blood pressure, he checks everything. And he says, 'Okay.'

INTERVIEWER: Cleared for action.

SIMENON: Exactly. Because I have to be sure that I am good for the eleven days.

INTERVIEWER: Does he come again at the end of the eleven days?

SIMENON: Usually.

INTERVIEWER: His idea or yours?

SIMENON: It's his idea.

INTERVIEWER: What does he find?

SIMENON: The blood pressure is usually down.

INTERVIEWER: What does he think of this? Is it all right?

SIMENON: He thinks it is all right but unhealthy to do it too often.

INTERVIEWER: Does he ration you?

SIMENON: Yes. Sometimes he will say, 'Look, after this novel take two months off.' For example, yesterday he said, 'Okay, but how many novels do you want to do before you go away for the summer?' I said, 'Two.' 'Okay,' he said.

INTERVIEWER: Fine. I'd like to ask now whether you see any pattern in the development of your views as they have worked out in your novels.

SIMENON: I am not the one who discovered it, but some critics in France did. All my life, my literary life, if I may say so, I have taken several problems for my novels, and about every ten years I have taken up the same problems from another point of view. I have the impression that I will never, probably, find the answer. I know of certain problems I have taken more than five times.

INTERVIEWER: And do you know that you will take those up again?

SIMENON: Yes, I will. And then there are a few problems – if I may call them problems – that I know I will never take again, because I have the impression that I went to the end of them. I don't any more care about them.

INTERVIEWER: What are some of the problems you have dealt with often and expect to deal with in future?

SIMENON: One of them, for example, which will probably haunt me more than any other is the problem of communication. I mean communication between two people. The fact that we are I don't know how many millions of people, yet communication, complete communication, is completely impossible between two of those people, is to me one of the biggest tragic themes in the world. When I was a young boy I was afraid of it. I would almost scream because of it. It gave me such a sensation of solitude, of loneliness. That is a theme I have taken I don't know how many times. But I know it will come again. Certainly it will come again.

INTERVIEWER: And another?

SIMENON: Another seems to be the theme of escape. Between two days changing your life completely; without caring at all what has happened before, just go on. You know what I mean?

INTERVIEWER: Starting over?

SIMENON: Not even starting over. Going to nothing.

INTERVIEWER: I see. Is either of these themes or another not far in the offing as a subject, do you suppose? Or is it harmful to ask this?

SIMENON: One is not very far away, probably. It is something on the theme of father and child, of two generations, man coming and man going. That's not completely it, but I don't see it neatly enough just yet to speak about it.

INTERVIEWER: This theme could be associated with the theme of lack of communication?

SIMENON: That's it; it is another branch of the same problem.

INTERVIEWER: What themes do you feel rather certain you will not deal with again?

SIMENON: One, I think, is the theme of the disintegration of a unit, and the unit was generally a family.

INTERVIEWER: Have you treated this theme often?

SIMENON: Two or three times, maybe more.

INTERVIEWER: In the novel *Pedigree*?

SIMENON: In *Pedigree* you have it, yes. If I had to choose one of my books to live and not the others, I would never choose *Pedigree*.

INTERVIEWER: What one might you choose?

SIMENON: The next one.

INTERVIEWER: And the next one after that?

SIMENON: That's it. It's always the next one. You see, even technically I have the feeling now that I am very far away from the goal.

INTERVIEWER: Apart from the next ones, would you be willing to nominate a published novel to survive?

SIMENON: Not one. Because when a novel is finished I have always the impression that I have not succeeded. I am not discouraged, but I see – I want to try again.

But one thing – I consider my novels about all on the same level, yet there are steps. After a group of five or six novels I have a kind of – I don't like the word 'progress' – but there seems to be a progress. There is a jump in quality, I think. So every five or six novels there is one I prefer to the others.

INTERVIEWER: Of the novels now available, which one would you say was one of these?

SIMENON: *The Brothers Rico*. The story might be the same if instead of a gangster you had the cashier of one of our banks or a teacher we might know.

INTERVIEWER: A man's position is threatened and so he will do anything to keep it?

SIMENON: That's it. A man who always wants to be on top with the small group where he lives. And who will sacrifice anything to stay there. And he may not be a very good man, but he made such an effort to be where he is that he will never accept not being there any more.

INTERVIEWER: I like the simple way that novel does so much.

SIMENON: I tried to do it very simply, simply. And there is not a single 'literary' sentence there, you know? It's written as if by a child.

INTERVIEWER: You spoke earlier about thinking of atmosphere when you first think of a novel.

SIMENON: What I mean by atmosphere might be translated by the 'poetic line'. You understand what I mean?

INTERVIEWER: Is 'mood' close enough?

SIMENON: Yes. And with the mood goes the season, goes the detail – at first it is almost like a musical theme.

INTERVIEWER: And so far in no way geographically located?

SIMENON: Not at all. That's the atmosphere for me, because I try – and I don't think I have done it, for otherwise the critics would have discovered it – I try to do it with prose, with the novel, what generally is done with poetry. I mean I try to go beyond the real, and the explainable ideas, and to explore the man – not doing it by the sound of the words as the poetical novels of the beginning of the century tried to do. I can't explain technically but – I try to put in my novels some things which you can't explain, to give some message which does not exist practically. You understand what I mean? I read a few days ago that T. S. Eliot, whom I admire very much, wrote that poetry is necessary in plays having one kind of story and not in plays having another, that it depends on the subject you treat. I don't think so. I think you may have the same secret message to give with any kind of subject. If your vision of the world is of a certain kind you will put poetry in everything, necessarily.

But I am probably the only one who thinks there is something of the kind in my books.

INTERVIEWER: One time you spoke about your wish to write the 'pure' novel. Is this what you were speaking of a while ago – about cutting out the 'literary' words and sentences – or does it also include the poetry you have just spoken of?

SIMENON: The 'pure' novel will do only what the novel can do. I mean that it doesn't have to do any teaching or any work of journalism. In a pure novel you wouldn't take sixty pages to describe the South or Arizona or some country in Europe. Just the drama, with only what is absolutely part of this drama. What I think about novels today is almost a translation of the rules of tragedy into the novel. I think the novel is the tragedy for our day.

INTERVIEWER: Is length important? Is it part of your definition of the pure novel?

SIMENON: Yes. That sounds like a practical question, but I think it is important, for the same reason you can't see a tragedy in more than one sitting. I think that the pure novel is too tense for the reader to stop in the middle and take it up the next day.

INTERVIEWER: Because television and movies and magazines are under the codes you have spoken of, I take it you feel the writer of the pure novel is almost obligated to write freely.

SIMENON: Yes. And there is a second reason why he should be. I think that now, for reasons probably political, propagandists are trying to create a type of man. I think the novelist has to show man as he is and not the man of propaganda; I mean the man they teach in the third grade of school, a man who has nothing to do with man as he really is.

INTERVIEWER: What is your experience with conversion of your books for movies and radio?

SIMENON: These are very important for the writer today. For they are probably the way the writer may still be independent. You asked me before whether I ever change anything in one of my novels commercially. I said, 'No.' But I would have to do it without the radio, television and movies.

INTERVIEWER: You once told me Gide made a helpful practical suggestion about one of your novels. Did he influence your work in any more general way?

SIMENON: I don't think so. But with Gide it was funny. In 1936 my publisher said he wanted to give a cocktail party so we could meet, for Gide had said he had read my novels and would like to meet me. So I went, and Gide asked me questions for more than two hours. After that I saw him many times, and he wrote me almost every month and sometimes oftener until he died – always to ask questions. When I went to visit him I always saw my books with so many notes in the margins that they were almost more Gide than Simenon. I never asked him about them; I was very shy about it. So now I will never know.

INTERVIEWER: Did he ask you any special kinds of questions?

SIMENON: Everything, but especially about the mechanism of my — may I use the word? it seems pretentious — creation. And I think I know why he was interested. I think Gide all his life had the dream of being the creator instead of the moralist, the philosopher. I was exactly his opposite, and I think that is why he was interested.

I had the same experience five years before with Count Keyserling. He wrote me exactly the way Gide did. He asked me to visit him at Darmstadt. I went there and he asked me questions for three days and three nights. He came to see me in Paris and asked me more questions and gave me a commentary on each of my books. For the same reason. Keyserling called me an *'imbécile de génie.'*

INTERVIEWER: I remember you once told me that in your commercial novels you would sometimes insert a non-commercial passage or chapter.

SIMENON: Yes, to train myself.

INTERVIEWER: How did that part differ from the rest of the novel?

SIMENON: Instead of writing just the story, in this chapter I tried to give a third dimension, not necessarily to the whole chapter, perhaps to a room, to a chair, to some object. It would be easier to explain it in the terms of painting.

INTERVIEWER: How?

SIMENON: To give the weight. A commercial painter paints flat; you can put your finger through. But a painter — for example, an apple by Cézanne has weight. And it has juice, everything, with just three strokes. I tried to give to my words just the weight that a stroke of Cézanne's gave to an apple. That is why most of the time I use concrete words. I try to avoid abstract words, or poetical words, you know, like 'crepuscule', for example. It is very nice, but it gives nothing. Do you understand? To avoid every stroke which does not give something to this third dimension.

On this point, I think that what the critics call my 'atmosphere' is nothing but the impressionism of the painter adapted to literature. My childhood was spent at the time of the impressionists and I was always in the museums and exhibitions. That gave me a kind of sense of it. I was haunted by it.

INTERVIEWER: Have you ever dictated fiction, commercial or any other?

SIMENON: No. I am an artisan; I need to work with my hands. I would like to carve my novel in a piece of wood. My characters – I would like to have them heavier, more three-dimensional. And I would like to make a man so that everybody, looking at him, would find his own problems in this man. That's why I spoke about poetry, because this goal looks more like a poet's goal than the goal of a novelist. My characters have a profession, have characteristics; you know – their age, their family situation, and everything. But I try to make each one of these characters heavy, like a statue, and to be the brother of everybody in the world. (*Pausing*) And what makes me happy is the letters I get. They never speak about my beautiful style; they are the letters a man would write to his doctor or his psychoanalyst. They say, 'You are one who undersands me. So many times I find myself in your novels.' Then there are pages of their confidences; and they are not crazy people. There are crazy people too, of course; but many are on the contrary people who – even important people. I am surprised.

INTERVIEWER: Early in your life did any particular book or author especially impress you?

SIMENON: Probably the one who impressed me most was Gogol. And certainly Dostoevski, but less than Gogol.

INTERVIEWER: Why do you think Gogol interested you?

SIMENON: Maybe because he makes characters who are just like everyday people but at the same time have what I called a few minutes ago the third dimension I am looking for. All of them have this poetic aura. But not the Oscar Wilde kind – a poetry which comes naturally, which is there, the kind Conrad has. Each character has the weight of sculpture, it is so heavy, so dense.

INTERVIEWER: Dostoevski said of himself and some of his fellow writers that they came out from Gogol's *Overcoat*, and now you feel you do too.

SIMENON: Yes. Gogol and Dostoevski.

INTERVIEWER: When you and I were discussing a particular trial while it was going on a year or two ago, you said you often followed such newspaper accounts with interest. Do you ever in following them say to yourself, 'This is something I might some day work into a novel'?

SIMENON: Yes.

INTERVIEWER: Do you consciously file it away?

SIMENON: No. I just forget I said it might be useful some day, and three or four or ten years later it comes. I don't keep a file.

INTERVIEWER: Speaking of trials, what would you say is the fundamental difference, if there is any, between your detective fiction – such as the Maigret which you finished a few days ago – and your more serious novels?

SIMENON: Exactly the same difference that exists between the painting of a painter and the sketch he will make for his pleasure or for his friends or to study something.

INTERVIEWER: In the Maigrets you look at the character only from the point of view of the detective?

SIMENON: Yes. Maigret can't go inside a character. He will see, explain, and understand; but he does not give the character the weight the character should have in another of my novels.

INTERVIEWER: So in the eleven days spent writing a Maigret novel your blood pressure does not change much?

SIMENON: No. Very little.

INTERVIEWER: You are not driving the detective to the limit of his endurance.

SIMENON: That's it. So I only have the natural fatigue of being so many hours at the typewriter. But otherwise, no.

INTERVIEWER: One more question, if I may. Has published general criticism ever in any way made you consciously change the way you write? From what you say I should imagine not.

SIMENON: Never. (*Pausing, and looking down*) I have a very, very strong will about my writing, and I will go my way. For instance, all the critics for twenty years have said the same thing: 'It is time for Simenon to give us a big novel, a novel with twenty or thirty characters.' They do not understand. I will never write a big novel. My big novel is the mosaic of my small novels. (*Looking up*) You understand?

Carvel Collins

ANGUS WILSON

A London apartment in Dolphin Square, just downriver from Chelsea. Dolphin Square – and this came as something of a surprise – is a huge block of service apartments, with restaurant (where we ate lunch), indoor swimming pool, shops, bars, etc. – the layout and décor of this part strongly reminiscent of an ocean liner. The apartment itself, on the ground floor and looking out on the central court, was small, comfortable, tidy, uneccentric; there were books but not great heaps of them; the pictures included a pair of patriotic prints from the First World War ('the period fascinates me'). For Wilson it is just a place to stay when he has to be in London: his real home is a cottage in Suffolk, five miles from the nearest village ('I find I hate cities more and more. I used to need people, but now I can be much more alone'). The electric fire was on, although the late September day was fine and quite mild. Wilson explained that he had just got back from Asia – Japan (where he had been a guest of honour at the P.E.N. Conference), the Philippines, Cambodia, Thailand – and found England cold.

Although one does not think of Wilson as a small man, he is rather below the average height. His face is mobile but somewhat plumper than in most of the published photographs, the hair white at the front shading to grey at the back, the forehead lined, the eyebrows rather prominent, the eyes pale grey and serious – but not solemn: Wilson's manner has a liveliness and warmth that is immediately engaging. He talks quickly, confidently yet unaffectedly, eagerly – obviously enjoying it. The conversation before and during lunch was mainly about Japan – it had been his first visit to Asia and he had clearly been impressed – and about other writers. Now, after lunch, Wilson agrees to talk about himself.

INTERVIEWER: When did you start writing?

WILSON: I never wrote anything – except for the school magazine – until November 1946. Then I wrote a short story one weekend – 'Raspberry Jam' – and followed that up by writing a short story every week-end for twelve weeks. I was then thirty-three. My writing started as a hobby: that seems a funny word to use – but, yes, hobby. During the war, when I was working at the Foreign Office, I had a bad nervous breakdown, and after the war I decided that simply to return to my job at the British Museum would be too depressing. Writing seemed a good way of diversifying my time. I was living in the country and commuting to London then and I could only do it at week-ends. That's why I started with short stories: this was something I could finish, realize completely, in a week-end.

INTERVIEWER: Had you never thought of becoming a writer before that time?

WILSON: No, I never had any intention of becoming a writer. I'd always thought that far too many things were written, and working in the Museum convinced me of it. But I showed some of my stories to Robin Ironside, the painter, and he asked if he could show them to Cyril Connolly, who took two for *Horizon*. Then a friend of mine at Secker and Warburg said, 'Let us have a look at them,' and they said that if I gave them twelve stories they would publish them. This was *The Wrong Set*. They told me there wasn't much sale for short stories and so on, but the book was surprisingly successful both here and in America. After that I went on writing – reviews, broadcasts, more short stories. The thing grew and grew, and when I came to write *Hemlock and After* I had to do it in one of my leaves. I did it in four weeks. But when I wanted to write a play – that was a different matter. I knew it would take longer to write and that I'd have to revise it, attend rehearsals, and so on. And I was still a full-time civil servant at the British Museum. To resolve the conflict I resigned. It was rather ironic really. When I left school I wanted a permanent job, and I got it at the Museum. Now at the age of forty-two I no longer wanted a permanent job. It meant giving up my pension, and that isn't easy at that age. But so far I haven't regretted it.

INTERVIEWER: Do you find writing comes easily to you?

WILSON: Yes. I write very easily. I told you *Hemlock* took four weeks. *Anglo-Saxon Attitudes* took four months, and an awful lot of that time was taken up just with thinking. The play – *The Mulberry Bush*, the only thing I've re-written several times – was different again. My latest book of short stories, *A Bit off the Map*, took longer too, and my new novel is proving a bit difficult. But I'm not unduly worried. When one starts writing it's natural for the stuff to come rolling off the stocks – is that the right image? – rather easily. And, of course, the fact that it comes harder doesn't necessarily mean that it's worse. When Dickens published his novels in serial form he always added in his letter to the reader: 'I send you this labour of love.' After *Bleak House* he couldn't; it hadn't been a labour of love. But the later Dickens novels are certainly none the worse for that.

INTERVIEWER: Do you work every day?

WILSON: Goodness, no. I did that when I was a civil servant and I don't propose to do so now. But when I'm writing a book I do work every day.

INTERVIEWER: To a schedule?

WILSON: Not really. No. I usually work from eight to two, but if it's going well I may go on to four. Only if I do I'm extremely exhausted. In fact, when the book is going well the only thing that stops me is sheer exhaustion. I wouldn't like to do what Elizabeth Bowen once told me she did – write something every day, whether I was working on a book or not.

INTERVIEWER: Do you usually work on one book at a time?

WILSON: Oh, yes. I've never worked on more than one book at a time, and I don't think it would be good.

INTERVIEWER: About how many words a day do you write?

WILSON: Oh – between one and two thousand. Sometimes more. But the average would be one or two thousand.

INTERVIEWER: Longhand, typewriter, or dictation?

WILSON: Longhand. I can't type. And I'm sure it wouldn't work for me to dictate, though I did think of it when I was doing the play; it might help with the dialogue. But the trouble is I'm too histrionic a person anyway, and even when I'm writing a novel I act out the scenes.

INTERVIEWER: Aloud?

WILSON: Very often. Especially dialogue.

INTERVIEWER: Do you make notes?

WILSON: Books of them. The gestatory period before I start to write is very important to me. That's when I'm persuading myself of the truth of what I want to say, and I don't think I could persuade my readers unless I'd persuaded myself first.

INTERVIEWER: What sort of notes?

WILSON: Oh, notes about the ages of the characters, where they live, little maps, facts about their lives before the book starts. Names are very important to me, too. Look at these notes for *The Mulberry Bush*, for example. There are statements of themes, like this: 'James and Rose are the core of the tradition.' And questions – I'm always asking myself questions – like 'What are Kurt's motives here?' I set myself problems and try to find ways out of them. Then the thing begins to take shape – this note, for example: 'The first act ends in row between Ann and Simon.' Then comes the first version of the first act. It's the same with the novels: I write notes like 'But this isn't what the book is really about. What it *is* about is . . .', and so on.

INTERVIEWER: Why do you feel the need for so many notes?

WILSON: Two reasons. To convince myself, as I said before. And to keep a kind of check on myself. Once one starts writing, the histrionic gifts – the divine passion or whatnot – are liable to take control and sweep you away. It's a matter of setting things on their right course. Then it's much easier to write as the spirit moves.

INTERVIEWER: Do you do careful or rapid first drafts?

WILSON: Oh, I only do one draft. I never do any other. I correct as I go along. And there is very little correction;

the changes in the draft are mainly deletions. Occasionally a new paragraph goes in. Take the end of *Hemlock*, for example. It's rather a Dickens ending, accounting for all the characters. At the end I found Ron's mother, Mrs Wrigley, wasn't accounted for, so I put in the paragraph about her. It's rather like Dickens at the end of *Dombey and Son*. After he'd sent the manuscript to his publishers he sent them a note: 'Please put in a paragraph about Diogenes the dog: something on these lines....' I like to have everyone accounted for too.

INTERVIEWER: What is the difference for you between a short story and a novel?

WILSON: Short stories and plays go together in my mind. You take a point in time and develop it from there; there is no room for development backwards. In a novel I also take a point in time, but feel every room for development backwards. All fiction for me is a kind of magic and trickery – a confidence trick, trying to make people believe something is true that isn't. And the novelist, in particular, is trying to convince the reader that he is seeing society as a whole.

This is why I use such a lot of minor characters and subplots, of course. It isn't wilful love of subplots for their own sake, wilful Victorianism, but because they enable me to suggest the existence of a wider society, the ripples of a society outside. And more important is this thing about fiction as trickery. The natural habit of any good and critical reader is to disbelieve what you are telling him and try to escape out of the world you are picturing. Some novelists try to make the magic work by taking you deep down inside one person. I try to multiply the worlds I put into the books – so that, like the ripples of the stone thrown into the brook, you feel the repercussions going farther and farther out, and at the same time bringing more in. The reader is more inclined to believe in Gerald and Ingeborg because someone so different as Mrs Salad is affected by them. I've always thought this had something to do with the endings of Shakespeare's tragedies. An entirely new lot of people come in – Fortinbras in *Hamlet*, for example, and it's the same

with *Macbeth* and *Lear*. You believe in the tragedies more
because these others from outside confirm them. The worst
kind of nightmare is the one where you dream you've
woken up and it's still going on. The third reason for all
the characters is the Proustian one, which seems to me
very good, that the strangest and most unlikely lives are in
fact interdependent. This is especially true in times like
our own when the old boundaries and demarcations are
becoming blurred.

INTERVIEWER: What about short stories?

WILSON: You can't do this sort of thing with short
stories. They have a kind of immediate ethical text. Many
of mine have punning titles. I take a platitude – 'the wrong
set', for example: the point is that no one knows what the
wrong set is, and one person's wrong set is another's right
set. And you get the pay-off, which is something I like. A
play is rather like this, but has more depth. And plays and
short stories are similar in that both start when all but the
action has finished.

INTERVIEWER: I think you've seen what Frank O'Connor said about *Anglo-Saxon Attitudes* when he was inter-
viewed for this series. He criticizes your 'exploitation of
every form of technique in the modern novel' – techniques
taken, he says, from the cinema and from *Point Counter
Point* – and the whole modern tendency to concentrate the
action of a novel around the actual moment of crisis instead of covering a longer period and 'demonstrating the
hero in all his phases'. *Anglo-Saxon Attitudes,* he says,
'would have been a good novel if it had begun twenty
years earlier'. I'm sure you will have something to say to
this.

WILSON: Yes, indeed. I thought his remarks very curious. He implies that I'm in the twentieth-century experimental tradition. It's very flattering, of course – 'every
known form of technique in the modern novel' – but I
wasn't aware of using any techniques, except that the book
was concerned with echoes of memory. I think the reader
should be unaware of techniques, though it's the critic's job
to see them, of course. O'Connor seems not to have noticed

that the techniques used in *Anglo-Saxon Attitudes* are not just flashbacks as in the cinema, nor just episodic as in *Point Counter Point* – I've recently re-read that and can see no shape in it at all. If you examine the flashbacks in *Anglo-Saxon Attitudes* – and they took me a lot of trouble, I may say – you'll see that it is an ironic picking up of phrases. Marie Hélène says, 'life consists, I believe, in accepting one's duty, and that means often to accept the second best.' This leads Gerald to remember his courtship of Ingeborg: he accepted the second best then, and it has ruined both his life and hers. This is an ironic comment on the cynical realism of Marie Hélène. It's not just cinema, you see, it's very carefully planned, though I say it myself.

INTERVIEWER: What about O'Connor's remark that it should have started twenty years earlier?

WILSON: If it had started twenty years earlier it would have been a simply enormous book – a kind of chronicle novel, I suppose: *The Story of a Disappointed Man*. Where O'Connor goes wrong is in thinking that I'm concerned at all with the hero as such. I'm only concerned with the hero as an illustration of the inevitability of decline if life is denied. After all, there's a definite statement in the book: Gerald's life goes wrong in two ways – with the historical fraud, and with his wife and children. And when he tries to 'face the truth' – in the conventional phrase – he can do this in relation to the fraud all right, but he can't remake his life with his wife and children. This shows up the platitude of 'facing the truth'. Gerald is only freed in that he faces the *result* of his *not* having faced the truth – he accepts his loneliness. A matter of theoretical morality can be put right, but this can't be done where human beings are involved.

INTERVIEWER: Other people besides O'Connor have commented on certain technical similarities between your work and Huxley's. I gather you don't feel you owe him any particular debt?

WILSON: Consciously, of course, I'm in great reaction against Huxley – and against Virginia Woolf. But I read them a great deal when young, and what you read in adolescence can go very deep. I've been much more influenced by Dickens, Proust, Zola. And the ceremony in *Hemlock* is obviously influenced by that scene in *The Possessed* where the poet, who is Turgenev, comes in and makes a fool of himself. Zola has certainly influenced me a great deal in the form and shape of my novels. From Proust I get the feeling about paradox and the truth of improbability – especially the latter.

INTERVIEWER: Are your characters based on observation?

WILSON: Oh, yes. I don't see how else you can do it. But not taken from life. Every character is a mixture of people you've known. Characters come to me – and I think this is behind the Madeleine business in Proust – when people are talking to me. I feel I have heard this, this tone of voice, in other circumstances. And, at the risk of seeming rude, I have to hold on to this and chase it back until it clicks with someone I've met before. The second secretary at the embassy in Bangkok may remind me of the chemistry assistant at Oxford. And I ask myself, what have they in common? Out of such mixtures I can create characters. All my life I've always known a lot of people. Some say my novels are narrow, but I really can't see what they mean. I thought they were pretty wide myself.

INTERVIEWER: Some people think you have an unnecessarily large number of vicious characters.

WILSON: I really don't know why people find my characters unpleasant. I believe – perhaps it would be different if I were religious – that life is very difficult for most people and that most people make a fair job of it. The opportunities for heroism are limited in this kind of world: the most people can do is sometimes not to be as weak as they've been at other times. When Evelyn Waugh reviewed *Hemlock and After* he was very percipient about techniques, but described the characters as 'young cad', 'mother's darling', and so on – terms it would never occur to me to use. I told him I thought the people he described in those terms had behaved rather well. Terence – the 'young cad' – is on the make, certainly, but he behaves rather well in spite of that. And Eric does half break away from his mother – which is quite an achievement in the circumstances.

Of course, all my characters are very self-conscious, aware of what they are doing and what they are like. There's heroism in going on at all while knowing how we are made. Simple, naïve people I'm impatient of, because they haven't faced up to the main responsibility of civilized man – that of facing up to what he is and to the Freudian motivations of his actions. Most of my characters have a Calvinistic conscience, and this is something which in itself makes action difficult. The heroism of my people, again, is in their success in making a relationship with other human beings, in a humanistic way, and their willingness to accept some sort of pleasure principle in life as against the gnawings of a Calvinist conscience and the awareness of Freudian motivations. These people are fully self-conscious, and the only ones who are at all evil – apart from Mrs Curry, who is something quite different, a kind of embodiment of evil – are those like Marie Hélène and Ingeborg who substitute for self-awareness and self-criticism a simple way of living, Marie Hélène's hard and practical, Ingeborg's soft and cosy. They accept a *pattern* of behaviour and morality instead of self-awareness. Characters can be heroic even though they can squeeze only a minimum of action out of the situation. That is how I see it, anyway, though I realize some people might find my characters rather inactive.

INTERVIEWER: I noticed earlier that you sometimes seem to speak of your characters as existing outside the novel – the kind of thing the Leavises so object to. And Elizabeth Sands makes a brief appearance in *Anglo-Saxon Attitudes*.

WILSON: Yes, my friends have criticized my putting Elizabeth Sands in there – 'Hugh Walpole,' they say. I told E. M. Forster this and he said, 'Ah yes – but Balzac too, you know.' I'm on Leavis's side really, but he always writes as a critic, never as a creator. And the writer can't visualize his characters within a framework, although the creation of a work of art demands putting them within a framework. The use of a character for artistic creation is one thing; the author's knowledge of that character is another. Otherwise you'd remove the element of choice, which is the essence of the creative act. What if George Eliot had seen *Middlemarch* whole, in a lump? There'd be no choice. At some point she must have imagined what Mr Casaubon's housekeeper was like and decided to leave her out. It's not instantaneous vision, and I don't think Leavis himself would expect it to be. Of course it was self-indulgence to bring Elizabeth Sands into *Anglo-Saxon Attitudes*: I felt that many people would like *Anglo-Saxon Attitudes* better than *Hemlock and After* – and for the wrong reasons – and I wanted to show them that the worlds of the two books were the same.

INTERVIEWER: You think *Hemlock and After* has been underrated?

WILSON: Yes. I think that in the long run *Hemlock and After* is a better book than *Anglo-Saxon Attitudes*, if not so competently carried out. *Hemlock* is both a more violent and a more compassionate book. I know this is a sentimental cliché, but I do feel towards my books very much as a parent must towards his children. As soon as someone says, 'I *did* like your short stories, but I don't like your novels,' or, 'Of course you only really came into your own with *Anglo-Saxon Attitudes*' – then immediately I want to defend all my other books. I feel this especially about *Hemlock and After* and *Anglo-Saxon Attitudes* – one child a bit odd but exciting, the other competent but not really so interesting. If people say they like one book and not the other, then I feel they can't have understood the one they don't like.

INTERVIEWER: The publisher's blurb for your new volume of short stories, *A Bit off the Map*, begins: 'In an England where the lines of class and caste are becoming blurred and the traditional values have lost much of their force, the characters in Angus Wilson's new stories seek – sometimes cheerfully, sometimes with desperation – to get their true bearings on the map of society.' Wouldn't this comment apply pretty much to all your books?

WILSON: Yes, I suppose it would. But you'll realize when

they appear that each of these stories is designed to show a specific example of such blurrings of the class lines and of the false answers people provide today to get back some sense of position in society. These new stories are all satirical of the old philosophies which have now become fashionable again – neo-Toryism, Colin Wilson's Nietzscheanism, and so on – of people seeking after values which now no longer apply.

INTERVIEWER: Do you think of yourself primarily as a satirist?

WILSON: No, I don't. Satire for me is something more abstract – *Animal Farm, Erewhon*, that sort of thing. I'm much more traditional than that – which is why I was so surprised at Frank O'Connor's putting me with the experimental writers. I've deliberately tried to get back to the Dickens tradition. I use irony as one main approach, perhaps overdoing it. It's been said that too much irony is one of the great dangers of the English tradition, and perhaps I've fallen into that trap. I don't think of *Point Counter Point* as satire: it's comedy of manners – and you could call my work that. But satire implies an abstract philosophy that I don't have; there's nothing I want to say in the way that Butler wanted to say something about machines, for example.

INTERVIEWER: In writing about Anglo-Saxon attitudes, then, you aren't seeking to change them?

WILSON: Oh, no. I don't think it's the novelist's job to give answers. He's only concerned with exposing the human situation, and if his books do good incidentally that's all well and good. It's rather like sermons.

INTERVIEWER: Isn't a sermon intended to do good?

WILSON: Only to the individual, not to society. It's designed to touch the heart – and I hope my books touch the heart now and again.

INTERVIEWER: But you definitely don't think a novelist should have a social purpose?

WILSON: I don't think a writer *should* have anything. I have certain social and political views, and I suppose these may appear in my work. But as a novelist I'm concerned with what I've discovered about human emotions. I attack not specific things, but only people who are set in one way of thinking. The people in my books who come out well may be more foolish, but they have retained an immediacy towards life, not a set of rules applied to life in advance.

INTERVIEWER: What do you think, then, of the 'angry young men'?

WILSON: Of course they don't really belong together – though it's largely their own fault that they have been lumped together. They thought popular journalism was a good way to propagate their ideas, and the popular journalists themselves have naturally written of them as a group. The only thing I have against them – while knowing and liking them personally – is the element of strong self-pity, which I do think is a very ruinous element in art. Whatever they write about – when Osborne writes about his feeling for the underprivileged, for example – you get the feeling that they are really complaining about the way *they* have been treated. And, apart from Colin Wilson, they are so concerned to say that they won't be taken in – we'll be honest and not lay claim to any higher feelings than those we're quite sure we have – that one sometimes wishes they'd be a bit more hypocritical. After all, if you think of yourself in that way, you come to think of everyone else in that way and reduce everything to the level of a commercial traveller talking in a bar, knowing life only too well – and in fact people are often better than they make themselves out to be. Their point of view is Iago's, and Iago disguised a very black heart – I don't accuse the angry young men of being blackhearted, of course – beneath his guise of a cynical plain man's point of view. It isn't quite good enough for serious artists.

INTERVIEWER: What do you feel about writing for the stage? Do you feel the novelist has anything to learn from it?

WILSON: Yes. One learns a great deal about what can be omitted, even from a novel, because the play is such a compact form. The best modern plays – by Tennessee Williams, John Osborne, and so on – have tremendous and wonderful power. But the play of ideas – Ibsen and so on – is a little too much at a discount these days.

INTERVIEWER: Do you intend to write for the stage again?

WILSON: Certainly. I want to try to produce more purely theatrical emotion. And I hope to do that and still try for the ideas and the wit of dialogue that I think I got in *The Mulberry Bush*, which seemed a little untheatrical to some people. I want to get more theatrical power, not to write like Williams, but to bring back something of the Ibsen and Shaw tradition.

INTERVIEWER: What about the cinema?

WILSON: I should be only too pleased if my books were turned into films, but I can't imagine myself writing original film scripts – I don't know the necessary techniques, and I rarely even go to the cinema these days. When writing a play you have to realize that the final production won't be only your own work. You have to co-operate with the producer, the actors, and so on. And I'm prepared for that. But in the cinema the writer is quite anonymous, and I feel – for good reasons or bad – that I must be responsible for what I've written and collect the praise or blame for it. Once a book is done I don't care what other people do with it. *The Mulberry Bush* is being televised soon, and the producer rang me up to say it would have to be cut to ninety minutes. I told him to go ahead and do what he wanted: he knows television and I don't. But I couldn't have made a sketch of *The Mulberry Bush* and let it be played about with, if you see the difference.

INTERVIEWER: What plans do you have for the future?

WILSON: I'm in the course of writing another novel. And, as I've just said, I want to do another play. Then I want to do a book of literary essays on nineteenth-century writers, about whom I have a lot to say that I think hasn't been said. And I want to do a book – not fiction – about the home front during the 1914 war. Of all the terrible things that have happened in my lifetime I still think of the trench warfare of the 1914 war as the worst. And the home front was in the strange position of being concerned and yet unconcerned at the same time. The predicament of these people seems likely to connect closely with the predicament of many of the characters in my novels: Bernard Sands and Gerald Middleton, for example, are both concerned with tragedy yet become observers of it by their withdrawal.

INTERVIEWER: Would you say something more about your new novel?

WILSON: I'm sorry, but I don't like to talk about my books in advance. It isn't just that any short account of a novel seems ridiculous by the side of the real thing. But, as I've said before, fiction writing is a kind of magic, and I don't care to talk about a novel I'm doing because if I communicate the magic spell, even in an abbreviated form, it loses its force for me. And so many people have talked out to me books they would otherwise have written. Once you have talked, the act of communication has been made.

Michael Millgate

ROBERT FROST

Mr Frost came into the front room of his house in Cambridge, Massachusetts, casually dressed, wearing high plaid slippers, offering greetings with a quiet, even diffident friendliness. But there was no mistaking the evidence of the enormous power of his personality. It makes you at once aware of the thick, compacted strength of his body, even now at eighty-six; it is apparent in his face, actually too alive and spontaneously expressive to be as ruggedly heroic as in his photographs.

The impression of massiveness, far exceeding his physical size, isn't separable from the public image he creates and preserves. That this image is invariably associated with unpopular conceptions of New England is no simple matter of his own geographical preferences. New England is of course evoked in the scenes and titles of many of his poems and, more importantly, in his Emersonian tendencies, including his habit of contradicting himself, his capacity to 'unsay' through the sound of his voice what his words seem to assert. His special resemblance to New England, however, is that he, like it, has managed to impose upon the world a wholly self-created image. It is not the critics who have defined him, it is Frost himself. He stood talking for a few minutes in the middle of the room, his remarkably ample, tousled white hair catching the late afternoon sun reflected off the snow in the road outside, and one wondered for a moment how he had managed over so long a life never to let his self-portrait be altered despite countless exposures to light less familiar and unintimidating. In the public world he has resisted countless chances to lose himself in some particular fashion, some movement, like the Georgians, or even in an area of his own work which, to certain critics or readers, happens for the moment to appear more exotically colourful than the whole. In one of the most revealing parts of this interview, *he says of certain of his poems that he doesn't 'want them out', the phrase itself, since all the poems involved have been published, offering an astonishing, even peculiar, evidence of the degree to which he feels in control of his poetic character. It indicates, too, his awareness that attempts to define him as a tragic philosophical poet of man and nature can be more constricting, because more painfully meaningful to him, than the simpler definitions they are designed to correct.*

More specifically, he seemed at various points to find the most immediate threat to his freedom in the tape recorder. Naturally, for a man both voluble and often mischievous in his recollections, Frost did not like the idea of being stuck, as he necessarily would be, with attitudes expressed in two hours of conversation. As an aggravation of this, he knew that no transcript taken from the tape could catch the subtleties of voice which give life and point to many of his statements. At a pause in the interview, Mr Robert O'Clair, a friend and colleague at Harvard who had agreed to sit in as a sort of witness, admitted that we knew very little about running a tape recorder. Frost, who'd moved from his chair to see its workings, readily agreed. 'Yes, I noticed that,' he laughed, 'and I respect you for it,' adding at once – and this is the point of the story – that 'they', presumably the people 'outside', 'like to hear me say nasty things about machines.' A thoroughly supple knowledge of the ways in which the world tries to take him and a confidence that his own ways are more just and liberating was apparent here and everywhere in the conversation.

Frost was seated most of the time in a blue overstuffed chair which he had bought to write in. It had no arms, he began, and this left him the room he needed.

FROST: I never write except with a writing board. I've never had a table in my life. And I use all sorts of things. Write on the sole of my shoe.

INTERVIEWER: Why have you never liked a desk? Is it because you've moved around so much and lived in so many places?

FROST: Even when I was younger I never had a desk. I've never had a writing room.

INTERVIEWER: Is Cambridge your home base now pretty much?

FROST: In the winter. But I'm nearly five months in Ripton, Vermont. I make a long summer up there. But this is my office and business place.

INTERVIEWER: Your place in Vermont is near the Bread Loaf School of Writing, isn't it?

FROST: Three miles away. Not so near I know it's there. I'm a way off from it, down the mountain and up a side road. They connect me with it a good deal more than I'm there. I give a lecture at the school and a lecture at the conference. That's about all.

INTERVIEWER: You were a co-founder of the school, weren't you?

FROST: They say that. I think I had more to do with the starting of the conference. In a very casual way, I said to the president [of Middlebury], 'Why don't you use the place for a little sociability after the school is over?' I thought of no regular business – no pay, no nothing, just inviting literary people, a few, for a week or two. The kitchen staff was still there. But then they started a regular business of it.

INTERVIEWER: When you were in England from 1912 to 1915, did you ever think you might possibly stay there?

FROST: No. No, I went over there to be poor for a while, nothing else. I didn't think of printing a book over there. I'd never offered a book to anyone here. I was thirty-eight years old, wasn't I? Something like that. And I thought the way to a book was the magazines. I hadn't too much luck with them, and nobody ever noticed me except to send me a cheque now and then. So I didn't think I was ready for a book. But I had written three books when I went over, the amount of three books – A Boy's Will, North of Boston, and part of the next [Mountain Interval] in a loose-leaf heap.

INTERVIEWER: What were the circumstances of your meeting Pound when you were in England?

FROST: That was through Frank Flint. The early Imagist and translator. He was a friend of Pound and belonged in that little group there. He met me in a bookstore, said, 'American?' And I said, 'Yes. How'd you know?' He said, 'Shoes.' It was the Poetry Book Shop, Harold Monro's, just being organized. He said, 'Poetry?' And I said, 'I accept the omen.' Then he said, 'You should know your fellow countryman, Ezra Pound.' And I said, 'I've never heard of him.' And I hadn't. I'd been skipping literary magazines – I don't ever read them very much – and the gossip, you know, I never paid much attention to. So he said, 'I'm going to tell him you're here.' And I had a card from Pound afterwards. I didn't use it for two or three months after that.

INTERVIEWER: He saw your book – *A Boy's Will* – just before publication, didn't he? How did that come about?

FROST: The book was already in the publisher's hands, but it hadn't come out when I met Pound, three or four months after he sent me his card. I didn't like the card very well.

INTERVIEWER: What did he say on it?

FROST: Just said, 'At home, sometimes.' Just like Pound. So I didn't feel that that was a very warm invitation. Then one day walking past Church Walk in Kensington, I took his card out and went in to look for him. And I found him there, a little put out that I hadn't come sooner, in his Poundian way. And then he said, 'Flint tells me you have a book.' And I said, 'Well, I ought to have.' He said, 'You haven't seen it?' And I said, 'No.' He said, 'What do you say we go and get a copy?' He was eager about being the first one to talk. That's one of the best things you can say about Pound: he wanted to be the first to jump. Didn't call people up on the telephone to see how they were going to jump. He was all silent with eagerness. We walked over to my publisher; he got the book. Didn't show it to me – put it in his pocket. We went back to his room. He said, 'You don't mind our liking this?' in his British accent, slightly. And I said, 'Oh, go ahead and like it.' Pretty soon he laughed at something, and I said I knew where that was in the book, what Pound would laugh at. And then pretty soon he said, 'You better run along home, I'm going to review it.' And I never touched it. I went home without my book and he kept it. I'd barely seen it in his hands.

INTERVIEWER: He wrote perhaps the first important favourable review, didn't he?

FROST: Yes. It was printed in the States, in Chicago, but it didn't help me much in England. The reviewing of the book there began right away, as soon as it was out. I guess most of those who reviewed it in England didn't know it had already been reviewed in Chicago. It didn't sound as though they did. But his review had something to do with the beginning of my reputation. I've always felt a little romantic about all that – that queer adventure he gave me. You know he had a mixed, a really curious position over there. He was friends with Yeats, Hueffer, and a very few others.

INTERVIEWER: Did you know Hueffer?

FROST: Yes, with him. And Yeats, with him.

INTERVIEWER: How much did you see of Yeats when you were in England?

FROST: Oh, quite a little, with him nearly always – I guess always.

INTERVIEWER: Did you feel when you left London to go to live on a farm in Gloucestershire that you were making a choice against the kind of literary society you'd found in the city?

FROST: No, my choices had been not connected with my going to England even. My choice was almost unconscious in those days. I didn't know whether I had any position in the world at all, and I wasn't choosing positions. You see, my instinct was not to belong to any gang, and my instinct was against being confused with the – what do you call them? – they called themselves Georgians, Edwardians, something like that, the people Edward Marsh was interested in. I understand that he speaks of me in his book, but I never saw him.

INTERVIEWER: Was there much of a gang feeling among the literary people you knew in London?

FROST: Yes. Oh, yes. Funny over there, I suppose it's the same over here. I don't know. I don't 'belong' here. But they'd say, 'Oh, he's that fellow that writes about homely things for that crowd, for those people. Have you anybody like that in America?' As if it were set, you know. Like Masefield – they didn't know Masefield in this gang, but, 'Oh, he's that fellow that does this thing, I believe, for that crowd.'

INTERVIEWER: Your best friend in those years was Edward Thomas?

FROST: Yes – quite separate again from everybody his age. He was as isolated as I was. Nobody knew he wrote poetry until he started to war, and that had something to do with my life with him. We got to be great friends. No, I had an instinct against belonging to any of those crowds. I've had friends, but very scattering, a scattering over there. You know, I could have ... Pound had an afternoon meeting once a week with Flint and Aldington and H. D. and at one time Hulme, I think. Hulme started with them. They met every week to re-write each other's poems.

INTERVIEWER: You saw Hulme occasionally? Was it at these re-writing sessions, or didn't you bother with them?

FROST: Yes, I knew Hulme, knew him quite well. But I never went to one of those meetings. I said to Pound, 'What do you do?' He said, 'Re-write each other's poems.' And I said, 'Why?' He said, 'To squeeze the water out of them.' 'That sounds like a parlour game to me,' I said, 'and I'm a serious artist' – kidding, you know. And he laughed and he didn't invite me any more.

INTERVIEWER: These personal associations that you had in England with Pound and Edward Thomas and what you call the Georgians – these had nothing to do with your establishing a sense of your own style, did they? You'd already written what were to be nearly the first three volumes of your poetry.

FROST: Two and a half books you might say. There are some poems out in Huntington Library that I must have written in the 'nineties. The first one of mine that's still in print was in '90. It's in print still, kicking round.

INTERVIEWER: Not in *A Boy's Will* – the earliest poem published in there was written in '94. I think.

FROST: No, it's not in there. First one I ever *sold* is in there. The first one I ever had printed was the first one I wrote. I never wrote prose or verse till 1890. Before that I wrote Latin and Greek sentences.

INTERVIEWER: Some of the early critics like Garnett and Pound talk a lot about Latin and Greek poetry with reference to yours. You'd read a lot in the classics?

FROST: Probably more Latin and Greek than Pound ever did.

INTERVIEWER: Didn't you teach Latin at one time?

FROST: Yes. When I came back to college after running away, I thought I could stand it if I stuck to Greek and Latin and philosophy. That's all I did those years.

INTERVIEWER: Did you read much in the Romantic poets? Wordsworth, in particular?

FROST: No, you couldn't pin me there. Oh, I read all sorts of things. I said to some Catholic priests the other day when they asked me about reading, I said, 'If you understand the word "catholic", I was very catholic in my taste.'

INTERVIEWER: What sort of things did your mother read to you?

FROST: That I wouldn't be able to tell you. All sorts of things, not too much, but some. She was a very hard-worked person – she supported us. Born in Scotland, but grew up in Columbus, Ohio. She was a teacher in Columbus for seven years – in mathematics. She taught with my father one year after he left Harvard and before he went to California. You know they began to teach in high schools in those days right after coming out of high school themselves. I had teachers like that who didn't go to college. I had two noted teachers in Latin and Greek who weren't college women at all. They taught Fred Robinson.* I had the same teachers he had. Fritz Robinson, the old scholar. My

* Editor of Chaucer, and formerly a professor of English at Harvard.

mother was just like that. Began teaching at eighteen in
the high school, then married along about twenty-five. I'm
putting all this together rather lately, finding out strolling
round like I do. Just dug up in Pennsylvania the date of her
marriage and all that, in Lewistown, Pennsylvania.

INTERVIEWER: Your mother ran a private school in
Lawrence, Massachusetts, didn't she?

FROST: Yes, she did, round Lawrence. She had a private
school. And I taught in that some, as well as taking some
other schools. I'd go out and teach in district schools whenever I felt like springtime.

INTERVIEWER: How old were you then?

FROST: Oh, just after I'd run away from Dartmouth,
along there in '93, '4, twenty years old. Every time I'd get
sick of the city I'd go out for the springtime and take
school for one term. I did that I think two or three times,
that same school. Little school with twelve children, about
a dozen children, all bare-footed. I did newspaper work in
Lawrence, too. I followed my father and mother in that, you
know. I didn't know what I wanted to do with myself to
earn a living. Taught a little, worked on a paper a little,
worked on farms a little, that was my own departure. But
I just followed my parents in newspaper work. I edited a
paper a while – a weekly paper – and then I was on a regular paper. I see its name still up there in Lawrence.

INTERVIEWER: When you started to write poetry, was
there any poet that you admired very much?

FROST: I was the enemy of that theory that idea of
Stevenson's that you should play the sedulous ape to anybody. That did more harm to American education than
anything ever got out.

INTERVIEWER: Did you ever feel any affinity between
your work and any other poet's?

FROST: I'll leave that for somebody else to tell me. I
wouldn't know.

INTERVIEWER: But when you read Robinson or Stevens,
for example, do you find anything that is familiar to you
from your own poetry?

FROST: Wallace Stevens? He was years after me.

INTERVIEWER: I mean in your reading of him, whether or not you felt any –

FROST: Any affinity, you mean? Oh, you couldn't say that. No. Once he said to me, 'You write on subjects.' And I said, 'You write on bric-à-brac.' And when he sent me his next book he'd written 'S'more bric-à-brac' in it. Just took it good-naturedly. No, I had no affinity with him. We were friends. Oh, gee, miles away. I don't know who you'd connect me with.

INTERVIEWER: Well, you once said in my hearing that Robert Lowell had tried to connect you with Faulkner, told you you were a lot like Faulkner.

FROST: Did I say that?

INTERVIEWER: No, you said that Robert Lowell told you that you were a lot like Faulkner.

FROST: Well, you know what Robert Lowell said once? He said, 'My uncle's dialect – the New England dialect, *The Biglow Papers* – was just the same as Burns's, wasn't it?' I said 'Robert! Burns's was not a dialect, Scotch is not a dialect. It's a language.' But he'd say anything, Robert, for the hell of it.

INTERVIEWER: You've never, I take it then, been aware of any particular line of preference in your reading?

FROST: Oh, I read 'em all. One of my points of departure is an anthology. I find a poet I admire, and I think, well, there must be a lot to that. Some old one – Shirley, for instance, 'The glories of our blood and state' – that sort of splendid poem. I go looking for more. Nothing. Just a couple like that and that's all. I remember certain boys took an interest in certain poems with me in old times. I remember Brower one day in somebody else's class when he was a student at Amherst – Reuben Brower, afterwards the Master of Adams House at Harvard. I remember I said, 'Anyone want to read that poem to me?' It was 'In going to my naked bed as one that would have slept', Edwards's old poem. He read it so well I said, 'I give you A for life.' And that's the way we joke with each other. I never had him regularly in a class of mine. I visited other classes up at Amherst and noticed him very early. Goodness sake, the way his voice fell into those lines, the natural way he did that very difficult poem with that old quotation – 'The falling out of faithful friends is the renewing of love.' I'm very catholic, that's about all you can say. I've hunted. I'm not thorough like the people educated in Germany in the old days. I've none of that. I hate the idea that you ought to read the whole of anybody. But I've done a lot of looking sometimes, read quite a lot.

INTERVIEWER: When you were in England did you find yourself reading the kind of poetry Pound was reading?

FROST: No. Pound was reading the troubadours.

INTERVIEWER: Did you talk to one another about any particular poets?

FROST: He admired at that time, when I first met him, Robinson and de la Mare. He got over admiring de la Mare anyway, and I think he threw out Robinson too. We'd just bring up a couple of little poems. I was around with him quite a little for a few weeks. I was charmed with his ways. He cultivated a certain rudeness to people that he didn't like, just like Willy Whistler. I thought he'd come under the influence of Whistler. They cultivated the French style of boxing. They used to kick you in the teeth.

INTERVIEWER: With grace.

FROST: You know the song, the nasty song: 'They fight with their feet –' Among other things, what Pound did was show me Bohemia.

INTERVIEWER: Was there much Bohemia to see at that time?

FROST: More than I had ever seen. I'd never had any. He'd take me to restaurants and things. Showed me ju-jitsu in a restaurant. Threw me over his head.

INTERVIEWER: Did he do that?

FROST: Wasn't ready for him at all. I was just as strong as he was. He said, 'I'll show you, I'll show you. Stand up.' So I stood up, gave him my hand. He grabbed my wrist, tipped over backwards and threw me over his head.

INTERVIEWER: How did you like that?

FROST: Oh, it was all right. Everybody in the restaurant

stood up. He used to talk about himself as a tennis player. I never played tennis with him. And then he'd show you all these places with these people that specialized in poets that dropped their aitches and things like that. Not like the 'beatniks', quite. I remember one occasion they had a poet in who had a poem in the *English Review* on Aphrodite, how he met Aphrodite at Leatherhead.* He was coming in and he was a navvy. I don't remember his name, never heard of him again – he may have gone on and had books. But he was a real navvy. Came in with his bicycle clips on. Tea party. Everybody horrified in a delighted way, you know. Horror, social horror. Red-necked, thick, heavy-built fellow, strong fellow, you know, like John L. Lewis or somebody. But he was a poet. And then I saw poets made out of whole cloth by Ezra. Ezra thought he did that. Take a fellow that had never written anything and think he could make a poet out of him. We won't go into that.

INTERVIEWER: I wonder about your reaction to such articles as the recent lead article by Karl Shapiro in the *New York Times Book Review* which praised you because presumably you're not guilty of 'Modernism' as Pound and Eliot are. [*Telephone rings.*]

FROST: Is that my telephone? Just wait a second. Halt! [*Interruption. Frost leaves for phone call.*]

FROST: Where were we? Oh yes, you were trying to trace me.

INTERVIEWER: I wasn't trying to trace you. I was –

FROST: Oh, this thing about Karl Shapiro. Yeah, isn't it funny? So often they ask me – I just been all around, you

* Frost is thinking of a poet named John Helston, author of 'Aphrodite at Leatherhead', which took up fourteen pages of the *English Review* for March 1913. Frost's recollection gives a special flavour, if one is needed, to the note appended to the poem by the editors of the magazine: 'Without presuming to "present" Mr Helston after the manner of fashionable actors, we think it will interest the public to know that he was for years a working mechanic – turner, fitter, etc. – in electrical, locomotive, motor-car, and other workshops.'

know, been out West, been all around – and so often they
ask me, 'What is a modern poet?' I dodge it often, but I
said the other night, 'A modern poet must be one that
speaks to modern people no matter when he lived in the
world. That would be one way of describing it. And it
would make him more modern, perhaps, if he were *alive*
and speaking to modern people.'

INTERVIEWER: Yes, but in their way of speaking, Eliot
and Pound seem to many people to be writing in a tradition that is very different from yours.

FROST: Yes. I suppose Eliot's isn't as far away as Pound's.
Pound seemed to me very like a troubadour, more like the
troubadours or a blend of several of them, Bertrand de
Born and Arnault Daniel. I never touched that. I don't
know Old French. I don't like foreign languages that I
haven't had. I don't read translations of things. I like to say
dreadful, unpleasant things about Dante. Pound, though,
he's supposed to know Old French.

INTERVIEWER: Pound was a good linguist, wasn't he?

FROST: I don't know that. There's a teacher of his down
in Florida that taught him at the University of Pennsylvania. He once said to me, 'Pound? I had him in Latin, and
Pound never knew the difference between a declension and
a conjugation.' He's death on him. Old man, still death on
Ezra. [*Breaks into laughter.*] Pound's gentle art of making
enemies.

INTERVIEWER: Do you ever hear from Pound? Do you
correspond with him now?

FROST: No. He wrote me a couple of letters when I got
him out of jail last year. Very funny little letters, but they
were all right.

INTERVIEWER: Whom did you speak to in Washington
about that?

FROST: Just the Attorney General. Just settled it with
him. I went down twice with Archie [MacLeish] and we
didn't get anything done because they were of opposite
parties, I think. And I don't belong to any party.

INTERVIEWER: Yes, but weren't you named Robert Lee
because your father was a staunch Democrat around the

time of the Civil War? That makes you a Democrat of sorts, doesn't it?

FROST: Yeah, I'm a Democrat. I was born a Democrat – and been unhappy ever since 1896. Somebody said to me, 'What's the difference between that and being a Republican?' Well, I went down after we'd failed, and after Archie thought we'd failed, I just went down alone, walked into the Attorney-General's office and said, 'I come down here to see what your mood is about Ezra Pound.' And two of them spoke up at once. 'Our mood's your mood; let's get him out.' Just like that, that's all. And I said, 'This week?' They said, 'This week if you say so. You go get a lawyer, and we'll raise no objection.' So, since they were Republicans, I went over and made friends with Thurman Arnold, that good leftish person, for my lawyer. I sat up that night and wrote an appeal to the court that I threw away, and, in the morning, just before I left town, I wrote another one, a shorter one. And that's all there was to it. Ezra thanked me in a very short note that read: 'Thanks for what you're doing. A little conversation would be in order.' Then signed, in large letters. And then he wrote me another one, a nicer one.

INTERVIEWER: Did you see him before he left for Italy?

FROST: No, no, I didn't want to high-hat him. I wanted him to feel kind of free from me. But he feels, evidently, a little gratitude of some kind. He's not very well, you know. Some of them didn't want ... [*What Frost was about to say here, it turned out later in the interview, not recorded, was that some friends of Pound – he mentioned Merrill Moore – felt Pound would be better off staying in St Elizabeth's Hospital. Moore said that Pound had a room to himself and a cabana!*] Well, it's a sad business. And he's a poet. I never, I never questioned that. We've been friends all the way along, but I didn't like what he did in war-time. I only heard it second-hand, so I didn't judge it too closely. But it sounded pretty bad. He was very foolish in what he bet on and whenever anybody really loses that way, I don't want to rub it into him.

INTERVIEWER: I've been asking a lot of questions about

the relationship of your poetry to other poetry, but of course there are many other non-literary things that have been equally important. You've been very much interested in science, for example.

FROST: Yes, you're influenced by the science of your time, aren't you? Somebody noticed that all through my book there's astronomy.

INTERVIEWER: Like 'The Literate Farmer and the Planet Venus'?

FROST: Yes, but it's all through the book, all through the book. Many poems – I can name twenty that have astronomy in them. Somebody noticed that the other day: 'Why has nobody ever seen how much you're interested in astronomy?' That's a bias, you could say. One of the earliest books I hovered over, hung around, was called *Our Place among the Infinities*, by an astronomer in England named Proctor, noted astronomer. It's a noted old book. I mention that in one of the poems: I use that expression 'our place among the infinities' from that book that I must have read as soon as I read any book, thirteen or fourteen years, right in there I began to read. That along with *Scottish Chiefs*. I remember that year when I first began to read a book through. I had a little sister who read everything through, lots of books, everybody's books – very young, precocious. Me, I was – they turned me out of doors for my health.

INTERVIEWER: While we're thinking about science and literature, I wonder if you have any reaction to the fact that Massachusetts Institute of Technology is beginning to offer a number of courses in literature?

FROST: I think they'd better tend to their higher mathematics and higher science. Pure science. They know I think that. I don't mean to criticize them too much. But you see it's like this: the greatest adventure of man is science, the adventure of penetrating into matter, into the material universe. But the adventure is our property, a human property, and the best description of us is the humanities. Maybe the scientists wanted to remind their students that the humanities describe you who are adventuring into science,

and science adds very little to that description of you, a
little tiny bit. Maybe in psychology, or in something like
that, but it's awful little. And so, the scientists to remind
their students of all this give them half their time over
there in the humanities now. And that seems a little unnecessary. They're worried about us and the pure sciences
all the time. They'd better get as far as they can into their
own subject. I was over there at the beginning of this and
expressed my little doubts about it. I was there with Comp-
ton one night – he was sitting on the platform beside me.
'We've been short' – I turned to him before the audience –
'we've been a little short in pure science, haven't we?' He
said, 'Perhaps – I'm afraid we may have been.' I said, 'I
think that better be tended to.' That's years ago.

INTERVIEWER: You just mentioned psychology. You
once taught psychology, didn't you?

FROST: That was entirely a joke. I could teach psychology. I've been asked to join a firm of psychiatrists, you
know [by Merrill Moore], and that's more serious. But I
went up there to disabuse the Teachers' College of the idea
that there is any immediate connection between any psychology and their classroom work, disabuse them of the
notion that they could mesmerize a class if they knew
enough psychology. That's what they thought.

INTERVIEWER: Weren't you interested at one time in
William James?

FROST: Yes, that was partly what drew me back to Harvard. But he was away all the time I was around here. I
had Santayana, Royce, and all that philosophy crowd, Mun-
sterberg, George Herbert Palmer, the old poetical one. I
had 'em all. But I was there waiting for James, and I lost
interest.

INTERVIEWER: Did Santayana interest you very much
at that time?

FROST: No, not particularly. Well, yes. I always wondered what he really meant, where he was headed, what it
all came to. Followed that for years. I never knew him personally. I never knew anybody personally in college. I was
kind of – went my own way. But I admired him. It was a

golden utterance – he was something to listen to, just like his written style. But I wondered what he really meant. I found years afterward somewhere in his words that all was illusion, of two kinds, true or false. And I decided false illusion would be the truth: two negatives make an affirmative.

INTERVIEWER: While we're on things other than poetry that you were and are interested in, we might get on to politics for a moment. I remember one evening your mentioning that Henry Wallace became somehow associated with your poem, 'Provide, Provide'.

FROST: People exaggerate such things. Henry Wallace was in Washington when I read the poem. Sat right down there in the first row. And when I got to the end of it where it says, 'Better to go down dignified – With boughten friendship at your side – Than none at all. Provide, Provide!' I added, 'Or somebody else will provide for ya.' He smiled; his wife smiled. They were right down there where I could see them.

INTERVIEWER: Well, you don't have a reputation for being a New Dealer.

FROST: They think I'm no New Dealer. But really and truly I'm not, you know, all that clear on it. In 'The Death of the Hired Man' that I wrote long, long ago, long before the New Deal, I put it two ways about home. One would be the manly way: 'Home is the place where, when you have to go there, They have to take you in.' That's the man's feeling about it. And then the wife says, 'I should have called it/Something you somehow hadn't to deserve.' That's the New Deal, the feminine way of it, the mother way. You don't have to deserve you mother's love. You have to deserve your father's. He's more particular. One's a Republican, one's a Democrat. The father is always a Republican towards his son, and his mother's always a Democrat. Very few have noticed that second thing: they've always noticed the sarcasm, the hardness of the male one.

INTERVIEWER: That poem is often anthologized, and I wonder if you feel that the poems of yours that appear most often in the anthologies represent you very well.

FROST: I'm always pleased when somebody digs up a new one. I don't know. I leave that in the lap of the gods, as they say.

INTERVIEWER: There are some I seldom see; for example, 'A Servant to Servants' or 'The Most of It' or 'The Subverted Flower'. All of these I noticed the other day are omitted, for instance, from Untermeyer's anthology of your poems. Strange, isn't it?

FROST: Well, he was making his own choice. I never said a word to him, never urged him. I remember he said [Edward Arlington] Robinson only did once. Robinson told him, 'If you want to please an old man you won't overlook my "Mr Flood's Party".' That is a beautiful poem.

INTERVIEWER: Do you feel that any particular area of your work hasn't been anthologized?

FROST: I wouldn't know that. 'The Subverted Flower', for instance, nobody's ever touched. No – I guess it is; it's in Matty's [F. O. Matthiessen's] anthology. That's the one he made for the Oxford people.

INTERVIEWER: Yes, but its appearance is extremely rare in any selection of your work. It doesn't seem to fit some people's preconceptions about you. Another neglected poem, and an especially good one, is 'Putting In the Seed'.

FROST: That's – sure. They leave that sort of thing out; they overlook that sort of thing with me. The only person ever noticed that was a hearty old friend of mine down at the University of Pennsylvania, Cornelius Weygandt.* He said, 'I know what *that's* about.'

INTERVIEWER: Do you ever read that poem in public?

FROST: No, I don't bother with those. No, there are certain ones. I wouldn't read 'The Subverted Flower' to anybody outside. It isn't that I'm afraid of them, but I don't want them out. I'm shy about certain things in my books, they're more – I'd rather they'd be read. A woman asked me, 'What do you mean by that "subverted flower"?' I said, 'Frigidity in women.' She left.

INTERVIEWER: Do you think that it was to correct the

* Author of historical and descriptive studies of New Hampshire.

public assumption that your poetry is represented by the most anthologized pieces such as 'Birches' that Lionel Trilling in his speech at your eighty-fifth birthday emphasized poems of a darker mood?

FROST: I don't know – I might run my eye over my book after Trilling, and wonder why he hadn't seen it sooner: that there's plenty to be dark about, you know. It's full of darkness.

INTERVIEWER: Do you suppose he imagined he was correcting some sort of public ignorance – some general mistake about your work?

FROST: He made the mistake himself. He was admitting he made it himself, wasn't he? He was telling what trouble he'd had to get at me. Sort of confession, but very pleasant.

INTERVIEWER: That's true, but many admirers of yours did object to his emphasis on the 'darkness' or 'terror' in your poems.

FROST: Yes, well, he took me a little by surprise that night. He was standing right beside me and I had to get up right after him. Birthday party. And it took me – it didn't hurt me, but I thought at first he was attacking me. Then when he began comparing me to Sophocles and D. H. Lawrence I was completely at sea. What the two of them had to do with me, you know. Might be I might like it about Sophocles, but I'd be puzzled, oh, utterly at sea about D. H. Lawrence. It's all right, though. I had to get up and recite soon after that, and so I was a little puzzled what to recite to illustrate what he was talking about. And right there – new to me: I hadn't read his paper. I'd never read him much. I don't read criticism. You see no magazines in the house.

INTERVIEWER: Did you feel better about his talk when you read his substantiation of it in the *Partisan Review*?

FROST: I read his defence of it. Very clever, very – very interesting. Admired him. He's a very – intellectual man. But I read very little, generally, in the magazines. Hadn't read that Shapiro thing you mentioned. That's news to me what he said. Is he a friend of mine?

INTERVIEWER: Oh, yes. He's a friend of yours, but he's

like many friends of yours: he chooses to see in you something more simple than your best friends see. It's a bit like J. Donald Adams, also in *The Times*, angrily defending you against Trilling, only J. Donald Adams doesn't understand you very well either.

FROST: What was Shapiro saying?

INTERVIEWER: He was saying that most modern poetry is obscure and over-difficult, that this is particularly true of Pound and Eliot, but that it isn't true of you.

FROST: Well, I don't want to be difficult. I like to fool – oh, you know, you like to be mischievous. But not in that dull way of just being dogged and doggedly obscure.

INTERVIEWER: The difficulty of your poetry is perhaps in your emphasis on variety in tones of voice. You once said that consciously or unconsciously it was tones of voice that you counted on to double the meaning of every one of your statements.

FROST: Yes, you could do that. Could unsay everything I said, nearly. Talking contraries – it's in one of the poems. Talk by contraries with people you're very close to. They know what you're talking about. This whole thing of suggestiveness and *double entendre* and hinting – comes down to the word 'hinting'. With people you can trust you can talk in hints and suggestiveness. Families break up when people take hints you don't intend and miss hints you do intend. You can watch that going on, as a psychologist. I don't know. No, don't ... no don't you ... don't think of me ... See, I haven't led a literary life. These fellows, they *really* work away with their prose trying to describe themselves and understand themselves, and so on. I don't do that. I don't want to know too much about myself. It interests me to know that Shapiro thinks I'm not difficult. That's all right. I never wrote a review in my life, never wrote articles. I'm constantly refusing to write articles. These fellows are all literary men. I don't have hours; I don't work at it, you know. I'm not a farmer, that's no pose of mine. But I have farmed some, and I putter around. And I walk and I live with other people. Like to talk a lot. But I haven't had a very literary life, and I'm never very much with the gang. I'm vice-president, no, I'm Honorary President of the Poetry Society of America. Once in a great while I go. And I wish them well. I wish the foundations would take them all, take care of them all.

INTERVIEWER: Speaking of foundations, why do you think big business, so long the object of literary ridicule for being philistine, should now be supporting so much literary effort?

FROST: It's funny they haven't sooner, because most of them have been to college and had poetry pushed into them. About half the reading they do in all languages will be in verse. Just think of it. And so they have a kind of respect for it all and they probably don't mind the abuse they've had from our quarter. They're people who're worried that we just don't have enough imagination – it's the lack of imagination they're afraid of in our system. If we had enough imagination we could lick the Russians. I feel like saying, 'Probably we won the Civil War with Emily Dickinson.' We didn't even know she was there. Poor little thing.

INTERVIEWER: Would you agree that there are probably more good prizes for poetry today than there are good poets?

FROST: I don't know. I hate to judge that. It's nice for them – it's so nice for them to be interested in us, with their foundations. You don't know what'll come of it. You know the real thing is that the sense of sacrifice and risk is one of the greatest stimuli in the world. And you take that all out of it – take that away from it so that there's no risk in being a poet, I bet you'd lose a lot of the pious spirits. They're in it for the – hell of it. Just the same as these fellows breaking through the sound barrier up there, just the same. I was once asked in public, in front of four or five hundred women, just how I found leisure to write. I said, 'Confidentially – since there's only five hundred of you here, and all women – like a sneak I stole some of it, like a man I seized some of it – and I had a little in my tin cup.' Sounds as if I'd been a beggar, but I've never been consciously a beggar. I've been at the mercy of ... I've been a beneficiary around colleges and all. And this is one of the advantages to the American way: I've never had to write a word of thanks to anybody I had a cent from. The colleges came between. Poetry has always been a beggar. Scholars have also been beggars, but they delegate their begging to the president of the college to do for them.

INTERVIEWER: I was suggesting just now that perhaps the number of emoluments for poets greatly exceeds the number of people whose work deserves to be honoured. Isn't this a situation in which mediocrity will necessarily be exalted? And won't this make it more rather than less difficult for people to recognize really good achievement when it does occur?

FROST: You know, I was once asked that, and I said I never knew how many disadvantages anyone needed to get anywhere in the world. And you don't know how to measure that. No psychology will ever tell you who needs a whip and who needs a spur to win races. I think the greatest thing about it with me has been this, and I wonder if others think it. I look at a poem as a performance. I look on the poet as a man of prowess, just like an athlete. He's a performer. And the things you can do in a poem are very various. You speak of figures, tones of voice varying all the time. I'm always interested, you know, when I have three or four stanzas, in the way I *lay* the sentences in them. I'd hate to have the sentences all lie the same in the stanzas. Every poem is like that: some sort of achievement in performance. Somebody has said that poetry among other things is the marrow of wit. That's probably way back somewhere – marrow of wit. There's got to be wit. And that's very, very much left out of a lot of this laboured stuff. It doesn't sparkle at all. Another thing to say is that every thought, poetical or otherwise, every thought is a feat of association. They tell of old Gibbon – as he was dying he was the same Gibbon as his historical parallels. All thought is a feat of association: having what's in front of you bring up something in your mind that you almost didn't know you knew. Putting this and that together. That click.

INTERVIEWER: Can you give an example of how this feat of association – as you call it – works?

FROST: Well, one of my masques turns on one association like that. God says, 'I was just showing off to the Devil, Job.' Job looks puzzled about it, distressed a little. God says, 'Do you mind?' And, 'No, no,' he says, 'No,' in that tone, you know, 'No,' and so on. That tone is everything, the way you say that 'no'. I noticed that – that's what made me write that. Just that one thing made that.

INTERVIEWER: Did your other masque – *Masque of Mercy* – have a similar impetus?

FROST: I noticed that the first time in the world's history when mercy is entirely the subject is in Jonah. It does say somewhere earlier in the Bible, 'If ten can be found in the city, will you spare it? Ten good people?' But in Jonah there is something worse than that. Jonah is told to go and prophesy against the city – and he *knows* God will let him down. He can't trust God to be unmerciful. You can trust God to be anything but unmerciful. So he ran away and – and got into a whale. That's the point of that and nobody notices it. They miss it.

INTERVIEWER: Why do you suppose, Mr Frost, that among religious groups the masques had their best reception among Jesuits and rabbis?

FROST: Amusing you say that – that's true. The other, the lesser sects without the law, you see, they don't get it. They're too apt to think there's rebellion in them – what they go through with their parents when they're growing up. But that isn't in them at all, you know. They're not rebellious. They're very doctrinal, very orthodox, both of them. But how'd you notice that? It's amusing to me too. You see, the rabbis have been fine to me and so have the S Js particularly, all over the country. I've just been in Kansas City staying with them. See, the masques are full of good orthodox doctrine. One of them turns on the thought that evil shows off to good and good shows off to evil. I made a couplet out of that for them in Kansas City, just the way I often do, offhand: 'It's from their having stood contrasted/That good and bad so long have lasted.'

INTERVIEWER: Making couplets 'offhand' is something like writing on schedule, isn't it? I know a young poet who claims he can write every morning from six to nine, presumably before class.

FROST: Well, there's more than one way to skin a cat. I don't know what that would be like, myself. When I get going on something, I don't want to just – you know ... Very first one I wrote I was walking home from school and I began to make it – a March day – and I was making it all afternoon and making it so I was late at my grandmother's for dinner. I finished it, but it burned right up, just burned right up, you know. And what started that? What burned it? So many talk, I wonder how falsely, about what it costs them, what agony it is to write. I've often been quoted: 'No tears in the writer, no tears in the reader. No surprise for the writer, no surprise for the reader.' But another distinction I made is: however sad, no grievance, grief without grievance. How could I, how could anyone have a good time with what cost me too much agony, how could they? What do I want to communicate but what a *hell* of a good time I had writing it? The whole thing is performance and prowess and feats of association. Why don't critics talk about those things – what a feat it was to turn that that way, and what a feat it was to remember that, to be reminded of that by this? Why don't they talk about that? Scoring. You've got to *score*. They say not, but you've got to score, in all the realms – theology, politics, astronomy, history, and the country life around you.

INTERVIEWER: What do you think of the performance of the poets who have made your birthplace, San Francisco, into their headquarters?

FROST: Have they? Somebody said I saw a lot of them in Kansas City at the end of my audience. They said, 'See that blur over there? That's whiskers.' No, I don't know much about that. I'm waiting for them to say something that I can get hold of. The worse the better. I like it anyway, you know. Like you say to somebody, 'Say something. Say something.' And he says, 'I burn.'

INTERVIEWER: Do young poets send you things?

FROST: Yes, some – not much, because I don't respond. I don't write letters and all that. But I get a little, and I meet them, talk with them. I get some books. I wonder what they're at. There's one book that sounded as if it might be good, 'Aw, hell'. The book was called 'Aw, hell'. Because 'aw', the way you say 'aw', you know, 'Aw, hell!' That might be something.

INTERVIEWER: Most of the titles are funny. One is called *Howl* and another *Gasoline*.

FROST: *Gasoline*, eh? I've seen a little of it, kicking round. I saw a bunch of nine of them in a magazine in Chicago when I was through there. They were all San Franciscans. Nothing I could talk about afterwards, though, either way. I'm always glad of anybody that says anything awful. I can use it. We're all like that. You've got to learn to enjoy a lot of things you don't like. And I'm always ready for somebody to say some outrageous thing. I feel like saying, 'Hold that now, long enough for me to go away and tell on you, won't you? Don't go back on it tomorrow.' Funny world.

INTERVIEWER: When you look at a new poem that might be sent to you, what is it usually that makes you want to read it all or not want to read it?

FROST: This thing of performance and prowess and feats of association – that's where it all lies. One of my ways of looking at a poem right away it's sent to me, right off, is to see if it's rhymed. Then I know just when to look at it. The rhymes come in pairs, don't they? And nine times out of ten with an ordinary writer, one of two of the terms is better than the other. One makeshift will do, and then they get another that's good, and then another makeshift, and then another one that's good. That is in the realm of performance, that's the deadly test with me. I want to be unable to tell which of those he thought of first. If there's any trick about it, putting the better one first so as to deceive me, I can tell pretty soon. That's all in the performance realm. They can belong to any school of thought they want to, Spinoza or Schopenhauer, it doesn't matter to me. A Cartesian I heard Poe called, a Cartesian philosopher, the other day ... tsssssss ...

INTERVIEWER: You once saw a manuscript of Dylan Thomas's where he'd put all the rhymes down first and then backed into them. That's clearly not what you mean by performance, is it?

FROST: See, that's very dreadful. It ought to be that you're thinking forward, with the feeling of strength that you're getting them good all the way, carrying out some intention more felt than thought. It begins. And what it is that guides us – what is it? Young people wonder about that, don't they? But I tell them it's just the same as when you feel a joke coming. You see somebody coming down the street that you're accustomed to abuse, and you feel it rising in you, something to say as you pass each other. Coming over him the same way. And where do these thoughts come from? Where does a thought? Something docs it to you. It's him coming toward you that gives you the animus, you know. When they want to know about inspiration, I tell them it's mostly animus.

Richard Poirier

EZRA POUND

Since his return to Italy, Ezra Pound has spent most of his time in the Tirol, staying at Castle Brunnenberg with his wife, his daughter Mary, his son-in-law Prince Boris de Rachewiltz, and his grandchildren. However, the mountains in this resort country near Merano are cold in the winter, and Mr Pound likes the sun. The interviewer was about to leave England for Merano, at the end of February, when a telegram stopped him at the door: 'Merano ice-bound. Come to Rome.'

Pound was alone in Rome, occupying a room in the apartment of an old friend named Ugo Dadone. It was the beginning of March and exceptionally warm. The windows and shutters of Pound's corner room swung open to the noises of the Via Angelo Poliziano. The interviewer sat in a large chair while Pound shifted restlessly from another chair to a sofa and back to the chair. Pound's impression on the room consisted of two suitcases and three books: the Faber Cantos, *a* Confucius, *and Robinson's edition of* Chaucer *which he was reading again.*

In the social hours of the evening – dinner at Crispi's, a tour among the scenes of his past, ice-cream at a café – Pound walked with the swaggering vigour of a young man. With his great hat, his sturdy stick, his tossed yellow scarf, and his coat, which he trailed like a cape, he was the lion of the Latin Quarter again. Then his talent for mimicry came forward, and laughter shook his grey beard.

During the daytime hours of the interview, which took three days, he spoke carefully and the questions sometimes tired him out. In the morning when the interviewer returned, Mr Pound was eager to revise the failures of the day before.

INTERVIEWER: You are nearly through the *Cantos* now, and this set me to wondering about their beginning. In

1916 you wrote a letter in which you talked about trying to write a version of Andreas Divus in Seafarer rhythms. This sounds like a reference to *Canto 1*. Did you begin the *Cantos* in 1916?

POUND: I began the Cantos about 1904, I suppose. I had various schemes, starting in 1904 or 1905. The problem was to get a form – something elastic enough to take the necessary material. It had to be a form that wouldn't exclude something merely because it didn't fit. In the first sketches, a draft of the present first *Canto* was the third.

Obviously you haven't got a nice little road map such as the middle ages possessed of Heaven. Only a musical form would take the material, and the Confucian universe as I see it is a universe of interacting strains and tensions.

INTERVIEWER: Had your interest in Confucius begun in 1904?

POUND: No, the first thing was this: you had six centuries that hadn't been packaged. It was a question of dealing with material that wasn't in the *Divina Commedia*. Hugo did a *Légende des Siècles* that wasn't an evaluative affair but just bits of history strung together. The problem was to build up a circle of reference – taking the modern mind to be the medieval mind with wash after wash of classical culture poured over it since the Renaissance. That was the psyche, if you like. One had to deal with one's own subject.

INTERVIEWER: It must be thirty or thirty-five years since you have written any poetry outside the *Cantos*, except for the Alfred Venison poems. Why is this?

POUND: I got to the point where, apart from an occasional lighter impulse, what I had to say fitted the general scheme. There has been a good deal of work thrown away because one is attracted to an historic character and then finds that he doesn't function within my form, doesn't embody a value needed. I have tried to make the *Cantos* historic (Vid. G. Giovannini, *re* relation history to tragedy. Two articles ten years apart in some philological periodical, not source material but relevant) but not fiction. The material one wants to fit in doesn't always work. If the stone isn't hard enough to maintain the form, it has to go out.

INTERVIEWER: When you write a *Canto* now, how do you plan it? Do you follow a special course of reading for each one?

POUND: One isn't necessarily reading. One is working on the life vouchsafed, I should think. I don't know about method. The *what* is so much more important than how.

INTERVIEWER: Yet when you were a young man, your interest in poetry concentrated on form. Your professionalism, and your devotion to technique, became proverbial. In the last thirty years, you have traded your interest in form for an interest in content. Was the change on principle?

POUND: I think I've covered that. Technique is the test of sincerity. If a thing isn't worth getting the technique to say, it is of inferior value. All that must be regarded as exercise. Richter in his *Treatise on Harmony*, you see, says, 'These are the principles of harmony and counterpoint; they have nothing whatever to do with composition, which is quite a separate activity.' The statement, which somebody made, that you couldn't write Provençal canzoni forms in English, is false. The question of whether it was advisable or not was another matter. When there wasn't the criterion of natural language without inversion, those forms were natural, and they realized them with music. In English the music is of a limited nature. You've got Chaucer's French perfection, you've got Shakespeare's Italian perfection, you've got Campion and Lawes. I don't think I got around to this kind of form until I got to the choruses in the *Trachiniae*. I don't know that I got to anything at all, really, but I thought it was an extension of the gamut. It may be a delusion. One was always interested in the implication of change of pitch in the union of *motz et son*, of the word and melody.

INTERVIEWER: Does writing the *Cantos*, now, exhaust all of your technical interest, or does the writing of translations, like the *Trachiniae* you just mentioned, satisfy you by giving you more fingerwork?

POUND: One sees a job to be done and goes at it. The *Trachiniae* came from reading the Fenollosa Noh plays for the new edition, and from wanting to see what would happen to a Greek play, given that same medium and the hope of its being performed by the Minorou company. The sight of Cathay in Greek, looking like poetry, stimulated crosscurrents.

INTERVIEWER: Do you think that free verse is particularly an American form? I imagine that William Carlos Williams probably does, and thinks of the iambic as English.

POUND: I like Eliot's sentence: 'No verse is *libre* for the man who wants to do a good job.' I think the best free verse comes from an attempt to get back to quantitative metre.

I suppose it may be *un*-English without being specifically *American*. I remember Cocteau playing drums in a jazz band as if it were a very difficult mathematical problem.

I'll tell you a thing that I think *is* an American form, and that is the Jamesian parenthesis. You realize that the person you are talking to hasn't got the different steps, and you go back over them. In fact the Jamesian parenthesis has immensely increased now. That I think is something that is definitely American. The struggle that one has when one meets another man who has had a lot of experience to find the point where the two experiences touch, so that he really knows what you are talking about.

INTERVIEWER: Your work includes a great range of experience, as well as of form. What do you think is the greatest quality a poet can have? Is it formal, or is it a quality of thinking?

POUND: I don't know that you can put the needed qualities in hierarchic order, but he must have a continuous curiosity, which of course does not make him a writer, but if he hasn't got that he will wither. And the question of doing anything about it depends on a persistent energy. A man like Agassiz is never bored, never tired. The transit from the reception of stimuli to the recording, to the correlation, that is what takes the whole energy of a lifetime.

INTERVIEWER: Do you think that the modern world has changed the ways in which poetry can be written?

POUND: There is a lot of competition that never was there before. Take the serious side of Disney, the Confucian side of Disney. It's in having taken an ethos, as he does in *Perri*, that squirrel film, where you have the values of courage and tenderness asserted in a way that everybody can understand. You have got an absolute genius there. You have got a greater correlation of nature than you have had since the time of Alexander the Great. Alexander gave orders to the fishermen that if they found out anything about fish that was interesting, a specific thing, they were to tell Aristotle. And with that correlation you got ichthyology to the scientific point where it stayed for two thousand years. And now one has got with the camera an *enormous* correlation of particulars. That capacity for making contact is a tremendous challenge to literature. It throws up the question of what needs to be done and what is superfluous.

INTERVIEWER: Maybe it's an opportunity, too. When you were a young man in particular, and even through the *Cantos*, you changed your poetic style again and again. You have never been content to stick anywhere. Were you consciously looking to extend your style? Does the artist *need* to keep moving?

POUND: I think the artist *has* to keep moving. You are trying to render life in a way that won't bore people and you are trying to put down what you see.

INTERVIEWER: I wonder what you think of contemporary movements. I haven't seen remarks of yours about poets more recent than Cummings, except for Bunting and Zukovsky. Other things have occupied you, I suppose.

POUND: One can't read everything. I was trying to find out a number of historic facts, and you can't see out of the back of your head. I do not think there is any record of a man being able to criticize the people that come after him. It is a sheer question of the amount of reading one man can do.

I don't know whether it is his own or whether it is a gem that he collected, but at any rate one of the things Frost said in London in 19 – whenever it was – 1912, was this: 'Summary of prayer: "Oh God, pay attention to *me*." ' And that is the approach of younger writers – not to divinity exactly! – and in general one has to limit one's reading to younger poets who are recommended by at least one other younger poet, as a sponsor. Of course a routine of that kind could lead to conspiracy, but at any rate . . .

As far as criticizing younger people, one has not the time to make a *comparative* estimate. People one is learning from, one does measure one against the other. I see a stirring now, but . . . For *general* conditions there is undoubtedly a *liveliness*. And Cal [Robert] Lowell is very good.

INTERVIEWER: You have given advice to the young all your life. Do you have anything special to say to them now?

POUND: To improve their curiosity and not to fake. But that is not enough. The mere registering of belly-ache and the mere dumping of the ash-can is not enough. In fact the University of Pennsylvania student *Punchbowl* used to have as its motto, 'Any damn fool can be spontaneous.'

INTERVIEWER: You once wrote that you had four useful hints from living literary predecessors, who were Thomas Hardy, William Butler Yeats, Ford Madox Ford, and Robert Bridges. What were these hints?

POUND: Bridges' was the simplest. Bridges' was a warning against homophones. Hardy's was the degree to which he would concentrate on the subject matter, not on the manner. Ford's in general was the *freshness* of language. And Yeats you say was the fourth? Well, Yeats by 1908 had written simple lyrics in which there were no departures from the natural order of words.

INTERVIEWER: You were secretary to Yeats in 1913 and 1914. What sort of thing did you go for?

POUND: Mostly reading aloud. Doughty's *Dawn in Britain*, and so on. And wrangling, you see. The Irish like contradiction. He tried to learn fencing at forty-five, which was amusing. He would thrash around with the foils like a whale. He sometimes gave the impression of being even a worse idiot than I am.

INTERVIEWER: There is an academic controversy about your influence on Yeats. Did you work over his poetry with him? Did you cut any of his poems in the way you cut *The Waste Land*?

POUND: I don't think I can remember anything like that.

I am sure I objected to particular expressions. Once out at Rapallo I tried for God's sake to prevent him from printing a thing. I told him it was rubbish. All he did was print it with a preface saying that I *said* it was rubbish.

I remember when Tagore had taken to doodling on the edge of his proofs, and they told him it was art. There was a show of it in Paris. 'Is this art?' Nobody was very keen on these doodlings, but of course so many people lied to him.

As far as the change in Yeats goes, I think that Ford Madox Ford might have some credit. Yeats never would have taken advice from Ford, but I think that Fordie helped him, via me, in trying to get towards a natural way of writing.

INTERVIEWER: Did anyone ever help you with your work as extensively as you helped others? I mean by criticism or cutting.

POUND: Apart from Fordie, rolling on the floor undecorously and holding his head in his hands, and groaning on one occasion, I don't think anybody helped me through my manuscripts. Ford's stuff appeared too loose then, but he led the fight against tertiary archaisms.

INTERVIEWER: You have been closely associated with visual artists — Gaudier-Brzeska and Wyndham Lewis in the vorticist movement, and later Picabia, Picasso, and Brancusi. Has this had anything to do with you as a writer?

POUND: I don't believe so. One looked at paintings in galleries and one might have found out something. 'The Game of Chess' poem shows the effect of modern abstract art, but vorticism from my angle was a renewal of the sense of construction. Colour went dead and Manet and the impressionists revived it. Then what I would call the sense of form was blurred, and vorticism, as distinct from cubism, was an attempt to revive the sense of form — the form you had in Piero della Francesca's *De Prospettive Pingendi*, his treatise on the proportions and composition. I got started on the idea of comparative forms before I left America. A fellow named Poole did a book on composition. I did have *some* things in my head when I got to London, and I *had* heard of

Catullus before I heard about modern French poetry. There's a bit of biography that might be rectified.

INTERVIEWER: I have wondered about your literary activities in America before you came to Europe. When did you first come over, by the way?

POUND: In 1898. At the age of twelve. With my great-aunt.

INTERVIEWER: Were you reading French poetry then?

POUND: No, I suppose I was reading Gray's 'Elegy in a Country Churchyard' or something. No, I wasn't reading French poetry. I was starting Latin next year.

INTERVIEWER: You entered college at fifteen, I believe?

POUND: I did it to get out of drill at Military Academy.

INTERVIEWER: How did you get started being a poet?

POUND: My grandfather on one side used to correspond with the local bank president in verse. My grandmother on the other side and her brothers used verse back and forth in their letters. It was taken for granted that anyone would write it.

INTERVIEWER: Did you learn anything in your university studies which helped you as a poet? I think you were a student for seven or eight years.

POUND: Only six. Well, six years and four months. I was writing all the time, especially as a graduate student. I started in freshman year studying Layamon's *Brut* and Latin. I got into college on my Latin; it was the only reason they *did* take me in. I did have the idea at fifteen, of making a general survey. Of course whether I was or wasn't a poet was a matter for the gods to decide, but at least it was up to me to find out what had been done.

INTERVIEWER: You taught for four months only, as I remember. But you know that now the poets in America are mostly teachers. Do you have any ideas on the connection of teaching in the university with writing poetry?

POUND: It is the economic factor. A man's got to get in his rent somehow.

INTERVIEWER: How did you manage all the years in Europe?

POUND: Oh, God. A miracle of God. My income gained

from October 1914 to October 1915 was £42.10.0. That figure is clearly engraved on my memory . . .

I was never too good a hand at writing for the magazines. I once did a satirical article for *Vogue*, I think it was. On a painter whom I did not admire. They thought I had got just the right tone and then Verhaeren died and they asked me to do a note on Verhaeren. And I went down and said, 'You want a nice bright snappy obituary notice of the gloomiest man in Europe.'

'What, a gloomy cuss, was he?'

'Yes,' I said. 'He wrote about peasants.'

'Peasants or pheasants?'

'Peasants.'

'Oh, I don't think we ought to touch it.'

That is the way I crippled my earning capacity by not knowing enough to keep quiet.

INTERVIEWER: I read somewhere – I think you wrote it – that you once tried to write a novel. Did that get anywhere?

POUND: It got, fortunately, into the fireplace at Langham Place. I think there were two attempts, before I had any idea whatever of what a novel ought to be.

INTERVIEWER: Did they have anything to do with 'Hugh Selwyn Mauberley?'

POUND: These were long before 'Mauberley'. 'Mauberley' was later, but it *was* the definite attempt to get the novel cut down to the size of verse. It really is 'Contacts and Life'. Wadsworth seemed to think 'Propertius' difficult because it was about Rome, so one applied the same thing to the contemporary outside.

INTERVIEWER: You said it was Ford who helped you towards a natural language, didn't you? Let's get back to London again.

POUND: One was hunting for a simple and natural language, and Ford was ten years older, and accelerated the process toward it. It was a continual discussion of that sort of thing. Ford knew the best of the people who were there before him, you see, and he had nobody to play with until Wyndham and I and my generation came along. He was definitely in opposition to the dialect, let us say, of Lionel Johnson and Oxford.

INTERVIEWER: You were for two or three decades at least in contact with all of the leading writers in English of the day and a lot of the painters, sculptors, and musicians. Of all these people, who were the most stimulating to you as an artist?

POUND: I saw most of Ford and Gaudier, I suppose. I should think that the people that I have written about were the most important to me. There isn't much revision to make there.

I may have limited my work, and limited the interest in it, by concentrating on the particular intelligence of particular people, instead of looking at the complete character and personality of my friends. Wyndham Lewis always claimed that I never *saw* people because I never noticed how wicked they were, what S.O.B.s they were. I wasn't the least interested in the vices of my friends, but in their intelligence.

INTERVIEWER: Was James a kind of standard for you in London?

POUND: When he died one felt there was no one to ask about anything. Up to then one felt someone knew. After I was sixty-five I had great difficulty in realizing that I was older than James had been when I met him.

INTERVIEWER: Did you know Remy de Gourmont personally? You've mentioned him frequently.

POUND: Only by letter. There was one letter, which Jean de Gourmont also considered important, where he said, 'Franchement d'écrire ce qu'on pense, seul plaisir d'un écrivain.'

INTERVIEWER: It is amazing that you could come to Europe and quickly associate yourself with the best living writers. Had you been aware of any of the poets writing in America before you left? Was Robinson anything to you?

POUND: Aiken tried to sell me Robinson and I didn't fall. This was in London too. I then dragged it out of him that there was a guy at Harvard doing funny stuff. Mr Eliot turned up a year or so later.

No, I should say that about 1900, you had Carman and

Hovey, Carwine and Vance Cheney. The impression then was that the American stuff wasn't *quite* as good as the English at any point. And you had Mosher's pirated editions of the English stuff. No, I went to London because I thought Yeats knew more about poetry than anybody else. I made my life in London by going to see Ford in the afternoons and Yeats in the evenings. By mentioning one to the other one could always start a discussion. That was the exercise. I went to study with Yeats and found that Ford disagreed with him. So then I kept on disagreeing with *them* for twenty years.

INTERVIEWER: In 1942, you wrote that you and Eliot disagreed by calling each other protestants. I wonder when you and Eliot diverged.

POUND: Oh, Eliot and I started diverging from the beginning. The fun of an intellectual friendship is that you diverge on something or other and agree on a few points. Eliot, having had the Christian patience of tolerance all his life and so forth, and working very hard, must have found me very trying. We started disagreeing about a number of things from the time we met. We also agreed on a few things and I suppose both of us must have been right about something or other.

INTERVIEWER: Well, was there a point at which poetically and intellectually you felt further apart than you had been?

POUND: There's the whole problem of the relation of Christianity to Confucianism, and there's the whole problem of the different brands of Christianity. There is the struggle for orthodoxy – Eliot for the Church, me gunning round for particular theologians. In one sense Eliot's curiosity would appear to have been focused on a smaller number of problems. Even that is too much to say. The actual outlook of the experimental generation was all a question of the private ethos.

INTERVIEWER: Do you think that as poets you felt a divergence on technical grounds, unrelated to your subject matter?

POUND: I should think the divergence was first a difference in subject matter. He has undoubtedly got a natural language. In the language in the plays, he seems to me to have made a very great contribution. And in being able to make contact with an extant milieu, and an extant state of comprehension.

INTERVIEWER: That reminds me of two operas – *Villon* and *Cavalcanti* – which you wrote. How did you come to compose music?

POUND: One wanted the word *and* the tune. One wanted great poetry *sung*, and the technique of the English opera libretto was not satisfactory. One wanted, with the quality of the texts of *Villon* and of *Cavalcanti*, to get something more extended than the single lyric. That's all.

INTERVIEWER: I suppose your interest in words to be sung was especially stimulated by your study of Provence. Do you feel that the discovery of Provençal poetry was your greatest breakthrough? Or perhaps the Fenollosa manuscripts?

POUND: The Provençal began with a very early interest, so that it wasn't really a discovery. And the Fenollosa was a windfall and one struggled against one's ignorance. One had the inside knowledge of Fenollosa's notes and the ignorance of a five-year-old child.

INTERVIEWER: How did Mrs Fenollosa happen to hit upon you?

POUND: Well, I met her at Sarojini Naidu's and she said that Fenollosa had been in opposition to all the profs and academes, and she had seen some of my stuff and said I was the only person who could finish up these notes as Ernest would have wanted them done. Fenollosa saw what needed to be done but he didn't have time to finish it.

INTERVIEWER: Let me change the subject now, and ask you some questions which are more biographical than literary. I have read that you were born in Hailey, Idaho, in 1885. I suppose it must have been pretty rough out there then?

POUND: I left at the age of eighteen months and I don't remember the roughness.

INTERVIEWER: You did not grow up in Hailey?

POUND: I did not grow up in Hailey.

INTERVIEWER: What was your family doing there when you were born?

POUND: Dad opened the Government Land Office out there. I grew up near Philadelphia. The suburbs of Philadelphia.

INTERVIEWER: The wild Indian from the West then was not . . .?

POUND: The wild Indian from the West is apocryphal, and the assistant assayer of the mint was not one of the most noted bandits of the frontier.

INTERVIEWER: I believe it's *true* that your grandfather built a railroad. What was the story of that?

POUND: Well, he got the railroad into Chippewa Falls, and they ganged up on him and would not let him buy any rails. That's in the *Cantos*. He went up to the north of New York State and found some rails on an abandoned road up there, bought them and had them shipped out, and then used his credit with the lumberjacks to get the road going to Chippewa Falls. What one learns in the home one learns in a way one doesn't learn in school.

INTERVIEWER: Does your particular interest in coinage start from your father's work at the mint?

POUND: You can go on for a long time on that. The government offices were more informal then, though I don't know that any other kids got in and visited. Now the visitors are taken through glass tunnels and see things from a distance, but you could then be taken around in the smelting room and see the gold piled up in the safe. You were offered a large bag of gold and told you could have it if you could take it away with you. You couldn't lift it.

When the Democrats finally came back in, they recounted all the silver dollars, four million dollars in silver. All the bags had rotted in these enormous vaults, and they were heaving it into the counting machines with shovels bigger than coal shovels. This spectacle of coin being shovelled around like it was litter – these fellows naked to the waist shovelling it around in the gas flares – things like that strike your imagination.

Then there's the whole technique of making metallic money. First, the testing of the silver is much more tricky than testing gold. Gold is simple. It is weighed, then refined and weighed again. You can tell the grade of the ore by the relative weights. But the test for silver is a cloudy solution; the accuracy of the eye in measuring the thickness of the cloud is an aesthetic perception, like the critical sense. I like the idea of the *fineness* of the metal. At that time, you see, gold bricks, and specimens of iron pyrites mistaken for gold, were brought up to Dad's office. You heard the talk about the last guy who brought a gold brick and it turned out to be fool's gold.

INTERVIEWER: I know you consider monetary reform the key to good government. I wonder by what process you moved from aesthetic problems toward governmental ones. Did the Great War, which slaughtered so many of your friends, do the moving?

POUND: The Great War came as a surprise, and certainly, to see the English – these people who had never done anything – get hold of themselves, fight it, was immensely impressive. But as soon as it was over they went dead, and then one spent the next twenty years trying to prevent the Second World War. I can't say exactly where my study of government started. I think the *New Age* office helped me to see the war not as a separate event but as part of a system, one war after another.

INTERVIEWER: One point of connection between literature and politics which you make in your writing interests me particularly. In the *A.B.C. of Reading* you say that good writers are those who keep the language efficient, and that this is their function. You dissociate this function from party. Can a man of the wrong party use language efficiently?

POUND: Yes. That's the whole trouble! A gun is just as good, no matter who shoots it.

INTERVIEWER: Can an instrument which is orderly be used to create disorder? Suppose good language is used to forward bad government? Doesn't bad government make bad language?

POUND: Yes, but bad language is *bound* to make in addition bad government, whereas good language is *not* bound to make bad government. That again is clear Confucius: if the orders aren't clear they can't be carried out. Lloyd George's laws were such a mess, the lawyers never knew what they meant. And Talleyrand proclaimed that they changed the meaning of words between one conference and another. The means of communication breaks down, and that of course is what we are suffering now. We are enduring the drive to work on the subconscious without appealing to the reason. They repeat a trade name with the music a few times, and then repeat the music without it so that the music will give you the name. I think of the *assault*. We suffer from the use of language to conceal thought and to withhold all vital and direct answers. There is the definite use of propaganda, forensic language, merely to conceal and mislead.

INTERVIEWER: Where do ignorance and innocence end and the chicanery begin?

POUND: There is natural ignorance and there is artificial ignorance. I should say at the present moment the artificial ignorance is about eighty-five per cent.

INTERVIEWER: What kind of action can you hope to take?

POUND: The only chance for victory over the brainwash is the right of every man to have his ideas judged one at a time. You never get clarity as long as you have these package words, as long as a word is used by twenty-five people in twenty-five different ways. That seems to me to be the first fight, if there is going to be any intellect left.

It is doubtful whether the individual soul is going to be allowed to survive at all. Now you get a Buddhist movement with everything *except* Confucius taken into it. An Indian Circe of negation and dissolution.

We are up against so many mysteries. There is the problem of benevolence, the point at which benevolence has ceased to be operative. Eliot says that they spend their time trying to imagine systems so perfect that nobody will have to be good. A lot of questions asked in that essay of Eliot's cannot be dodged, like the question of whether there need be any change from the Dantesquan scale of values or the Chaucerian scale of values. If so, how much? People who have lost reverence have lost a great deal. That was where I split with Tiffany Thayer. All these large words fall into clichés.

There is the mystery of the scattering, the fact that the people who presumably understand each other are geographically scattered. A man who fits in his milieu as Frost does, is to be considered a happy man.

Oh, the luck of a man like Mavrocordato, who is in touch with other scholars, so that there is somewhere where he can verify a point! Now for certain points where I want verification there is a fellow named Dazzi in Venice that I write to and he comes up with an answer, as it might be about the forged Donation of Constantine. But the advantages which were supposed to inhere in the university – where there are other people to *contrôl** opinion or to *contrôl* the data – were very great. It is crippling not to have had them. Of course I have been trying over a ten year period to get any member of an American faculty to mention any other member of his same faculty, in his own department or outside it, whose intelligence he respects or with whom he will discuss serious matters. In one case the gentleman regretted that someone else had *left* the faculty.

I have been unable to get straight answers out of people on what appeared to me to be vital questions. That may have been due to my violence or obscurity with which I framed the questions. Often, I think, so-called obscurity is not obscurity in the language but in the other person's not being able to make out *why* you are saying a thing. For instance the attack on 'Endymion' was complicated because Gifford and company couldn't see why the deuce Keats was doing it.

Another struggle has been the struggle to keep the value of a local and particular character, of a particular culture in this awful maelstrom, this awful avalanche toward uniformity. The whole fight is for the conservation of the individual soul. The enemy is the suppression of history;

* Pound indicates that he is using the French *contrôler*: 'to verify, check information, a fact.'

against us is the bewildering propaganda and brainwash, luxury and violence. Sixty years ago, poetry was the poor man's art: a man off on the edge of the wilderness, or Frémont, going off with a Greek text in his pocket. A man who wanted the best could have it on a lonely farm. Then there was the cinema, and now television.

INTERVIEWER: The political action of yours that everybody remembers is your broadcasts from Italy during the war. When you gave these talks, were you conscious of breaking the American law?

POUND: No, I was completely surprised. You see I had that promise. I was given the freedom of the microphone twice a week. 'He will not be asked to say anything contrary to his conscience or contrary to his duty as an American citizen.' I thought that covered it.

INTERVIEWER: Doesn't the law of treason talk about 'giving aid and comfort to the enemy', and isn't the enemy the country with whom we are at war?

POUND: I thought I was fighting for a constitutional point. I mean to say, I may have been completely nuts, but I certainly *felt* that it wasn't committing treason.

Wodehouse went on the air and the British asked him not to. Nobody asked me not to. There was no announcement until the collapse that the people who had spoken on the radio would be prosecuted.

Having worked for years to prevent war, and seeing the folly of Italy and America being at war –! I certainly wasn't telling the troops to revolt. I thought I was fighting an internal question of constitutional government. And if any man, any individual man, can say he has had a bad deal from me because of race, creed, or colour, let him come out and state it with particulars. The *Guide to Kulchur* was dedicated to Basil Bunting and Louis Zukovsky, a Quaker and a Jew.

I don't know whether you think the Russians ought to be in Berlin or not. I don't know whether I was doing any good or not, whether I was doing any harm. Oh, I was probably offside. But the ruling in Boston was that there is no treason without treasonable intention.

What I was right about was the conservation of individual

rights. If, when the executive or any other branch exceeds its legitimate powers, no one protests, you will lose all your liberties. My method of opposing tyranny was wrong over a thirty-year period; it had nothing to do with the Second World War in particular. If the individual, or heretic, gets hold of some essential truth, or sees some error in the system being practised, he commits so many marginal errors himself that he is worn out before he can establish his point.

The world in twenty years has piled up hysteria – anxiety over a third war, bureaucratic tyranny, and hysteria from paper forms. The immense and undeniable loss of freedoms, as they were in 1900, is undeniable. We have seen the acceleration in efficiency of the tyrannizing factors. It's enough to keep a man worried. Wars are made to make debt. I suppose there's a possible out in space satellites and other ways of making debt.

INTERVIEWER: When you were arrested by the Americans, did you then expect to be convicted? To be hanged?

POUND: At first I puzzled over having missed a cog somewhere. I expected to turn myself in and be asked about what I learned. I did and I wasn't. I know that I checked myself, on several occasions during the broadcasts, on reflecting that it was not up to me to do certain things, or to take service with a foreign country. Oh, it was paranoia to think one could argue against the usurpations, against the folks who got the war started to get America into it. Yet I hate the idea of obedience to something which is wrong.

Then later I was driven into the courtyard at Chiavari. They had been shooting them, and I thought I was finished then and there. Then finally a guy came in and said he was damned if he would hand me over to the Americans unless I wanted to be handed over to them.

INTERVIEWER: In 1942, when the war started for America, I understand you tried to leave Italy and come back to the United States. What were the circumstances of the refusal?

POUND: Those circumstances were by hearsay. I am a bit hazy in my head about a considerable period, and I think that ... I know that I had a chance to get as far as Lisbon, and be cooped up there for the rest of the war.

INTERVIEWER: Why did you want to get back to the States at that time?

POUND: I wanted to get back during the election, before the election.

INTERVIEWER: The election was in 1940, wasn't it?

POUND: That would be 1940. I don't honestly remember what happened. My parents were too old to travel. They would have had to stay there in Rapallo. Dad retired there on his pension.

INTERVIEWER: During those years in the war in Italy did you write poetry? The *Pisan Cantos* were written when you were interned. What did you write during those years?

POUND: Arguments, arguments, and arguments. Oh, I did some of the Confucius translation.

INTERVIEWER: How was it that you began to write poetry again only after you were interned? You didn't write any cantos at all during the war, did you?

POUND: Let's see — the Adams stuff came out just before the war shut off. No. There was *Oro e Lavoro*. I was writing economic stuff in Italian.

INTERVIEWER: Since your internment, you've published three collections of *Cantos*, *Thrones* just recently. You must be near the end. Can you say what you are going to do in the remaining *Cantos*?

POUND: It is difficult to write a paradiso when all the superficial indications are that you ought to write an apocalypse. It is obviously much easier to find inhabitants for an inferno or even a purgatorio. I am trying to collect the record of the top flights of the mind. I might have done better to put Agassiz on top instead of Confucius.

INTERVIEWER: Are you more or less stuck?

POUND: Okay, I am stuck. The question is, am I dead, as Messrs. A.B.C. might wish? In case I conk out, this is provisionally what I have to do: I must clarify obscurities; I must make clearer definite ideas or dissociations. I must find a verbal formula to combat the rise of brutality — the principle of order versus the split atom. There was a man in

the bughouse, by the way, who insisted that the atom had
never been split.

An epic is a poem containing history. The modern mind
contains heteroclite elements. The past epos has succeeded
when all or a great many of the answers were assumed, at
least between author and audience, or a great mass of
audience. The attempt in an experimental age is therefore
rash. Do you know the story: 'What are you drawing,
Johnny?'

'God.'

'But nobody knows what He looks like.'

'They will when I get through!'

That confidence is no longer obtainable.

There *are* epic subjects. The struggle for individual rights
is an epic subject, consecutive from jury trial in Athens to
Anselm versus William Rufus, to the murder of Becket and
to Coke and through John Adams.

Then the struggle appears to come up against a block. The
nature of sovereignty is epic matter, though it may be a bit
obscured by circumstance. Some of this *can* be traced,
pointed; obviously it has to be condensed to get into the
form. The nature of the individual, the heteroclite contents
of contemporary consciousness. It's the fight for light versus
subconsciousness; it demands obscurities and penumbras. A
lot of contemporary writing avoids inconvenient areas of
the subject.

I am writing to resist the view that Europe and civilization are going to Hell. If I am being 'crucified for an idea' –
that is, the coherent idea around which my muddles accumulated – it is probably the idea that European culture
ought to survive, that the best qualities of it ought to survive
along with whatever other cultures, in whatever universality.
Against the propaganda of terror and the propaganda of
luxury, have you a nice simple answer? One has worked on
certain materials trying to establish bases and axes of reference. In writing so as to be understood, there is always the
problem of rectification without giving up what is correct.
There is the struggle not to sign on the dotted line for the
opposition.

INTERVIEWER: Do the separate sections of the *Cantos*, now – the last three sections have appeared under separate names – mean that you are attacking particular problems in particular sections?

POUND: No. *Rock Drill* was intended to imply the necessary resistance in getting a certain main thesis across – hammering. I was not following the three divisions of the *Divine Comedy* exactly. One can't follow the Dantesquan cosmos in an age of experiment. But I have made the division between people dominated by emotion, people struggling upwards, and those who have some part of the divine vision. The thrones in Dante's *Paradiso* are for the spirits of the people who have been responsible for good government. The thrones in the Cantos are an attempt to move out from egoism and to establish some definition of an order possible or at any rate conceivable on earth. One is held up by the low percentage of reason which seems to operate in human affairs. *Thrones* concerns the states of mind of people responsible for something more than their personal conduct.

INTERVIEWER: Now that you come near the end, have you made any plans for revising the *Cantos*, after you've finished?

POUND: I don't know. There's need of elaboration, of clarification, but I don't know that a comprehensive revision is in order. There is no doubt that the writing is too obscure as it stands, but I hope that the order of ascension in the *Paradiso* will be towards a greater limpidity. Of course there ought to be a corrected edition because of errors that have crept in.

INTERVIEWER: Let me change the subject again, if I may. In all those years in St Elizabeth's, did you get a sense of contemporary America from your visitors?

POUND: The trouble with visitors is that you don't get enough of the opposition. I suffer from the cumulative isolation of not having had enough contact – fifteen years living more with ideas than with persons.

INTERVIEWER: Do you have any plans for going back to the States? Do you want to?

POUND: I undoubtedly want to. But whether it is nostalgia for America that isn't there any more or not I don't know. This is a difference between an abstract Adams-Jefferson-Adams-Jackson America, and whatever is really going on. I undoubtedly have moments when I should like very much to live in America. There are these concrete difficulties against the general desire. Richmond is a beautiful city, but you can't live in it unless you drive an automobile. I'd like at least to spend a month or two a year in the U.S.

INTERVIEWER: You said the other day that as you grew older you felt more American all the time. How does this work?

POUND: It works. Exotics were necessary as an attempt at a foundation. One is transplanted and grows, and one is pulled up and taken back to what one has been transplanted from and it is no longer there. The contacts aren't there and I suppose one reverts to one's organic nature and finds it merciful. Have you ever read Andy White's memoirs? He's the fellow who founded Cornell University. That was the period of euphoria, when everybody thought that all the good things in America were going to function, before the decline, about 1900. White covers a period of history that goes back to Buchanan on one side. He alternated between being Ambassador to Russia and head of Cornell.

INTERVIEWER: Your return to Italy has been a disappointment, then?

POUND: Undoubtedly. Europe was a shock. The shock of no longer feeling oneself in the centre of something is probably part of it. Then there is the incomprehension, Europe's incomprehension, of organic America. There are so many things which I, as an American, cannot say to a European with any hope of being understood. Somebody said that I am the last American living the tragedy of Europe.

Donald Hall

Note: Mr Pound's health made it impossible for him to finish proof-reading this interview. The text is complete, but may contain details which Mr Pound would have changed under happier circumstances.

T. S. ELIOT

The interview took place in New York, at the apartment of Mrs Louis Henry Cohn, of House of Books, Ltd., who is a friend of Mr and Mrs Eliot. The bookcases of the attractive living-room contain a remarkable collection of modern authors. On a wall near the entrance hangs a drawing of Mr Eliot, done by his sister-in-law, Mrs Henry Ware Eliot. An inscribed wedding photograph of the Eliots stands in a silver frame on a table. Mrs Cohn and Mrs Eliot sat on a sofa at one end of the room, while Mr Eliot and the interviewer faced each other in the centre. The microphone of a tape recorder lay on the floor between them.

Mr Eliot looked particularly well. He was visiting the United States briefly on his way back to London from a holiday in Nassau. He was tanned, and he seemed to have put on weight in the three years since the interviewer had seen him. Altogether, he looked younger and seemed jollier. He frequently glanced at Mrs Eliot during the interview, as if he were sharing with her an answer which he was not making.

The interviewer had talked with Mr Eliot previously in London. The small office at Faber and Faber, a few flights above Russell Square, displays a gallery of photographs on its walls: here is a large picture of Virginia Woolf, with an inset portrait of Pius XII; here are I. A. Richards, Paul Valéry, W. B. Yeats, Goethe, Marianne Moore, Charles Whibley, Djuna Barnes, and others. Many young poets have stared at the faces there, during a talk with Mr Eliot. One of them has told a story which illustrates some of the unsuspected in Mr Eliot's conversation. After an hour of serious literary discussion, Mr Eliot paused to think if he had a final word of advice; the young poet, an American, was about to go up to Oxford as Mr Eliot had done forty years before. Then, as gravely as if he were recommending salvation, Mr Eliot advised the purchase of long woollen under-

*wear because of Oxford's damp stone. Mr Eliot is able to
be avuncular while he is quite aware of comic disproportion
between manner and message.*

*Similar combinations modified many of the comments
which are reported here, and the ironies of gesture are in-
visible on the page. At times, actually, the interview moved
from the ironic and the mildly comic to the hilarious. The
tape is punctuated by the head-back Boom Boom of Mr
Eliot's laughter, particularly in response to mention of his
early derogation of Ezra Pound, and to a question about the
unpublished, and one gathers improper, King Bolo poems of
his Harvard days.*

INTERVIEWER: Perhaps I can begin at the beginning. Do
you remember the circumstances under which you began to
write poetry in St Louis when you were a boy?

ELIOT: I began I think about the age of fourteen, under
the inspiration of FitzGerald's *Omar Khayyam*, to write a
number of very gloomy and atheistical and despairing quatrains in the same style, which fortunately I suppressed completely – so completely that they don't exist. I never showed
them to anybody. The first poem that shows is one which
appeared first in the *Smith Academy Record*, and later in
The Harvard Advocate, which was written as an exercise for
my English teacher and was an imitation of Ben Jonson. He
thought it very good for a boy of fifteen or sixteen. Then I
wrote a few at Harvard, just enough to qualify for election
to an editorship on *The Harvard Advocate*, which I enjoyed. Then I had an outburst during my junior and senior
years. I became much more prolific, under the influence first
of Baudelaire and then of Jules Laforgue, whom I discovered
I think in my junior year at Harvard.

INTERVIEWER: Did anyone in particular introduce you
to the French poets? Not Irving Babbitt, I suppose?

ELIOT: No, Babbitt would be the last person! The one
poem that Babbitt always held up for admiration was Gray's
'Elegy'. And that's a fine poem but I think this shows certain limitations on Babbitt's part, God bless him. I have ad-
vertized my source, I think; it's Arthur Symons's book on

French poetry,* which I came across in the Harvard Union. In those days the Harvard Union was a meeting place for any undergraduate who chose to belong to it. They had a very nice little library, like the libraries in many Harvard houses now. I liked his quotations and I went to a foreign bookshop somewhere in Boston (I've forgotten the name and I don't know whether it still exists) which specialized in French and German and other foreign books and found Laforgue, and other poets. I can't imagine why that bookshop should have had a few poets like Laforgue in stock. Goodness knows how long they'd had them or whether there were any other demands for them.

INTERVIEWER: When you were an undergraduate, were you aware of the dominating presence of any older poets? Today the poet in his youth is writing in the age of Eliot and Pound and Stevens. Can you remember your own sense of the literary times? I wonder if your situation may not have been extremely different.

ELIOT: I think it was rather an advantage not having any living poets in England or America in whom one took any particular interest. I don't know what it would be like but I think it would be a rather troublesome distraction to have such a lot of domineering presences, as you call them, about. Fortunately we weren't bothered by each other.

INTERVIEWER: Were you aware of people like Hardy or Robinson at all?

ELIOT: I was slightly aware of Robinson because I read an article about him in *The Atlantic Monthly* which quoted some of his poems, and that wasn't my cup of tea at all. Hardy was hardly known to be a poet at that time. One read his novels, but his poetry only really became conspicuous to a later generation. Then there was Yeats, but it was the early Yeats. It was too much Celtic twilight for me. There was really nothing except the people of the '90s who had all died of drink or suicide or one thing or another.

INTERVIEWER: Did you and Conrad Aiken help each other with your poems, when you were co-editors on the *Advocate*?

* *The Symbolist Movement in Literature.*

ELIOT: We were friends but I don't think we influenced each other at all. When it came to foreign writers, he was more interested in Italian and Spanish, and I was all for the French.

INTERVIEWER: Were there any other friends who read your poems and helped you?

ELIOT: Well, yes. There was a man who was a friend of my brother's, a man named Thomas H. Thomas who lived in Cambridge and who saw some of my poems in *The Harvard Advocate*. He wrote me a most enthusiastic letter and cheered me up. And I wish I had his letters still. I was very grateful to him for giving me that encouragement.

INTERVIEWER: I understand that it was Conrad Aiken who introduced you and your work to Pound.

ELIOT: Yes it was. Aiken was a very generous friend. He tried to place some of my poems in London, one summer when he was over, with Harold Monro and others. Nobody would think of publishing them. He brought them back to me. Then in 1914, I think, we were both in London in the summer. He said, 'You go to Pound. Show him your poems.' He thought Pound might like them. Aiken liked them, though they were very different from his.

INTERVIEWER: Do you remember the circumstances of your first meeting with Pound?

ELIOT: I think I went to call on him first. I think I made a good impression, in his little triangular sitting-room in Kensington. He said, 'Send me your poems.' And he wrote back, 'This is as good as anything I've seen. Come around and have a talk about them.' Then he pushed them on Harriet Monroe, which took a little time.

INTERVIEWER: In an article about your *Advocate* days, for the book in honour of your sixtieth birthday, Aiken quotes an early letter from England in which you refer to Pound's verse as 'touchingly incompetent'. I wonder when you changed your mind.

ELIOT: Hah! That was a bit brash, wasn't it? Pound's verse was first shown me by an editor of *The Harvard Advocate*, W. G. Tinckom-Fernandez, who was a crony of mine and Conrad Aiken's and the other Signet* poets of the period. He showed me those little things of Elkin Mathews, *Exultations* and *Personae*.† He said, 'This is up your street; you ought to like this.' Well, I didn't, really. It seemed to me rather fancy old-fashioned romantic stuff, cloak-and-dagger kind of stuff. I wasn't very much impressed by it. When I went to see Pound, I was not particularly an admirer of his work, and though I now regard the work I saw then as very accomplished, I am certain that in his later work is to be found the grand stuff.

INTERVIEWER: You have mentioned in print that Pound cut *The Waste Land* from a much larger poem into its present form. Were you benefited by his criticism of your poems in general? Did he cut other poems?

ELIOT: Yes. At that period, yes. He was a marvellous critic because he didn't try to turn you into an imitation of himself. He tried to see what you were trying to do.

INTERVIEWER: Have you helped to rewrite any of your friends' poems? Ezra Pound's, for instance?

ELIOT: I can't think of any instances. Of course I have made innumerable suggestions on manuscripts of young poets in the last twenty-five years or so.

INTERVIEWER: Does the manuscript of the original, un-cut *Waste Land* exist?

ELIOT: Don't ask me. That's one of the things I don't know. It's an unsolved mystery. I sold it to John Quinn. I also gave him a notebook of unpublished poems, because he had been kind to me in various affairs. That's the last I heard of them. Then he died and they didn't turn up at the sale.

INTERVIEWER: What sort of thing did Pound cut from *The Waste Land*? Did he cut whole sections?

ELIOT: Whole sections, yes. There was a long section about a shipwreck. I don't know what that had to do with anything else, but it was rather inspired by the Ulysses Canto in *The Inferno*, I think. Then there was another section which was an imitation *Rape of the Lock*. Pound said,

* Harvard's literary club.

† Early books of Pound, published by Elkin Mathews in 1909.

'It's no use trying to do something that somebody else has done as well as it can be done. Do something different.'

INTERVIEWER: Did the excisions change the intellectual structure of the poem?

ELIOT: No. I think it was just as structureless, only in a more futile way, in the longer version.

INTERVIEWER: I have a question about the poem which is related to its composition. In *Thoughts after Lambeth* you denied the allegation of critics who said that you expressed 'the disillusionment of a generation' in *The Waste Land*, or you denied that it was your intention. Now F. R. Leavis, I believe, has said that the poem exhibits no progression; yet on the other hand, more recent critics, writing after your later poetry, found *The Waste Land* Christian. I wonder if this was part of your intention.

ELIOT: No, it wasn't part of my conscious intention. I think that in *Thoughts after Lambeth* I was speaking of intentions more in a negative than in a positive sense, to say what was not my intention. I wonder what an 'intention' means! One wants to get something off one's chest. One doesn't know quite what it is that one wants to get off the chest until one's got it off. But I couldn't apply the word 'intention' positively to any of my poems. Or to any poem.

INTERVIEWER: I have another question about you and Pound and your earlier career. I have read somewhere that you and Pound decided to write quatrains, in the late teens, because *vers libre* had gone far enough.

ELIOT: I think that's something Pound said. And the suggestion of writing quatrains was his. He put me on to *Emaux et Camées*.*

INTERVIEWER: I wonder about your ideas about the relation of form to subject. Would you then have chosen the form before you knew quite what you were going to write in it?

ELIOT: Yes, in a way. One studied originals. We studied Gautier's poems and then we thought, 'Have I anything to say in which this form will be useful?' And we experimented. The form gave the impetus to the content.

* Poems by Théophile Gautier.

INTERVIEWER: Why was *vers libre* the form you chose to use in your early poems?

ELIOT: My early *vers libre*, of course, was started under the endeavour to practise the same form as Laforgue. This meant merely rhyming lines of irregular length, with the rhymes coming in irregular places. It wasn't quite so *libre* as much as *vers*, especially the sort which Ezra called 'Amygism'.* Then, of course, there were things in the next phase which were freer, like 'Rhapsody on a Windy Night'. I don't know whether I had any sort of model or practice in mind when I did that. It just came that way.

INTERVIEWER: Did you feel, possibly, that you were writing against something, more than from any model? Against the poet laureate perhaps?

ELIOT: No. no, no. I don't think one was constantly trying to reject things, but just trying to find out what was right for oneself. One really ignored poet laureates as such, the Robert Bridges. I don't think good poetry can be produced in a kind of political attempt to overthrow some existing form. I think it just supersedes. People find a way in which they can say something. 'I can't say it that way, what way can I find that will do?' One didn't really *bother* about the existing modes.

INTERVIEWER: I think it was after 'Prufrock' and before 'Gerontion' that you wrote the poems in French which appear in your *Collected Poems*. I wonder how you happened to write them. Have you written any since?

ELIOT: No, and I never shall. That was a very curious thing which I can't altogether explain. At that period I thought I'd dried up completely. I hadn't written anything for some time and was rather desperate. I started writing a few things in French and found I *could*, at that period. I think it was that when I was writing in French I didn't take the poems so seriously, and that, not taking them seriously, I wasn't so worried about not being able to write. I did these things as a sort of *tour de force* to see what I could do. That went on for some months. The best of them have been

* A reference to Amy Lowell, who captured and transformed imagism.

printed. I must say that Ezra Pound went through them, and Edmond Dulac, a Frenchman we knew in London, helped with them a bit. We left out some, and I suppose they disappeared completely. Then I suddenly began writing in English again and lost all desire to go on with French. I think it was just something that helped me get started again.

INTERVIEWER: Did you think at all about becoming a French symbolist poet like the two Americans of the last century?

ELIOT: Stuart Merrill and Viélé-Griffin. I only did that during the romantic year I spent in Paris after Harvard. I had at that time the idea of giving up English and trying to settle down and scrape along in Paris and gradually write French. But it would have been a foolish idea even if I'd been much more bilingual than I ever was, because, for one thing, I don't think that one can be a bilingual poet. I don't know of any case in which a man wrote great or even fine poems equally well in two languages. I think one language must be the one you express yourself in in poetry, and you've got to give up the other for that purpose. And I think that the English language really has more resources in some respects than the French. I think, in other words, I've probably done better in English than I ever would have in French even if I'd become as proficient in French as the poets you mentioned.

INTERVIEWER: Can I ask you if you have any plans for poems now?

ELIOT: No, I haven't any plans for anything at the moment, except that I think I would like, having just got rid of *The Elder Statesman* (I only passed the final proofs just before we left London), to do a little prose writing of a critical sort. I never think more than one step ahead. Do I want to do another play or do I want to do more poems? I don't know until I find I want to do it.

INTERVIEWER: Do you have any unfinished poems that you look at occasionally?

ELIOT: I haven't much in that way, no. As a rule, with me an unfinished thing is a thing that might as well be rubbed out. It's better, if there's something good in it that I might make use of elsewhere, to leave it at the back of my mind than on paper in a drawer. If I leave it in a drawer it remains the same thing but if it's in the memory it becomes transformed into something else. As I have said before, *Burnt Norton* began with bits that had to be cut out of *Murder in the Cathedral*. I learned in *Murder in the Cathedral* that it's no use putting in nice lines that you think are good poetry if they don't get the action on at all. That was when Martin Browne was useful. He would say, 'There are very nice lines here, but they've nothing to do with what's going on on stage.'

INTERVIEWER: Are any of your minor poems actually sections cut out of longer works? There are two that sound like 'The Hollow Men'.

ELIOT: Oh, those were the preliminary sketches. Those things were earlier. Others I published in periodicals but not in my collected poems. You don't want to say the same thing twice in one book.

INTERVIEWER: You seem often to have written poems in sections. Did they begin as separate poems? I am thinking of 'Ash Wednesday', in particular.

ELIOT: Yes, like 'The Hollow Men', it originated out of separate poems. As I recall, one or two early drafts of parts of 'Ash Wednesday' appeared in *Commerce* and elsewhere. Then gradually I came to see it as a sequence. That's one way in which my mind does seem to have worked throughout the years poetically – doing things separately and then seeing the possibility of fusing them together, altering them, and making a kind of whole of them.

INTERVIEWER: Do you write anything now in the vein of *Old Possum's Book of Practical Cats* or *King Bolo*?

ELIOT: Those things do come from time to time! I keep a few notes of such verse, and there are one or two incomplete cats that probably will never be written. There's one about a glamour cat. It turned out too sad. This would never do. I can't make my children weep over a cat who's gone wrong. She had a very questionable career, did this cat. It wouldn't do for the audience of my previous volume of cats.

I've never done any dogs. Of course dogs don't seem to lend themselves to verse quite so well, collectively, as cats. I may eventually do an enlarged edition of my cats. That's more likely than another volume. I did add one poem, which was originally done as an advertisement for Faber and Faber. It seemed to be fairly successful. Oh, yes, one wants to keep one's hand in, you know, in every type of poem, serious and frivolous and proper and improper. One doesn't want to lose one's skill.

INTERVIEWER: There's a good deal of interest now in the process of writing. I wonder if you could talk more about your actual habits in writing verse. I've heard you composed on the typewriter.

ELIOT: Partly on the typewriter. A great deal of my new play, *The Elder Statesman*, was produced in pencil and paper, very roughly. Then I typed it myself first before my wife got to work on it. In typing myself I make alterations, very considerable ones. But whether I write or type, composition of any length, a play for example, means for me regular hours, say ten to one. I found that three hours a day is about all I can do of actual composing. I could do polishing perhaps later. I sometimes found at first that I wanted to go on longer, but when I looked at the stuff the next day, what I'd done after the three hours were up was never satisfactory. It's much better to stop and think about something else quite different.

INTERVIEWER: Did you ever write any of your non-dramatic poems on schedule? Perhaps the *Four Quartets*?

ELIOT: Only 'occasional' verse. The *Quartets* were not on schedule. Of course the first one was written in '35, but the three which were written during the war were more in fits and starts. In 1939 if there hadn't been a war I would probably have tried to write another play. And I think it's a very good thing I didn't have the opportunity. From my personal point of view, the one good thing the war did was to prevent me from writing another play too soon. I saw some of the things that were wrong with *Family Reunion*, but I think it was much better that any possible play was blocked for five years or so to get up a head of steam. The form of the

Quartets fitted in very nicely to the conditions under which I was writing, or could write at all. I could write them in sections and I didn't have to have quite the same continuity; it didn't matter if a day or two elapsed when I did not write, as they frequently did, while I did war jobs.

INTERVIEWER: We have been mentioning your plays without talking about them. In *Poetry and Drama* you talked about your first plays. I wonder if you could tell us something about your intentions in *The Elder Statesman*.

ELIOT: I said something, I think, in *Poetry and Drama* about my ideal aims, which I never expect fully to realize. I started, really, from *The Family Reunion*, because *Murder in the Cathedral* is a period piece and something out of the ordinary. It is written in rather a special language, as you do when you're dealing with another period. It didn't solve any of the problems I was interested in. Later I thought that in *The Family Reunion* I was giving so much attention to the versification that I neglected the structure of the play. I think *The Family Reunion* is still the best of my plays in the way of poetry, although it's not very well constructed.

In *The Cocktail Party* and again in *The Confidential Clerk*, I went further in the way of structure. *The Cocktail Party* wasn't altogether satisfactory in that respect. It sometimes happens, disconcertingly, at any rate with a practitioner like myself, that it isn't always the things constructed most according to plan that are the most successful. People criticized the third act of *The Cocktail Party* as being rather an epilogue, so in *The Confidential Clerk* I wanted things to turn up in the third act which were fresh events. Of course, *The Confidential Clerk* was so well constructed in some ways that people thought it was just meant to be farce.

I wanted to get to learn the technique of the theatre so well that I could then forget about it. I always feel it's not wise to violate rules until you know how to observe them.

I hope that *The Elder Statesman* goes further in getting more poetry in, at any rate, than *The Confidential Clerk* did. I don't feel that I've got to the point I aim at and I don't think I ever will, but I would like to feel I was getting a little nearer to it each time.

INTERVIEWER: Do you have a Greek model behind *The Elder Statesman*?

ELIOT: The play in the background is the *Oedipus at Colonus*. But I wouldn't like to refer to my Greek originals as models. I have always regarded them more as points of departure. That was one of the weaknesses of *The Family Reunion*; it was rather too close to the *Eumenides*. I tried to follow my original too literally and in that way led to confusion by mixing pre-Christian and post-Christian attitudes about matters of conscience and sin and guilt.

So in the subsequent three I have tried to take the Greek myth as a sort of springboard, you see. After all, what one gets essential and permanent, I think, in the old plays, is a situation. You can take the situation, rethink it in modern terms, develop your own characters from it, and let another plot develop out of that. Actually you get farther and farther away from the original. *The Cocktail Party* had to do with Alcestis simply because the question arose in my mind, what would the life of Admetus and Alcestis be, after she'd come back from the dead; I mean if there'd been a break like that, it couldn't go on just as before. Those two people were the centre of the thing when I started and the other characters only developed out of it. The character of Celia, who came to be really the most important character in the play, was originally an appendage to a domestic situation.

INTERVIEWER: Do you still hold to the theory of levels in poetic drama (plot, character, diction, rhythm, meaning) which you put forward in 1932?

ELIOT: I am no longer very much interested in my own theories about poetic drama, especially those put forward before 1934. I have thought less about theories since I have given more time to writing for the theatre.

INTERVIEWER: How does the writing of a play differ from the writing of poems?

ELIOT: I feel that they take quite different approaches. There is all the difference in the world between writing a play for an audience and writing a poem, in which you're writing primarily for yourself – although obviously you wouldn't be satisfied if the poem didn't mean something to other people afterwards. With a poem you can say, 'I got my feeling into words for myself. I now have the equivalent in words for that much of what I have felt.' Also in a poem you're writing for your own voice, which is very important. You're thinking in terms of your own voice, whereas in a play from the beginning you have to realize that you're preparing something which is going into the hands of other people, unknown at the time you're writing it. Of course I won't say there aren't moments in a play when the two approaches may not converge, when I think ideally they should. Very often in Shakespeare they do, when he is writing a poem and thinking in terms of the theatre and the actors and the audience all at once. And the two things are one. That's wonderful when you can get that. With me it only happens at odd moments.

INTERVIEWER: Have you tried at all to control the speaking of your verse by the actors? To make it seem more like verse?

ELIOT: I leave that primarily to the producer. The important thing is to have a producer who has the feeling of verse and who can guide them in just how emphatic to make the verse, just how far to depart from prose or how far to approach it. I only guide the actors if they ask me questions directly. Otherwise I think that they should get their advice through the producer. The important thing is to arrive at an agreement with him first, and then leave it to him.

INTERVIEWER: Do you feel that there's been a general tendency in your work, even in your poems, to move from a narrower to a larger audience?

ELIOT: I think that there are two elements in this. One is that I think that writing plays (that is *Murder in the Cathedral* and *The Family Reunion*) made a difference to the writing of the *Four Quartets*. I think that it led to a greater simplification of language and to speaking in a way which is more like conversing with your reader. I see the later *Quartets* as being much simpler and easier to understand than *The Waste Land* and 'Ash Wednesday'. Sometimes the thing I'm trying to say, the subject matter, may be difficult, but it seems to me that I'm saying it in a simpler way.

The other element that enters into it, I think, is just experience and maturity. I think that in the early poems it was a question of not being able to – of having more to say than one knew how to say, and having something one wanted to put into words and rhythm which one didn't have the command of words and rhythm to put in a way immediately apprehensible.

That type of obscurity comes when the poet is still at the stage of learning how to use language. You have to say the thing the difficult way. The only alternative is not saying it at all, at that stage. By the time of the *Four Quartets*, I couldn't have written in the style of *The Waste Land*. In *The Waste Land*, I wasn't even bothering whether I understood what I was saying. These things, however, become easier to people with time. You get used to having *The Waste Land*, or *Ulysses*, about.

INTERVIEWER: Do you feel that the *Four Quartets* are your best work?

ELIOT: Yes, and I'd like to feel that they get better as they go on. The second is better than the first, the third is better than the second, and the fourth is the best of all. At any rate, that's the way I flatter myself.

INTERVIEWER: This is a very general question, but I wonder if you could give advice to a young poet about what disciplines or attitudes he might cultivate to improve his art.

ELIOT: I think it's awfully dangerous to give general advice. I think the best one can do for a young poet is to criticize in detail a particular poem of his. Argue it with him if necessary; give him your opinion, and if there are any generalizations to be made, let him do them himself. I've found that different people have different ways of working and things come to them in different ways. You're never sure when you're uttering a statement that's generally valid for all poets or when it's something that only applies to yourself. I think nothing is worse than to try to form people in your own image.

INTERVIEWER: Do you think there's any possible generalization to be made about the fact that all the better poets now, younger than you, seem to be teachers?

ELIOT: I don't know. I think the only generalization that can be made of any value will be one which will be made a generation later. All you can say at this point is that at different times there are different possibilities of making a living, or different limitations on making a living. Obviously a poet has got to find a way of making a living apart from his poetry. After all, artists do a great deal of teaching, and musicians too.

INTERVIEWER: Do you think that the optimal career for a poet would involve no work at all but writing and reading?

ELIOT: No, I think that would be – but there again one can only talk about oneself. It is very dangerous to give an optimal career for everybody, but I feel quite sure that if I'd started by having independent means, if I hadn't had to bother about earning a living and could have given all my time to poetry, it would have had a deadening influence on me.

INTERVIEWER: Why?

ELIOT: I think that for me it's been very useful to exercise other activities, such as working in a bank, or publishing even. And I think also that the difficulty of not having as much time as I would like has given me a greater pressure of concentration. I mean it has prevented me from writing too much. The danger, as a rule, of having nothing else to do is that one might write too much rather than concentrating and perfecting smaller amounts. That would be *my* danger.

INTERVIEWER: Do you consciously attempt, now, to keep up with the poetry that is being written by young men in England and America?

ELIOT: I don't now, not with any conscientiousness. I did at one time when I was reading little reviews and looking out for new talents as a publisher. But as one gets older, one is not quite confident in one's own ability to distinguish new genius among younger men. You're always afraid that you are going as you have seen your elders go. At Faber and Faber now I have a younger colleague who reads poetry manuscripts. But even before that, when I came across new stuff that I thought had real merit, I would show it to younger friends whose critical judgement I trusted and get their opinion. But of course there is always the danger that there is merit where you don't see it. So I'd rather have younger people to look at things first. If they like it, they will show it to me, and see whether I like it too. When you get something that knocks over younger people of taste and judgement and older people as well, then that's likely to be something important. Sometimes there's a lot of resistance. I shouldn't like to feel that I was resisting, as my work was resisted when it was new, by people who thought that it was imposture of some kind or other.

INTERVIEWER: Do you feel that younger poets in general have repudiated the experimentalism of the early poetry of this century? Few poets now seem to be resisted the way you were resisted, but some older critics like Herbert Read believe that poetry after you has been a regression to out-dated modes. When you talked about Milton the second time, you spoke of the function of poetry as a retarder of change, as well as a maker of change, in language.

ELIOT: Yes, I don't think you want a revolution every ten years.

INTERVIEWER: But is it possible to think that there has been a counter-revolution rather than an exploration of new possibilities?

ELIOT: No, I don't see anything that looks to me like a counter-revolution. After a period of getting away from the traditional forms, comes a period of curiosity in making new experiments with traditional forms. This can produce very good work if what has happened in between has made a difference: when it's not merely going back, but taking up an old form, which has been out of use for a time, and making something new with it. That is not counter-revolution. Nor does mere regression deserve the name. There is a tendency in some quarters to revert to Georgian scenery and sentiments: and among the public there are always people who prefer mediocrity, and when they get it, say, 'What a relief! Here's some real poetry again.' And there are also people who like poetry to be modern but for whom the really creative stuff is too strong – they need something diluted.

What seems to me the best of what I've seen in young poets is not reaction at all. I'm not going to mention any names, for I don't like to make public judgements about younger poets. The best stuff is a further development of a less revolutionary character than what appeared in earlier years of the century.

INTERVIEWER: I have some unrelated questions that I'd like to end with. In 1945 you wrote, 'A poet must take as his material his own language as it is actually spoken around him.' And later you wrote, 'The music of poetry, then, will be a music latent in the common speech of his time.' After the second remark, you disparaged 'standardized B.B.C. English'. Now isn't one of the changes of the last fifty years, and perhaps even more of the last five years, the growing dominance of commercial speech through the means of communication? What you referred to as 'B.B.C. English' has become immensely more powerful through the I.T.A. and B.B.C. television, not to speak of C.B.S., N.B.C., and A.B.C. Does this development make the problem of the poet and his relationship to common speech more difficult?

ELIOT: You've raised a very good point there. I think you're right, it does make it more difficult.

INTERVIEWER: I wanted *you* to make the point.

ELIOT: Yes, but you wanted the point to be *made*. So I'll take the responsibility of making it: I do think that where you have these modern means of communication and means of imposing the speech and idioms of a small number on the mass of people at large, it does complicate the problem very much. I don't know to what extent that goes for film speech, but obviously radio speech has done much more.

INTERVIEWER: I wonder if there's a possibility that what you mean by common speech will disappear.

ELIOT: That is a very gloomy prospect. But very likely indeed.

INTERVIEWER: Are there other problems for a writer in

our time which are unique? Does the prospect of human annihilation have any particular effect on the poet?

ELIOT: I don't see why the prospect of human annihilation should affect the poet differently from men of other vocations. It will affect him as a human being, no doubt in proportion to his sensitiveness.

INTERVIEWER: Another unrelated question: I can see why a man's criticism is better for his being a practising poet, better although subject to his own prejudices. But do you feel that writing criticism has helped you as a poet?

ELIOT: In an indirect way it has helped me somehow as a poet – to put down in writing my critical valuation of the poets who have influenced me and whom I admire. It is merely making an influence more conscious and more articulate. It's been a rather natural impulse. I think probably my best critical essays are essays on the poets who had influenced me, so to speak, long before I thought of writing essays about them. They're of more value, probably, than any of my more generalized remarks.

INTERVIEWER: G. S. Fraser wonders, in an essay about the two of you, whether you ever met Yeats. From remarks in your talk about him, it would seem that you did. Could you tell us the circumstances?

ELIOT: Of course I had met Yeats many times. Yeats was always very gracious when one met him and had the art of treating younger writers as if they were his equals and contemporaries. I can't remember any one particular occasion.

INTERVIEWER: I have heard that you consider that your poetry belongs in the tradition of American literature. Could you tell us why?

ELIOT: I'd say that my poetry has obviously more in common with my distinguished contemporaries in America than with anything written in my generation in England. That I'm sure of.

INTERVIEWER: Do you think there's a connection with the American past?

ELIOT: Yes, but I couldn't put it any more definitely than that, you see. It wouldn't be what it is, and I imagine it wouldn't be so good; putting it as modestly as I can, it wouldn't be what it is if I'd been born in England, and it wouldn't be what it is if I'd stayed in America. It's a combination of things. But in its sources, in its emotional springs, it comes from America.

INTERVIEWER: One last thing. Seventeen years ago you said, 'No honest poet can ever feel quite sure of the permanent value of what he has written. He may have wasted his time and messed up his life for nothing.' Do you feel the same now, at seventy?

ELIOT: There may be honest poets who feel sure. I don't.

Donald Hall

BORIS PASTERNAK

I decided to visit Boris Pasternak about ten days after my arrival in Moscow one January. I had heard much about him from my parents, who had known him for many years, and I had heard and loved his poems since my earliest years.

I had messages and small presents to take to him from my parents and from other admirers. But Pasternak had no phone, I discovered in Moscow. I dismissed the thought of writing a note as too impersonal. I feared that in view of the volume of his correspondence he might have some sort of standard rejection form for requests to visit him. It took a great effort to call unannounced on a man so famous. I was afraid that Pasternak in later years would not live up to my image of him suggested by his poems – lyric, impulsive, above all youthful.

My parents had mentioned that when they saw Pasternak in 1957, just before he received the Nobel Prize, he had held open house on Sundays – a tradition among Russian writers which extends to Russians abroad. As an adolescent in Paris, I remember being taken to call on the writer Remizov and the famous philosopher Berdyaev on Sunday afternoons.

On my second Sunday in Moscow I suddenly decided to go to Peredelkino. It was a radiant day, and in the centre of the city, where I stayed, the fresh snow sparkled against the Kremlin's gold cupolas. The streets were full of sightseers – out-of-town families bundled in peasant-like fashion walking towards the Kremlin. Many carried bunches of fresh mimosa – sometimes one twig at a time. On winter Sundays large shipments of mimosa are brought to Moscow. Russians buy them to give to one another or simply to carry, as if to mark the solemnity of the day.

I decided to take a taxi to Peredelkino, although I knew of an electric train which went from the Kiev railroad station near the outskirts of Moscow. I was suddenly in a great hurry to get there, although I had been warned time and

again by knowledgeable Muscovites of Pasternak's unwill-
ingness to receive foreigners. I was prepared to deliver my
messages and perhaps shake his hand and turn back.

The cab driver, a youngish man with the anonymous air
of taxi-drivers everywhere, assured me that he knew Peredelkino very well – it was about thirty kilometres out on the
Kiev highway. The fare would be about thirty roubles (about
three dollars). He seemed to find it completely natural that
I should want to drive out there on that lovely sunny
day.

But the driver's claim to know the road turned out to be
a boast, and soon we were lost. We had driven at fair speed
along the four-lane highway free of snow and of billboards
or petrol stations. There were a few discreet road signs but
they failed to direct us to Peredelkino, and so we began stopping whenever we encountered anyone to ask directions.
Everyone was friendly and willing to help, but nobody
seemed to know of Peredelkino. We drove for a long time
on an unpaved, frozen road through endless white fields.
Finally we entered a village from another era, in complete
contrast with the immense new apartment houses in the
outskirts of Moscow – low, ancient-looking cottages border-
ing a straight main street. A horse-drawn sled went by; ker-
chiefed women were grouped near a small wooden church.
We found we were in a settlement very close to Peredelkino.
After a ten-minute drive on a small winding road through
dense evergreens I was in front of Pasternak's house. I had
seen photographs of it in magazines and suddenly there it
was on my right: brown, with bay windows, standing on a
slope against a background of fir trees and overlooking the
road by which we had accidentally entered the town.

Peredelkino is a loosely settled little town, hospitable-
looking and cheerful at sunny midday. Many writers and
artists live in it year round in houses provided, as far as I
know, for their lifetimes, and there is a large rest home for
writers and journalists run by the Soviet Writers' Union.
But part of the town still belongs to small artisans and
peasants and there is nothing 'arty' in the atmosphere.

Tchoukovsky, the famous literary critic and writer of

children's books, lives there in a comfortable and hospitable house lined with books – he runs a lovely small library for the town's children. Constantin Fedine, one of the best known of living Russian novelists, lives next door to Pasternak. He is now the first secretary of the Writers' Union – a post long held by Alexander Fadeyev, who also lived here until his death in 1956. Later, Pasternak showed me Isaac Babel's house where he was arrested in the late 1930s and to which he never returned.

Pasternak's house was on a gently curving country road which leads down the hill to a brook. On that sunny afternoon the hill was crowded with children on skis and sleds, bundled like teddy bears. Across the road from the house was a large fenced field – a communal field cultivated in summer; now it was a vast white expanse dominated by a little cemetery on a hill, like a bit of background out of a Chagall painting. The tombs were surrounded by wooden fences painted a bright blue, the crosses were planted at odd angles, and there were bright pink and red paper flowers half buried in the snow. It was a cheerful cemetery.

The house's veranda made it look much like an American frame house of forty years ago, but the firs against which it stood marked it as Russian. They grew very close together and gave the feeling of deep forest, although there were only small groves of them around the town.

I paid the driver and with great trepidation pushed open the gate separating the garden from the road and walked up to the dark house. At the small veranda to one side there was a door with a withered, half-torn note in English pinned on it saying, 'I am working now. I cannot receive anybody, please go away.' After a moment's hesitation I chose to disregard it, mostly because it was so old-looking and also because of the little packages in my hands. I knocked, and almost immediately the door was opened – by Pasternak himself.

He was wearing an astrakhan hat. He was strikingly handsome; with his high cheek-bones and dark eyes and fur-hat he looked like someone out of a Russian tale. After the mounting anxiety of the trip I suddenly felt relaxed – it seemed to me that I had never really doubted that I would meet Pasternak.

I introduced myself as Olga Andreyev, Vadim Leonido-vitch's daughter, using my father's semi-formal name. It is made up of own first name and his father's, the short-story writer and playwright, Leonid, author of the play *He Who Gets Slapped* and *The Seven Who Were Hanged*, etc. Andreyev is a fairly common Russian name.

It took Pasternak a minute to realize that I had come from abroad to visit him. He greeted me with great warmth, taking my hand in both of his, and asking about my mother's health and my father's writing, and when I was last in Paris, and looking closely into my face in search of family resemblances. He was going out to pay some calls. Had I been a moment later I would have missed him. He asked me to walk part of the way with him – as far as his first stop, at the Writers' Club.

While Pasternak was getting ready to go I had a chance to look around the simply furnished dining-room into which I had been shown. From the moment I had stepped inside I had been struck by the similarity of the house to Leo Tolstoy's house in Moscow, which I had visited the day before. The atmosphere in both combined austerity and hospitality in a way which I think must have been characteristic of a Russian intellectual's home in the nineteenth century. The furniture was comfortable, but old and unpretentious. The rooms looked ideal for informal entertaining, for children's gatherings, for the studious life. Although it was extremely simple for its period Tolstoy's house was bigger and more elaborate than Pasternak's, but the unconcern about elegance or display was the same.

Usually one walked into Pasternak's house through the kitchen, where one was greeted by a tiny, smiling, middle-aged cook who helped to brush the snow off one's clothes. Then came the dining-room with a bay window where geraniums grew. On the walls hung charcoal studies by Leonid Pasternak, the writer's painter father. There were life-studies and portraits. One recognized Tolstoy, Gorki, Scriabin, Rachmaninoff. There were sketches of Boris Pasternak and his brother and sisters as children, of ladies in big hats with veils. . . . It was very much the world of Pasternak's early reminiscences, that of his poems about adolescent love.

Pasternak was soon ready to go. We stepped out into the brilliant sunlight and walked through the evergreen grove behind the house in rather deep snow which sifted into my low-cut boots.

Soon we were on a packed road, much more comfortable for walking although it had treacherous icy patches. Pasternak took long, lanky steps. On particularly perilous spots he would take my arm; otherwise he gave all his attention to the conversation. Walks are an established part of life in Russia – like drinking tea or lengthy philosophical discussions – a part he apparently loved. We took what was obviously a very roundabout path to the Writers' Club. The stroll lasted about forty minutes. He first plunged into an elaborate discussion of the art of translating. He would stop from time to time to ask about the political and literary situations in France and in the United States. He said that he rarely read papers – 'Unless I sharpen my pencil and glance over the sheet of newspaper into which I collect the shavings. This is how I learned last autumn that there was a near revolution against de Gaulle in Algeria, and that Soustelle was ousted – *Sous*telle was *oust*ed', he repeated – a rough translation of his words, emphasizing both approval of de Gaulle's decision and the similarity in the words as he spoke them. But actually he seemed remarkably well informed about literary life abroad; it seemed to interest him greatly.

From the first moment I was charmed and impressed by the similarity of Pasternak's speech to his poetry – full of alliterations and unusual images. He related words to each other musically, without however at any time sounding affected or sacrificing the exact meaning. For somebody acquainted with his verse in Russian, to have conversed with Pasternak is a memorable experience. His word sense was so personal that one felt the conversation was somehow the continuation, the elaboration of a poem, a rushed speech, with waves of words and images following one another in a crescendo.

Later I remarked to him on the musical quality of his speech. 'In writing as in speaking,' he said, 'the music of the word is never just a matter of sound. It does not result from the harmony of vowels and consonants. It results from the relation between the speech and its meaning. And meaning – content – must always lead.'

Often I found it difficult to believe that I was speaking to a man of seventy; Pasternak appeared remarkably young and in good health. There was something a little strange and forbidding in this youthfulness as if something – was it art? – had mixed itself with the very substance of the man to preserve him. His movements were completely youthful – the gestures of the hands, the manner in which he threw his head back. His friend, the poetess Marina Tsvetayeva, once wrote, 'Pasternak looks at the same time like an Arab and like his horse.' And indeed, with his dark complexion and somehow archaic features Pasternak did have something of an Arabic face. At certain moments he seemed suddenly to become aware of the impact of his own extraordinary face, of his whole personality. He seemed to withdraw for an instant, half closing his slanted brown eyes, turning his head away, vaguely reminiscent of a horse baulking.

I had been told by some writers in Moscow – most of them didn't know him personally – that Pasternak was a man in love with his own image. But then I was told many contradictory things about him in the few days I spent in Moscow. Pasternak seemed a living legend – a hero for some, a man who had sold out to the enemies of Russia for others. Intense admiration for his poetry among writers and artists was universal. It was the title character of Dr Zhivago that seemed most controversial. 'Nothing but a worn-out intellectual of no interest whatsoever', said a well-known young poet, otherwise very liberal-minded and a great admirer of Pasternak's poetry.

In any event, I found that there was no truth to the charge that Pasternak was an egocentric. On the contrary, he seemed intensely aware of the world around him and reacted to every change of mood in people near him. It is hard to imagine a more perceptive conversationalist. He grasped the most elusive thought at once. The conversation lost all heaviness. Pasternak asked questions about my parents. Although he had seen them but a few times in his life, he remembered everything about them and their tastes. He recalled with surprising exactness some of my father's poems which he had liked. He wanted to know about writers I knew – Russians in Paris, and French, and Americans. American literature seemed particularly to interest him, although he knew only the important names. I soon discovered that it was difficult to make him talk about himself, which I had hoped he would do.

As we walked in the sunshine, I told Pasternak what interest and admiration *Dr Zhivago* had aroused in the West and particularly in the United States, despite the fact that in my and many others' opinion the translation into English did not do justice to his book.

'Yes,' he said, 'I am aware of this interest and I am immensely happy and proud of it. I get an enormous amount of mail from abroad about my work. In fact, it is quite a burden at times, all those inquiries that I have to answer, but then it is indispensible to keep up relations across boundaries. As for the translators of *Dr Zhivago*, do not blame them too much. It's not their fault. They are used, like translators everywhere, to reproduce the literal sense rather than the tone of what is said – and of course it is the tone that matters. Actually, the only interesting sort of translation is that of classics. There is challenging work. As far as modern writing is concerned, it is rarely rewarding to translate it, although it might be easy. You said you were a painter. Well, translation is very much like copying paintings. Imagine yourself copying a Malevitch; wouldn't it be boring? And that is precisely what I have to do with the well-know Czech surrealist Nezval. He is not really bad, but all this writing of the 'twenties has terribly aged. This translation which I have promised to finish and my own correspondence take much too much of my time.'

Do you have difficulty receiving your mail?

'At present I receive all of it, everything sent me, I assume. There's a lot of it – which I'm delighted to receive, though

I'm troubled by the volume of it and the compulsion to answer it all.

'As you can imagine, some of the letters I get about *Dr Zhivago* are quite absurd. Recently somebody writing about *Dr Zhivago* in France was inquiring about the plan of the novel. I guess it baffles the French sense of order. ... But how silly, for the plan of the novel is outlined by the poems accompanying it. This is partly why I chose to publish them alongside the novel. They are there also to give the novel more body, more richness. For the same reason I used religious symbolism – to give warmth to the book. Now some critics have got so wrapped up in those symbols – which are put in the book the way stoves go into a house, to warm it up – they would like me to commit myself and climb into the stove.'

Have you read Edmund Wilson's critical essays on Dr Zhivago?

'Yes, I have read them and appreciated their perception and intelligence, but you must realize that the novel must not be judged on theological lines. Nothing is further removed from my understanding of the world. One must live and write restlessly, with the help of the new reserve that life offers. I am weary of this notion of faithfulness to a point of view at all cost. Life around us is ever changing, and I believe that one should try to change one's slant accordingly – at least once every ten years. The great heroic devotion to one point of view is very alien to me – it's a lack of humility. Mayakovsky killed himself because his pride would not be reconciled with something new happening within himself – or around him.'

We had reached a gate beside a long, low wooden fence. Pasternak stopped. He was due there, our conversation had already made him slightly late. I said goodbye with regret. There were so many things that I wanted to ask him right then. Pasternak showed me the way to the railway station, very close by, downhill behind the little cemetery. A little electric train took me into Moscow in less than an hour. It is the one described so accurately by Pasternak in *Early Trains*:

> *... And, worshipful, I humbly watch*
> *Old peasant women, Muscovites,*
> *Plain artisans, plain labourers*
> *Young students and suburbanites.*
>
> *I see no traces of subjection*
> *Born of unhappiness, dismay*
> *Or want. They bear their daily trials*
> *Like masters who have come to stay.*
>
> *Disposed in every sort of posture*
> *In little knots, in quiet nooks*
> *The children and the young sit still*
> *Engrossed, like experts, reading books.*
>
> *Then Moscow greets us in a mist*
> *Of darkness turning silver grey ...*

My subsequent two visits with Pasternak merge in my memory into one long literary conversation. Although he declined to give me a formal interview ('For this, you must come back when I am less busy, next autumn perhaps') he seemed interested in the questions which I wanted to ask him. Except for meals, we were alone, and there were no interruptions. Both times, as I was about to leave, Pasternak kissed my hand in the old-fashioned Russian manner, and asked me to come back the following Sunday.

I remember coming to Pasternak's house from the railway station at dusk, taking a short cut I had learned near the cemetery. Suddenly the wind grew very strong; a snowstorm was beginning. I could see snow flying in great round waves past the station's distant lights. It grew dark very quickly; I had difficulty walking against the wind. I knew this to be customary Russian weather, but it was the first real *metol* – snowstorm – I had seen. It recalled poems by Pushkin and Blok, and it brought to mind Pasternak's early poems, and the snowstorms of *Dr Zhivago*. To be in his house a few minutes later, and to hear his elliptical sentences so much like his verse, seemed strange.

I arrived too late to attend the midday dinner; Pasternak's family had retired, the house seemed deserted. Pasternak insisted that I have something to eat and the cook brought some venison and vodka into the dining-room. It was about four o'clock and the room was dark and warm, shut off from the world with only the sound of snow and wind outside. I was hungry and the food delicious. Pasternak sat across the table from me discussing my grandfather, Leonid Andreyev. He had recently re-read some of his stories and liked them. 'They bear the stamp of those fabulous Russian nineteen-hundreds. Those years are now receding in our memory, and yet they loom in the mind like great mountains seen in the distance, enormous. Andreyev was under a Nietzschean spell, he took from Nietzsche his taste for excesses. So did Scriabin. Nietzsche satisfied the Russian longing for the extreme, the absolute. In music and writing men had to have this enormous scope before they acquired specificity, became themselves.'

Pasternak told me about a piece he had recently written for a magazine, on the subject of 'What is man?' 'How old-fashioned Nietzsche seems, he who was the most important thinker of the days of my youth! What enormous influence – on Wagner, on Gorki ... Gorki was impregnated with his ideals. Actually, Nietzsche's principal function was to be the transmitter of the bad taste of his period. It is Kierkegaard, barely known in those years, who was destined to influence deeply our own years. I would like to know the works of Berdyaev better; he is in the same line of thought, I believe – truly a writer of our time.'

It grew quite dark in the dining-room and we moved to a little sitting-room on the same floor where a light was on. Pasternak brought me tangerines for dessert. I ate them with a strange feeling of something already experienced; tangerines appear in Pasternak's work very often – in the beginning of *Dr Zhivago*, in early poems. They seem to stand for a sort of ritual thirst-quenching. And then there was another vivid evocation of a Pasternak poem, like the snowstorm which blew outside – an open grand piano, black and enormous, filling up most of the room:

. . . and yet we are nearest
In twilight here, the music tossed upon
*the fire, year after year, like pages of a diary.**

On these walls, as in the dining-room, there were sketches by Leonid Pasternak. The atmosphere was both serious and relaxed.

It seemed a good time to ask Pasternak a question which interested me especially. I had heard from people who had seen him while he was working on *Dr Zhivago* that he rejected most of his early verse as too tentative and dated. I had difficulty believing it. There is a classical perfection to *Themes and Variations* and *My Sister, Life*, experimental as they were in the 1920s. I found that writers and poets in Russia knew them by heart and would recite them with fervour. Often one would detect the influence of Pasternak in the verse of young poets. Mayakovsky and Pasternak, each in his own manner, are the very symbol of the years of the Revolution and the 1920s. Then art and the revolutionary ideas seemed inseparable. It was enough to let oneself be carried by the wave of overwhelming events and ideas. There were fewer heart-breaking choices to make (and I detected a longing for those years on the part of young Russian intellectuals). Was it true that Pastnerak rejected those early works?

In Pasternak's reply I sensed a note of slight irritation. It might have been because he didn't like to be solely admired for those poems – did he realize perhaps that they are unsurpassable? Or was it the more general weariness of the artist dissatisfied with past achievements, concerned with immediate artistic problems only?

'These poems were like rapid sketches – just compare them with the works of our elders. Dostoevski and Tolstoy were not just novelists. Blok not just a poet. In the midst of literature – the world of commonplaces, conventions, established names – they were three voices which spoke because they had something to say . . . and it sounded like thunder. As for the facility of the 'twenties, take my father for example. How much search, what efforts to finish one of his

* 'The Trembling Piano', *Themes and Variations*.

paintings! Our success in the 'twenties was partly due to chance. Our works were dictated by the times. They lacked universality; now they have aged. Moreover, I believe that it is no longer for lyric poetry to express the immensity of our experience. Life has grown too cumbersome, too complicated. We have acquired values which are best expressed in prose. I have tried to express them through my novel, I have them in mind as I write my play.'

What about Zhivago? Do you still feel, as you told my parents in 1957, that he is the most significant figure of your work?

'When I wrote *Dr Zhivago* I had the feeling of an immense debt towards my contemporaries. It was an attempt to repay it. This feeling of debt was overpowering as I slowly progressed with the novel. After so many years of just writing lyric poetry or translating, it seemed to me that it was my duty to make a statement about our epoch – about those years, remote and yet looming so closely over us. Time was pressing. I wanted to record the past and to honour in *Dr Zhivago* the beautiful and sensitive aspects of the Russia of those years. There will be no return of those days of our fathers and forefathers, but in the great blossoming of the future I foresee their values will revive. I have tried to describe them. I don't know whether *Dr Zhivago* is fully successful as a novel, but then with all its faults I feel it has more value than those early poems. It is richer, more humane than the works of my youth.'

Among your contemporaries in the 'twenties which ones do you think have best endured?

'You know how I feel about Mayakovsky. I have told it at great length in my autobiography, *Safe Conduct*. I am indifferent to most of his later works, with the exception of his last unfinished poem, "At the Top of My Voice". The falling apart of form, the poverty of thought, the unevenness which is characteristic of poetry in that period are alien to me. But there are exceptions. I love all of Essenin, who captures so well the smell of Russian earth. I place Tsvetayeva highest – she was a formed poet from her very beginning. In an age of affectations she had her own voice – human, classical. She was a woman with a man's soul. Her struggle with everyday life gave her strength. She strove and reached perfect clarity. She is a greater poet than Ahmatova, whose simplicity and lyricism I have always admired. Tsvetayeva's death was one of the great sadnesses of my life.'

What about Andrei Beily, so influential in those years?

'Beily was too hermetic, too limited. His scope is comparable to that of chamber music – never greater. If he had really suffered, he might have written the major work of which he was capable. But he never came into contact with real life. It is perhaps the fate of writers who die young like Beily, this fascination with new forms? I have never understood those dreams of a new language, of a completely original form of expression. Because of this dream much of the work of the 'twenties which was but stylistic experimentation has ceased to exist. The most extraordinary discoveries are made when the artist is overwhelmed by what he has to say. Then he uses the old language in his urgency and the old language is transformed from within. Even in those years one felt a little sorry for Beily because he was so cut off from the real life which could have helped his genius to blossom.'

What about today's young poets?

'I am impressed by the extent that poetry seems a part of everyday life for Russians. Printings of twenty thousand volumes of poetry by young poets are amazing to a Westerner, but actually poetry in Russia is not as alive as you might think. It is fairly limited to a group of intellectuals. And today's poetry is often rather ordinary. It is like the pattern of a wallpaper, pleasant enough but without real *raison d'être*. Of course some young people show talent – for example Evtuchenko.'

Wouldn't you say, however, that the first half of the Russian twentieth century is a time of high achievement in poetry rather than in prose?

'I don't think that's so any longer. I believe that prose is today's medium – elaborate, rich like Faulkner's. Today's work must re-create whole segments of life. This is what I am trying to do in my new play. I say trying because everyday life has grown very complicated for me. It must be so anywhere for a well-known writer, but I am unprepared for such a role. I don't like life deprived of secrecy and quiet. It seems to me that in my youth there was work, an integral part of life which illuminated everything else in it. Now it is something I have to fight for. All those demands by scholars, editors, readers cannot be ignored, but together with the translations they devour my time. ... You must tell people abroad who are interested in me that this is my only serious problem – this terrible lack of time.'

My last visit with Pasternak was a very long one. He had asked me to come early, in order to have a talk before the dinner which was to be a family feast. It was again a sunny Sunday. I arrived shortly before Pasternak returned from his morning stroll. As I was shown into his study, the house echoed with cheerful voices. Somewhere in the back of it, members of his family were assembled.

Pasternak's study was a large, rather bare room on the second floor. Like the rest of the house it had little furniture – a large desk near the bay window, a couple of chairs, a sofa. The light coming from the window looking over the large snowy field was brilliant. Pinned on the light grey wooden walls there was a multitude of art postcards. When he came in, Pasternak explained to me that those were all sent to him by readers, mostly from abroad. Many were reproductions of religious scenes – medieval Nativities, St George killing the dragon, St Magdalene. ... They were related to *Dr Zhivago's* themes.

After his walk Pasternak looked especially well. He was wearing a collegiate-looking navy-blue blazer and was obviously in a good mood. He sat at the desk by the window and placed me across from him. As on other occasions, the atmosphere was relaxed and yet of great concentration. I remember vividly feeling happy – Pasternak looked so gay and the sun through the window was warm. As we sat there for two or more hours, I felt a longing to prolong those moments – I was leaving Moscow the next day – but the bright sunlight flooding the room inexorably faded as the day advanced.

Pasternak decided to tell me about his new play. He seemed to do so on the spur of the moment. Quite fascinated, I listened to him – there were few interruptions on my part. Once or twice, unsure of some historical or literary allusion, I asked him for explanation.

'I think that on account of your background – so close to the events of the Russian nineteenth century – you will be interested in the outlines of my new work. I am working on a trilogy. I have about a third of it written.

'I want to re-create a whole historical era, the nineteenth century in Russia with its main event, the liberation of the serfs. We have, of course, many works about that time, but there is no modern treatment of it. I want to write something panoramic, like Gogol's *Dead Souls*. I hope that my plays will be as real, as involved with everyday life as *Dead Souls*. Although they will be long, I hope that they can be played in one evening. I think that most plays should be cut for staging. I admire the English for knowing how to cut Shakespeare, not just to keep what is essential, but rather to emphasize what is significant. The Comédie Française came to Moscow recently. They don't cut Racine and I feel it is a serious mistake. Only what is expressive today, what works dramatically should be staged.

'My trilogy deals with three meaningful moments in the long process of liberating the serfs. The first play takes place in 1840 – that is when unrest caused by serfdom is first felt throughout the country. The old feudal system is outlived, but no tangible hope is yet to be seen for Russia. The second deals with the 1860s. Liberal landowners have appeared and the best among Russian aristocrats begin to be deeply stirred by Western ideas. Unlike the first two plays, which are set in a great country estate, the third part will take place in St Petersburg in the 1880s. But this part is but a project yet, while the first and second plays are partially written. I can tell you in more detail about those if you like.

'The first play describes life at its rawest, most trivial, in the manner of the first part of *Dead Souls*. It is existence before it has been touched by any form of spirituality.

'Imagine a large estate lost in the heart of rural Russia

around 1840. It is in a state of great neglect, nearly bankrupt. The masters of the estate, the Count and his wife, are away. They have gone on a trip to spare themselves the painful spectacle of the designation – by means of a lottery – of those among their peasants who must go into the Army. As you know, military service lasted for twenty-five years in Russia in those times. The masters are about to return and the household is getting ready to receive them. In the opening scene we see the servants cleaning house – sweeping, dusting, hanging fresh curtains. There is a lot of confusion, of running around – laughter and jokes among the young servant girls.

'Actually, the times are troubled in this part of the Russian countryside. Soon the mood among the servants becomes more sombre. From their conversations we learn that there are hidden bandits in the neighbouring woods; they are probably runaway soldiers. We also hear of legends surrounding the estate, like that of the "house killer" from the times of Catherine the Great. She was a sadistic woman, an actual historical figure who took delight in terrifying and torturing her serfs – her crimes so extreme at a time when almost anything was permitted to serf-owners that she was finally arrested.

'The servants also talk about a plaster bust standing high on a cupboard. It is a beautiful young man's head in eighteenth-century hair dress. This bust is said to have a magical meaning. Its destinies are linked to those of the estate. It must therefore be dusted with extreme care, lest it be broken.

'The main character in the play is Prokor, the keeper of the estate. He is about to leave for town to sell wood and wheat – the estate lives off such sales – but he joins in the general mood instead of going. He remembers some old masquerade costumes stored away in a closet and decides to play a trick on his superstitious fellow servants. He dresses himself like a devil – big bulging eyes like a fish. Just as he emerges in his grotesque costume, the master's arrival is announced. In haste the servants group themselves at the entrance to welcome the Count and his wife. Prokor has no other alternative but to hide himself in a closet.

'As the Count and Countess come in, we begin at once to sense that there is a great deal of tension between them, and we find out that during their trip home the Count has been trying to get his wife to give him her jewels – all that's left besides the mortgaged estate. She has refused, and when he threatened her with violence a young valet travelling with them defended her – an unbelievable defiance. He hasn't been punished yet, but it's only a question of time before the Count's wrath is unleashed against him.

'As the Count renews his threats against the Countess, the young valet, who has nothing to lose anyway, suddenly reaches for one of the Count's pistols which have just been brought in from the carriage. He shoots at the Count. There is a great panic – servants rushing around and screaming. The plaster statue tumbles down from the cupboard and breaks into a thousand pieces. It wounds one of the young servant girls, blinding her. She is "The Blind Beauty" after whom the trilogy is named. The title is, of course, symbolic of Russia, oblivious for so long of its own beauty and its own destinies. Although she is a serf, the blind beauty is also an artist; she is a marvellous singer, an important member of the estate's chorus of serfs.

'As the wounded Count is carried out of the room, the Countess, unseen in the confusion, hands her jewels to the young valet, who manages to make his escape. It is poor Prokor, still costumed as a devil and hidden in the closet, who is eventually accused of having stolen them. As the Countess does not reveal the truth, he is convicted of the theft and sent to Siberia ...

'As you see, all this is very melodramatic, but I think that the theatre *should* try to be emotional, colourful. I think everybody's tired of stages where nothing happens. The theatre is the art of emotions – it is also that of the concrete. The trend should be towards appreciating melodrama again: Victor Hugo, Schiller ...

'I am working now on the second play. As it stands, it's broken into separate scenes. The setting is the same estate, but times have changed. We are in 1860, on the eve of the liberation of the serfs. The estate now belongs to a nephew of the Count. He would have already freed his serfs but for his fears of hurting the common cause. He is impregnated with liberal ideas and loves the arts. And his passion is theatre. He has an outstanding theatrical company. Of course, the actors are his serfs, but their reputation extends to all of Russia.

'The son of the young woman blinded in the first play is the principal actor of the group. He is also the hero of this part of the trilogy. His name is Agafon, a marvellously talented actor. The Count has provided him with an outstanding education.

'The play opens with a snowstorm.' Pasternak described it with large movements of his hands. 'An illustrious guest is expected at the estate – none other than Alexandre Dumas, then travelling in Russia. He is invited to attend the première of a new play. The play is called *The Suicide*. I might write it – a play within a play as in *Hamlet*. I would love to write a melodrama in the taste of the middle of the nineteenth century ...

'Alexandre Dumas and his entourage are snowed in at a relay station not too far from the estate. A scene takes place there, and who should the relay-master be but Prokor, the former estate keeper? He has been back from Siberia for some years – released when the Countess disclosed his innocence on her death-bed. He has become increasingly prosperous running the relay station. And yet despite the advent of new times, the scene at the inn echoes the almost medieval elements of the first play: we see the local executioner and his aides stop at the inn. They are travelling from the town to their residence deep in the woods – by custom they are not allowed to live near other people.

'A very important scene takes place at the estate when the guests finally arrive there. There is a long discussion about art between Alexandre Dumas and Agafon. This part will illustrate my own ideas about art – not those of the 1860s, needless to say. Agafon dreams of going abroad, of becoming a Shakespearean actor, to play Hamlet.

'This play has a denouement somehow similar to that of the first one. An obnoxious character whom we first meet at the relay station is the local police chief. He is a sort of Sobakevitch, the character in *Dead Souls* who personifies humanity at its crudest. Backstage, after the performance of *The Suicide*, he tries to rape one of the young actresses. Defending her, Agafon hits the police chief with a champagne bottle, and has to flee for fear of persecution. The Count, however, helps him, and eventually gets him to Paris.

'In the third play, Agafon comes back to Russia to live in St Petersburg. No longer a serf (we are now in 1880) he's an extremely successful actor. Eventually he has his mother cured of her blindness by a famous European doctor.

'As for Prokor, in the last play he has become an affluent merchant. I want him to represent the middle class which did so much for Russia at the end of the nineteenth century. Imagine someone like Schukine, who collected all those beautiful paintings in Moscow at the turn of the century. Essentially, what I want to show at the end of the trilogy is just that: the birth of an enlightened and affluent middle-class, open to occidental influences, progressive, intelligent, artistic ...'

It was typical of Pasternak to tell me about his plays in concrete terms, like a libretto. He didn't emphasize the ideas behind the trilogy, though it became apparent, after a while, that he was absorbed in ideas about art – not in its historical context, but as an element ever present in life. As he went on, I realized that what he was describing was simply the frame of his new work. Parts of it were completed, others were still to be filled in.

'At first I consulted all sorts of documents on the nineteenth century. Now I'm finished with research. After all, what is important is not the historical accuracy of the work, but the successful re-creation of an era. It is not the object described that matters, but the light that falls on it like that from a lamp in a distant room.'

Towards the end of his description of his trilogy, Pasternak was obviously hurried. Dinner time was long past. He would glance at his watch from time to time. But, despite the fact that he didn't have the opportunity to clarify philosophical implications which would have given body to the

strange framework of the dramas, I felt I had been witness
to a remarkable evocation of the Russian past.

The story of our fathers sounds like the days of the Stuarts
*Further away than Pushkin and can be seen only in dream.**

As we came down to the dining-room the family already
was seated around the large table. 'Don't they look like an
impressionist painting?' said Pasternak. 'With the geraniums in the background and this mid-afternoon light? There
is a painting by Simon just like this . . .'

Everyone stood as we entered and remained standing
while Pasternak introduced me around the table. Besides
Mme Pasternak, two of Pasternak's sons were there – his
oldest son by his first marriage, and his youngest son, who
was eighteen or twenty years old – a handsome boy, dark,
with quite a strong resemblance to his mother. He was a
student in physics at the Moscow University. Professor
Nihaus was also a guest. He is a famous Chopin teacher at
the Moscow Conservatory to whom Mme Pasternak had
once been married. He was quite elderly, with an old-
fashioned moustache, very charming and refined. He asked
about Paris and musicians we knew there in common. There
were also two ladies at the table whose exact relationship to
the Pasternak family I didn't learn.

I was seated to the right of Pasternak. Mme Pasternak
was at his left. The table was simply set, covered with a
white linen Russian table-cloth embroidered with red cross-
stitches. The silverware and china were very simple. There
was a vase with mimosa in the middle, and bowls of oranges
and tangerines. The hors d'oeuvres were already set on the
table. Guests passed them to each other while Pasternak
poured the vodka. There were caviare, marinated herring,
pickles, macedoine of vegetables. . . . The meal progressed
slowly. Soon kvass was poured out – a home-made fermented
drink usually drunk in the country. Because of fermenta-
tion the kvass corks would sometimes pop during the night
and wake everybody up – just like a pistol shot, said Mme

* From *The Year 1905*.

Pasternak. After the hors d'oeuvres the cook served a succulent stew made of game.

The conversation was general. Hemingway's works were discussed. Last winter he was one of the most widely read authors in Moscow. A new collection of his writings had just been published. Mme Pasternak and the ladies at the table remarked that they found Hemingway monotonous – all those endless drinks with little else happening to the heroes.

Pasternak, who had fallen silent for a while, took exception.

'The greatness of a writer has nothing to do with subject matter itself, only with how much the subject matter touches the author. It is the density of style which counts. Through Hemingway's style you feel matter, iron, wood.' He was punctuating his words with his hands, pressing them against the wood of the table. 'I admire Hemingway but I prefer what I know of Faulkner. *Light in August* is a marvellous book. The character of the little pregnant woman is unforgettable. As she walks from Alabama to Tennessee something of the immensity of the United States, of its essence, is captured for us who have never been there.'

Later the conversation turned to music. Professor Nihaus and Pasternak discussed fine points of interpretation of Chopin. Pasternak said how much he loved Chopin – 'a good example of what I was saying the other day – Chopin used the old Mozartian language to say something completely new – the form was reborn from within. Nonetheless, I am afraid that Chopin is considered a little old-fashioned in the United States. I gave a piece on Chopin to Stephen Spender which was not published.'

I told him how much Gide loved to play Chopin – Pasternak didn't know this and was delighted to hear it. The conversation moved on to Proust, whom Pasternak was slowly reading at that time.

'Now that I am coming to the end of *A la Recherche du Temps Perdu*, I am struck by how it echoes some of the ideas which absorbed us in 1910. I put them into a lecture about "Symbolism and Immortality" which I gave on the day before Leo Tolstoy died and I went to Astapovo with my father. Its text has long been lost, but among many other things on the nature of symbolism it said that, although the artist will die, the happiness of living which he has experienced is immortal. If it is captured in a personal and yet universal form it can actually be relived by others through his work.

'I have always liked French literature,' he continued. 'Since the war I feel that French writing has acquired a new accent, less rhetoric. Camus' death is a great loss for all of us.' (Earlier, I had told Pasternak of Camus' tragic end, which took place just before I came to Moscow. It was not written up in the Russian press. Camus is not translated into Russian.) 'In spite of differences of themes, French literature is now much closer to us. But French writers when they commit themselves to political causes are particularly unattractive. Either they are cliquish and insincere or with their French sense of logic they feel they have to carry out their beliefs to their conclusion. They fancy they must be absolutists like Robespierre or Saint-Just.'

Tea and cognac were served at the end of the meal. Pasternak looked tired suddenly and became silent. As always during my stay in Russia I was asked many questions about the West – about its cultural life and our daily existence.

Lights were turned on. I looked at my watch to discover that it was long past six o'clock. I had to go. I felt very tired, too.

Pasternak walked me to the door, through the kitchen. We said good-bye outside on the little porch in the blue snowy evening. I was terribly sad at the thought of not returning to Peredelkino. Pasternak took my hand in his and held it for an instant, urging me to come back very soon. He asked me once again to tell his friends abroad that he was well, that he remembered them even though he hadn't time to answer their letters. I had already walked down the porch and into the path when he called me back. I was happy to have an excuse to stop, to turn back, to have a last glimpse of Pasternak standing bare-headed, in his blue blazer under the door light.

'Please,' he called, 'don't take what I have said about letters personally. Do write to me, in any language you prefer. I will answer you.'

Olga Carlisle

ALDOUS HUXLEY

Among serious novelists, Aldous Huxley is surely the wittiest and most irreverent. Ever since the early 'twenties his name has been a byword for a particular kind of social satire; in fact, he has immortalized in satire a whole period and a way of life. In addition to his ten novels, Huxley has written, during the course of an extremely prolific career, poetry, drama, essays, travel, biography, and history.

Descended from two of the most eminent Victorian families, he inherited science and letters from his grandfather T. H. Huxley and his great-uncle Matthew Arnold respectively. He absorbed both strains in an erudition so unlikely that it has sometimes been regarded as a kind of literary gamesmanship. (In conversation his learning comes out spontaneously, without the slightest hint of premeditation; if someone raises the topic of Victorian gastronomy, for example, Huxley will recite a typical daily menu of Prince Edward, meal by meal, course by course, down to the last crumb.) The plain fact is that Aldous Huxley is one of the most prodigiously learned writers not merely of this century but of all time.

After Eton and Balliol, he became a member of the postwar intellectual upper crust, the society he set out to vivisect and anatomize. He first made his name with such brilliant satires as Antic Hay *and* Point Counter Point, *writing in the process part of the social history of the 'twenties. In the 'thirties he wrote his most influential novel,* Brave New World, *combining satire and science fiction in the most successful of futuristic utopias. Since 1937, when he settled in Southern California, he has written fewer novels and turned his attention more to philosophy, history, and mysticism. Although remembered best for his early satires, he is still productive and provocative as ever.*

It is rather odd to find Aldous Huxley in a suburb of Los Angeles called Hollywoodland. He lives in an unpretentious hilltop house that suggests the Tudor period of American real-estate history. On a clear day he can look out across miles of cluttered, sprawling city at a broad sweep of the Pacific. Behind him dry brown hills rise to a monstrous sign that dominates the horizon, proclaiming HOLLYWOOD-LAND *in aluminium letters twenty feet high.*

Mr Huxley is a very tall man – he must be six feet four – and, though lean, very broad across the shoulders. He carries his years lightly indeed; in fact he moves so quietly as to appear weightless, almost wraithlike. His eyesight is limited, but he seems to find his way about instinctively, without touching anything.

In manner and speech he is very gentle. Where one might have been led to expect the biting satirist or the vague mystic, one is impressed by how quiet and gentle he is on the one hand, how sensible and down-to-earth on the other. His manner is reflected in his lean, grey, emaciated face: attentive, reflective, and for the most part unsmiling. He listens patiently while others speak, then answers deliberately.

INTERVIEWERS: Would you tell us something first about the way you work?

HUXLEY: I work regularly. I always work in the mornings, and then again a little bit before dinner. I'm not one of those who work at night. I prefer to read at night. I usually work four or five hours a day. I keep at it as long as I can, until I feel myself going stale. Sometimes, when I bog down, I start reading – fiction or psychology or history, it doesn't much matter what – not to borrow ideas or materials, but simply to get started again. Almost anything will do the trick.

INTERVIEWERS: Do you do much rewriting?

HUXLEY: Generally, I write everything many times over. All my thoughts are second thoughts. And I correct each page a great deal, or rewrite it several times as I go along.

INTERVIEWERS: Do you keep a notebook, like certain characters in your novels?

HUXLEY: No, I don't keep notebooks. I have occasionally kept diaries for short periods, but I'm very lazy, I mostly don't. One should keep notebooks, I think, but I haven't.

INTERVIEWERS: Do you block out chapters or plan the over-all structure when you start out on a novel?

HUXLEY: No, I work away a chapter at a time, finding my way as I go. I know very dimly when I start what's going to happen. I just have a very general idea, and then the thing develops as I write. Sometimes – it's happened to me more than once – I will write a great deal, then find it just doesn't work, and have to throw the whole thing away. I like to have a chapter finished before I begin on the next one. But I'm never entirely certain what's going to happen in the next chapter until I've worked it out. Things come to me in driblets, and when the driblets come I have to work hard to make them into something coherent.

INTERVIEWERS: Is the process pleasant or painful?

HUXLEY: Oh, it's not painful, though it is hard work. Writing is a very absorbing occupation and sometimes exhausting. But I've always considered myself very lucky to be able to make a living at something I enjoy doing. So few people can.

INTERVIEWERS: Do you ever use maps or charts or diagrams to guide you in your writing?

HUXLEY: No, I don't use anything of that sort, though I do read up a good deal on my subject. Geography books can be a great help in keeping things straight. I had no trouble finding my way around the English part of *Brave New World*, but I had to do an enormous amount of reading up on New Mexico, because I'd never been there. I read all sorts of Smithsonian reports on the place and then did the best I could to imagine it. I didn't actually go there until six years later, in 1937, when we visited Frieda Lawrence.

INTERVIEWERS: When you start out on a novel, what sort of a general idea do you have? How did you begin *Brave New World*, for example?

HUXLEY: Well, that started out as a parody of H. G. Wells' *Men Like Gods*, but gradually it got out of hand and turned into something quite different from what I'd originally intended. As I became more and more interested in the subject, I wandered farther and farther from my original purpose.

INTERVIEWERS: What are you working on now?

HUXLEY: At the moment I'm writing a rather peculiar kind of fiction. It's a kind of fantasy, a kind of reverse *Brave New World*, about a society in which real efforts are made to realize human potentialities. I want to show humanity can make the best of both Eastern and Western worlds. So the setting is an imaginary island between Ceylon and Sumatra, at a meeting place of Indian and Chinese influence. One of my principal characters is, like Darwin and my grandfather, a young scientist on one of those scientific expeditions the British Admiralty sent out in the 1840s; he's a Scotch doctor, who rather resembles James Esdaile, the man who introduced hypnosis into medicine. And then, as in *News from Nowhere* and other utopias, I have another intruder from the outside world, whose guided tour provides a means of describing the society. Unfortunately, he's also the serpent in the garden, looking enviously at this happy, prosperous state. I haven't worked out the ending yet, but I'm afraid it must end with paradise lost – if one is to be realistic.

INTERVIEWERS: In the 1946 preface to *Brave New World* you make certain remarks that seem to prefigure this new utopia. Was the work already incubating then?

HUXLEY: Yes, the general notion was in the back of my mind at that time, and it has preoccupied me a good deal ever since – though not necessarily as the theme for a novel. For a long time I had been thinking a great deal about various ways of realizing human potentialities; then about three years ago I decided to write these ideas into a novel. It's gone very slowly because I've had to struggle with the fable, the framework to carry the expository part. I know what I want to say clearly enough; the problem is how to embody the ideas. Of course, you can always talk them out in dialogue, but you can't have your characters talking indefinitely without becoming transparent – and tiresome. Then there's always the problem of point of view: who's going to tell the story or live the experiences? I've had a great deal of trouble working out the plot and rearranging sections that I've already written. Now I think I can see my way clear to the end. But I'm afraid it's getting hopelessly long. I'm not sure what I'm going to do with it all.

INTERVIEWERS: Some writers hesitate to talk about their work in progress for fear they'll talk it away. You aren't afraid of that?

HUXLEY: No, I don't mind talking about my writing at all. In fact, it might be a good practice; it might give me a clearer notion of what I was trying to do. I've never discussed my writing with others much, but I don't believe it can do any harm. I don't think that there's any risk that ideas or materials will evaporate.

INTERVIEWERS: Some writers – Virginia Woolf, for example – have been painfully sensitive to criticism. Have you been much affected by your critics?

HUXLEY: No, they've never had any effect on me, for the simple reason that I've never read them. I've never made a point of writing for any particular person or audience; I've simply tried to do the best job I could and let it go at that. The critics don't interest me because they're concerned with what's past and done, while I'm concerned with what comes next. I've never re-read my early novels, for example. Perhaps I should read them one of these days.

INTERVIEWERS: How did you happen to start writing? Do you remember?

HUXLEY: I started writing when I was seventeen, during a period when I was almost totally blind and could hardly do anything else. I typed out a novel by the touch system; I couldn't even read it. I've no idea what's become of it; I'd be curious to see it now, but it's lost. My aunt, Mrs Humphry Ward, was a kind of literary godmother to me. I used to have long talks with her about writing; she gave me no end of sound advice. She was a very sound writer herself, rolled off her plots like sections of macadamized road. She had a curious practice: every time she started work on a new novel she read Diderot's *Le Neveu de Rameau*. It seemed to act as a kind of trigger or release mechanism. Then later, during the war and after, I met a great many writers through Lady Ottoline Morrell. She used to invite all kinds of people out to her country house. I met Katherine

Mansfield there, and Siegfried Sassoon, and Robert Graves, and all the Bloomsburies. I owe a great debt of gratitude to Roger Fry. Listening to his talk about the arts was a liberal education. At Oxford I began writing verse. I had several volumes of verse published before I turned to writing stories. I was very lucky; I never had any difficulty getting published. After the war, when I came down from Oxford, I had to make my living. I had a job on the *Athenaeum*, but that paid very little, not enough to live on; so in spare moments I worked for the Condé Nast publications. I worked for *Vogue* and *Vanity Fair*, and for *House and Garden*. I used to turn out articles on everything from decorative plaster to Persian rugs. And that wasn't all. I did dramatic criticism for the *Westminster Review*. Why – would you believe it? – I even did music criticism. I heartily recommend this sort of journalism as an apprenticeship. It forces you to write on everything under the sun, it develops your facility, it teaches you to master your material quickly, and it makes you look at things. Fortunately, though, I didn't have to keep at it very long. After *Crome Yellow* – that was in 1921 – I didn't have to worry so much about making a living. I was already married, and we were then able to live on the Continent – in Italy until the Fascists made life unpleasant, then in France. We had a little house outside Paris, where I could write without being disturbed. We'd be in London part of every year, but there was always too much going on; I couldn't get much writing done there.

INTERVIEWERS: Do you think that certain occupations are more conducive to creative writing than others? In other words, does the work you do or the company you keep affect your writing?

HUXLEY: I don't believe there is an ideal occupation for the writer. He could write under almost any circumstance, even in complete isolation. Why, look at Balzac, locked up in a secret room in Paris, hiding from his creditors, and producing the *Comédie Humaine*. Or think of Proust in his cork-lined room (although of course he had plenty of visitors). I suppose the best occupation is just meeting a great many different kinds of people and seeing what interests them. That's one of the disadvantages of getting older; you're inclined to make intimate contacts with fewer people.

INTERVIEWERS: What would you say makes the writer different from other people?

HUXLEY: Well, one has the urge, first of all, to order the facts one observes and to give meaning to life; and along with that goes the love of words for their own sake and a desire to manipulate them. It's not a matter of intelligence; some very intelligent and original people don't have the love of words or the knack to use them effectively. On the verbal level they express themselves very badly.

INTERVIEWERS: What about creativeness in general?

HUXLEY: Yes, what about it? Why is it that in most children education seems to destroy the creative urge? Why do so many boys and girls leave school with blunted perceptions and a closed mind? A majority of young people seem to develop mental arteriosclerosis forty years before they get the physical kind. Another question: why do some people remain open and elastic into extreme old age, whereas others become rigid and unproductive before they're fifty? It's a problem in biochemistry and adult education.

INTERVIEWERS: Some psychologists have claimed that the creative urge is a kind of neurosis. Would you agree?

HUXLEY: Most emphatically not. I don't believe for a moment that creativity is a neurotic symptom. On the contrary, the neurotic who succeeds as an artist has had to overcome a tremendous handicap. He creates in spite of his neurosis, not because of it.

INTERVIEWERS: You've never had much use for Freud, have you?

HUXLEY: The trouble with Freudian psychology is that it is based exclusively on a study of the sick. Freud never met a healthy human being – only patients and other psycho-analysts. Then too, Freudian psychology is only concerned with the past. Other systems of psychology, that concern themselves with the present state of the subject or his future potentialities, seem to me to be more realistic.

INTERVIEWERS: Do you see any relation between the creative process and the use of such drugs as lysergic acid?

HUXLEY: I don't think there is any generalization one can make on this. Experience has shown that there's an enormous variation in the way people respond to lysergic acid. Some people probably could get direct aesthetic inspiration for painting or poetry out of it. Others I don't think could. For most people it's an extremely significant experience, and I suppose in an indirect way it could help the creative process. But I don't think one can sit down and say, 'I want to write a magnificent poem, and so I'm going to take lysergic acid.' I don't think it's by any means certain that you would get the result you wanted – you might get almost any result.

INTERVIEWERS: Would the drug give more help to the lyric poet than the novelist?

HUXLEY: Well, the poet would certainly get an extraordinary view of life which he wouldn't have had in any other way, and this might help him a great deal. But, you see (and this is the most significant thing about the experience), during the experience you're really not interested in doing anything practical – even writing lyric poetry. If you were making love to a woman, would you be interested in writing about it? Of course not. And during the experience you're not particularly interested in words, because the experience transcends words and is quite inexpressible in terms of words. So the whole notion of conceptualizing what is happening seems very silly. *After* the event, it seems to me quite possible that it might be of great assistance; people would see the universe around them in a very different way and would be inspired, possibly, to write something about it.

INTERVIEWERS: But is there much carry-over from the experience?

HUXLEY: Well, there's always a complete memory of the experience. You remember something extraordinary having happened. And to some extent you can relive the experience, particularly the transformation of the outside world. You get hints of this, you see the world in this transfigured way now and then – not to the same pitch of intensity, but something of the kind. It does help you to look at the world in a new way. And you come to understand very clearly the way that certain specially gifted people have seen the world. You are actually introduced into the kind of world that Van Gogh lived in, or the kind of world that Blake lived in. You begin to have a direct experience of this kind of world while you're under the drug, and afterwards you can remember and to some slight extent recapture this kind of world, which certain privileged people have moved in and out of, as Blake obviously did all the time.

INTERVIEWERS: But the artist's talents won't be any different from what they were before he took the drug?

HUXLEY: I don't see why they should be different. Some experiments have been made to see what painters can do under the influence of the drug, but most of the examples I have seen are very uninteresting. You could never hope to reproduce to the full extent the quite incredible intensity of colour that you get under the influence of the drug. Most of the things I have seen are just rather tiresome bits of expressionism, which correspond hardly at all, I would think, to the actual experience. Maybe an immensely gifted artist – someone like Odilon Redon (who probably saw the world like this all the time, anyhow) – maybe such a man could profit by the lysergic-acid experience, could use his visions as models, could reproduce on canvas the external world as it is transfigured by the drug.

INTERVIEWERS: Here this afternoon, as in your book, *The Doors of Perception*, you've been talking chiefly about the visual experience under the drug, and about painting. Is there any similar gain in psychological insight?

HUXLEY: Yes, I think there is. While one is under the drug one has penetrating insights into the people around one, and also into one's own life. Many people get tremendous recalls of buried material. A process which may take six years of psychoanalysis happens in an hour – and considerably cheaper! And the experience can be very liberating and widening in other ways. It shows that the world one habitually lives in is merely a creation of this conventional, closely conditioned being which one is, and that there are quite other kinds of worlds outside. It's a very salutary thing to realize that the rather dull universe in which most of us spend our time is not the only universe there is. I think it's healthy that people should have this experience.

INTERVIEWERS: Could such psychological insight be helpful to the fiction writer?

HUXLEY: I doubt it. After all, fiction is the fruit of sustained effort. The lysergic-acid experience is a revelation of something outside of time and the social order. To write fiction, one needs a whole series of inspirations about people in an actual environment, and then a whole lot of hard work on the basis of those inspirations.

INTERVIEWERS: Is there any resemblance between lysergic acid, or mescaline, and the 'soma' of your *Brave New World*?

HUXLEY: None whatever. Soma is an imaginary drug, with three different effects – euphoric, hallucinant, or sedative – an impossible combination. Mescalin is the active principle of the peyote cactus, which has been used for a long time by the Indians of the South-west in their religious rites. It is now synthesized. Lysergic acid diethylamide (LSD-25) is a chemical compound with effects similar to mescalin; it was developed about twelve years ago, and it is only being used experimentally at present. Mescalin and lysergic acid transfigure the external world and in some cases produce visions. Most people have the sort of positive and enlightening experience I've described; but the visions may be infernal as well as celestial. These drugs are physiologically innocuous, except to people with liver damage. They leave most people with no hangover, and they are not habit-forming. Psychiatrists have found that, skilfully used, they can be very helpful in the treatment of certain kinds of neuroses.

INTERVIEWERS: How did you happen to get involved in experiments with mescalin and lysergic acid?

HUXLEY: Well, I'd been interested in it for some years, and I had been in correspondence with Humphrey Osmond, a very gifted young British psychiatrist working in Canada. When he started testing its effects on different kinds of people, I became one of his guinea pigs. I've described all this in *The Doors of Perception*.

INTERVIEWERS: To return to writing, in *Point Counter Point* you have Philip Quarles say, 'I am not a congenital novelist.' Would you say the same of yourself?

HUXLEY: I don't think of myself as a congenital novelist – no. For example, I have great difficulty in inventing plots. Some people are born with an amazing gift for story-telling; it's a gift which I've never had. One reads, for example, Stevenson's accounts of how all the plots for his stories were provided in dreams by his subconscious mind (what he calls the 'Brownies' working for him), and that all he had to do was to work up the material they had provided. I've never had any Brownies. The great difficulty for me has always been creating situations.

INTERVIEWERS: Developing character has been easier for you than creating plots?

HUXLEY: Yes, but even then I'm not very good at creating people; I don't have a very wide repertory of characters. These are difficult things for me. I suppose it's largely a question of temperament. I don't happen to have the right kind of temperament.

INTERVIEWERS: By the phrase 'congenital novelist' we thought you meant one who is only interested in writing novels.

HUXLEY: I suppose this is another way of saying the same thing. The congenital novelist doesn't have other interests. Fiction for him is an absorbing thing which fills up his mind and takes all his time and energy, whereas someone else with a different kind of mind has these other, extracurricular activities going on.

INTERVIEWERS: As you look back on your novels, which are you most happy with?

HUXLEY: I personally think the most successful was *Time Must Have a Stop*. I don't know, but it seemed to me that I integrated what may be called the essay element with the fictional element better there than in other novels. Maybe this is not the case. It just happens to be the one that I like best, because I feel that it came off best.

INTERVIEWERS: As you see it, then, the novelist's problem is to fuse the 'essay element' with the story?

HUXLEY: Well, there are lots of excellent story-tellers who are simply story-tellers, and I think it's a wonderful gift, after all. I suppose the extreme example is Dumas: that extraordinary old gentleman, who sat down and thought nothing of writing six volumes of *The Count of Monte Cristo* in a few months. And my God, *Monte Cristo* is damned good! But it isn't the last word. When you can find story-telling which carries at the same time a kind of parable-like meaning (such as you get, say, in Dostoevski or in the best of Tolstoy), this is something extraordinary, I feel. I'm always flabbergasted when I re-read some of the short things of Tolstoy, like *The Death of Ivan Ilyich*. What an astounding work that is! Or some of the short things of Dostoevski, like *Notes from Underground*.

INTERVIEWERS: What other novelists have especially affected you?

HUXLEY: It's awfully difficult for me to answer such a question. I read individual books that I like and take things from and am stimulated by.... As a very young man, as an undergraduate, I used to read a lot of French novels. I was very fond of a novelist who is now very much out-of-date – Anatole France. I haven't read him now for forty years; I don't know what he's like. Then I remember reading the first volume of Proust in 1915 and being tremendously impressed by it. (I re-read it recently and was curiously disappointed.) Gide I read at that time too.

INTERVIEWERS: Several of your early novels, *Point Counter Point* especially, appear to have been written under the influence of Proust and Gide. It this so?

HUXLEY: I suppose some of my early novels are faintly Proustian. I don't think I shall ever experiment again with the kind of treatment of time and remembrance of things past that I used in *Eyeless in Gaza*, shifting back and forth in time to show the pressure of the past on the present.

INTERVIEWERS: Then in some of those early novels you also make use of musical effects, much as Gide does.

HUXLEY: The marvellous thing about music is that it does so easily and rapidly what can be done only very laboriously in words, or really can't be done at all. It's futile to even attempt to write musically. But I've tried in some of my essays – in *Themes and Variations*, for instance. Then I've used the equivalent of musical variations in some of my stories, where I take certain traits of character and treat them seriously in one personage and comically, in a sort of parody, in another.

INTERVIEWERS: Were you much taken with Joyce?

HUXLEY: Never very much – no. I never got very much out of *Ulysses*. I think it's an extraordinary book, but so much of it consists of rather lengthy demonstrations of how a novel ought *not* to be written, doesn't it? He does show nearly every conceivable way it should not be written, and then goes on to show how it might be written.

INTERVIEWERS: What do you think of Virginia Woolf's fiction?

HUXLEY: Her works are very strange. They're very beautiful, aren't they? But one gets such a curious feeling from them. She sees with incredible clarity, but always as though through a sheet of plate glass; she never touches anything. Her books are not immediate. They're very puzzling to me.

INTERVIEWERS: How about Henry James? Or Thomas Mann?

HUXLEY: James leaves me very cold. And I find Mann a little boring. He's obviously an admirable novelist. You know, I used to go every summer to the place described in *Mario and the Magician*, and it seemed to me that I never got any sense of the place out of Mann. I knew it very well: the coast where Shelley was washed up, under the mountains of Carrara, where the marble comes from. It was an incredibly beautiful place then. Now, needless to say, it's all become like Coney Island, with millions of people there.

INTERVIEWERS: Speaking of places, do you think your own writing was affected when you transplanted yourself from England to America?

HUXLEY: I don't know – I don't think so. I never strongly felt that the place where I lived had great importance to me.

INTERVIEWERS: Then you don't think the social climate makes much difference to fiction?

HUXLEY: Well, what is 'fiction'? So many people talk

about 'fiction' or 'the writer' as though you could generalize about them. There are always many diverse members of the group; and fiction is a genus of which there are many species. I think that certain species of fiction quite clearly call for a certain locale. It's impossible that Trollope could have written except where he did write. He couldn't have gone off to Italy like Byron or Shelley. He required the English middle-class life. But then look at Lawrence. At the beginning you would have said that he had to stay in the Midlands of England, near the coal mines. But he could write anywhere.

INTERVIEWERS: Now, thirty years later, would you care to say what you think of Lawrence as a novelist and as a man?

HUXLEY: I occasionally re-read some of his books. How good he is! Especially in the short stories. And the other day I read part of *Women in Love*, and that again seemed very good. The vividness, the incredible vividness of the descriptions of nature is amazing in Lawrence. But sometimes one doesn't know what he's getting at. In *The Plumed Serpent*, for instance, he'll glorify the Mexican Indians with their dark life of the blood on one page, and then on the next he'll damn the lazy natives like a British colonel in the days of Kipling. That book is a mass of contradictions. I was very fond of Lawrence as a man. I knew him very well the last four years of his life. I had met him during the First World War and saw him a certain amount then, but I didn't get to know him really well until 1926. I was a little disturbed by him. You know, he *was* rather disturbing. And to a conventionally brought up young bourgeois he was rather difficult to understand. But later on I got to know and like him. My first wife became very friendly with him and understood him and they got on very well together. We saw the Lawrences often during those last four years; they stayed with us in Paris, then we were together in Switzerland, and we visited them at the Villa Mirenda near Florence. My wife typed out the manuscript of *Lady Chatterley's Lover* for him, even though she was a bad typist and had no patience with English spelling – she was a Belgian, you know. Then she didn't always appreciate the nuances of the language she was typing. When she started using some of those four-letter words in conversation, Lawrence was profoundly shocked.

INTERVIEWERS: Why did Lawrence keep moving around so much?

HUXLEY: One reason he was for ever moving on is that his relations with people would become so complicated that he'd have to get away. He was a man who loved and hated too intensely; he both loved and hated the same people at the same time. Then, like a great many tubercular people, he was convinced that climate had a great effect on him – not only the temperature, but the direction of the wind, and all sorts of atmospheric conditions. He had invented a whole mythology of climate. In his last years he wanted to go back to New Mexico. He had been very happy there on the ranch in Taos. But he wasn't strong enough to make the trip. By all the rules of medicine he should have been dead; but he lived on, supported by some kind of energy that seemed to be independent of his body. And he kept on writing to the end. ... We were there, in Vence, when he died. ... He actually died in my first wife's arms. After his death his wife Frieda was utterly helpless and didn't know what to do with herself. Physically she was very strong, but in the practical affairs of life she depended on Lawrence entirely. For instance, when she went back to London after his death to settle his affairs, she stayed in a particularly dreary old hotel, simply because she had stayed there once with him and didn't feel secure in any other place.

INTERVIEWERS: Certain characters in your novels seem to have been based on people you knew – on Lawrence and Norman Douglas and Middleton Murry, for instance. Is this true? And how do you convert a real person into a fictional character?

HUXLEY: I try to imagine how certain people I know would behave in certain circumstances. Of course I base my characters partly on the people I know – one can't escape it – but fictional characters are over-simplified; they're much less complex than the people one knows. There is something of Murry in several of my characters, but I wouldn't say I'd put Murry in a book. And there is something of Norman

Douglas in old Scogan of *Crome Yellow*. I knew Douglas quite well in the 'twenties in Florence. He was a remarkably intelligent and highly educated man, but he had deliberately limited himself to the point where he would talk about almost nothing but drink and sex. He became quite boring after a time. Did you ever see that collection of pornographic limericks that he had privately printed? It was the only way, poor fellow, that he could make some money. It was a terribly unfunny book. I didn't see him at all in his later years.

INTERVIEWERS: Lawrence and Frieda are represented in Mark and Mary Rampton of *Point Counter Point*, aren't they? You even follow the story of the Lawrences quite closely in many particulars.

HUXLEY: Yes, I suppose so, but only a small part of Lawrence is in that character. Isn't it remarkable how everyone who knew Lawrence has felt compelled to write about him? Why, he's had more books written about him than any writer since Byron!

INTERVIEWERS: How do you name your characters? Do you pick them at random, like Simenon, out of telephone directories? Or are the names meant to convey something? Some of your characters in *After Many a Summer Dies the Swan* have odd names; do these have any particular significance?

HUXLEY: Yes, names are very important, aren't they? And the most unlikely names keep turning up in real life, so one must be careful. I can explain some of the names in *After Many a Summer*. Take Virginia Maunciple. That name was suggested to me by Chaucer's manciple. What is a manciple, anyhow? A kind of steward. It's the sort of name that a movie starlet would choose, in the hope of being unique, custom-made. She's called Virginia because she appears so virginal to Jeremy and so obviously isn't in fact; also because of her devotion to the Madonna. Dr Sigmund Obispo; here the first name obviously refers to Freud, and Obispo I took from San Luis Obispo for local colour and because it has a comical sound. And Jeremy Pordage. There's a story connected with that name. When I was an undergraduate at Oxford,

Professor Walter Raleigh (who was a marvellous teacher) had me do a piece of research on the literature connected with the Popish Plot. One of the authors mentioned by Dryden under the name of 'lame Mephibosheth' was called Pordage. His poetry, when I read it at the Bodleian, turned out to be unbelievably bad. But the name was a treasure. As for Jeremy, that was chosen for the sound; combined with Pordage it has a rather spinsterish ring. Propter came from the Latin for 'on account of' – because, as a wise man, he is concerned with ultimate causes. Another reason why I chose the name was its occurrence in a poem of Edward Lear, 'Incidents in the Life of My Uncle Arly'. Let's see, how does it go now?

> *Like the ancient Medes and Persians,*
> *Always by his own exertions*
> *He subsisted on those hills;*
> *Whiles, by teaching children spelling,*
> *Or at times by merely yelling,*
> *Or at intervals by selling*
> *'Propter's Nicodemus Pills'.*

Pete Boone doesn't mean anything in particular. It's just a straightforward American name that suits the character. Jo Stoyte, too – the name simply means what it sounds like.

INTERVIEWERS: You seem to have turned away from satire in recent years. What do you think of satire now?

HUXLEY: Yes, I suppose I have changed in that respect. But I'm all for satire. We need it. People everywhere take things much too seriously, I think. People are much too solemn about things. I'm all for sticking pins into episcopal behinds, and that sort of thing. It seems to me a most salutary proceeding.

INTERVIEWERS: Were you fond of Swift as a young man?

HUXLEY: Oh, yes, I was very fond of Swift. And of another book, a wonderfully funny book, one of the few old books that have stayed funny: *The Letters of Obscure Men*, the *Epistolae Obscurorum Virorum*. I'm sure Swift must have read it; it is so much his method. In general, I get a great deal out of the eighteenth century: Hume, Law, Crébillon, Diderot, Fielding, Pope – though I'm old-fashioned enough to think the Romantics are better poets than Pope.

INTERVIEWERS: You praised Fielding long ago in your essay 'Tragedy and the Whole Truth'. Do you still believe that fiction can give a fuller view of life than tragedy?

HUXLEY: Yes, I still believe that tragedy is not necessarily the highest form. The highest form does not yet exist, perhaps. I can conceive of something much more inclusive and yet equally sublime, something which is adumbrated in the plays of Shakespeare. I think that in some way the tragic and comic elements can be more totally fused. I don't know how. Don't ask me how. If we get another Shakespeare one of these days – as I hope we will – perhaps we'll see. As I say in that essay, Homer has a kind of fusion of these elements, but on a very simple-minded level. But, my goodness, how good Homer is, anyhow! And there's another really sublime writer who has this quality – Chaucer. Why, Chaucer invented a whole psychology out of absolutely nothing: an incredible achievement. It's one of the great misfortunes of English literature that Chaucer wrote at a time when his language was to become incomprehensible. If he had been born two or three hundred years later I think the whole course of English literature would have been changed. We wouldn't have had this sort of Platonic mania – separating mind from body and spirit from matter.

INTERVIEWERS: Then, even though you have been writing fewer novels in recent years, you don't think less highly of the art of fiction than you used to?

HUXLEY: Oh, no, no no. I think fiction, and biography and history, are *the* forms. I think one can say much more about general abstract ideas in terms of concrete characters and situations, whether fictional or real, than one can in abstract terms. Several of the books I like best of what I've written are historical and biographical things: *Grey Eminence*, and *The Devils of Loudun*, and the biography of Maine de Biran, the 'Variations on a Philosopher'. These are all discussions of what are to me important general ideas in terms of specific lives and incidents. And I must say I think that probably *all* philosophy ought to be written in this form; it would be much more profound and much more edifying. It's awfully easy to write abstractly, without attaching much meaning to the big words. But the moment you have to express ideas in the light of a particular context, in a particular set of circumstances, although it's a limitation in some ways, it's also an invitation to go much further and much deeper. I think that fiction and, as I say, history and biography are *immensely* important, not only for their own sake, because they provide a picture of life now and of life in the past, but also as vehicles for the expression of general philosophic ideas, religious ideas, social ideas. My goodness, Dostoevski is six times as profound as Kierkegaard, because he writes *fiction*. In Kierkegaard you have this Abstract Man going on and on – like Coleridge – why, it's *nothing* compared with the really profound Fictional Man, who has always to keep these tremendous ideas *alive* in a concrete form. In fiction you have the reconciliation of the absolute and the relative, so to speak, the expression of the general in the particular. And this, it seems to me, is the exciting thing – both in life and in art.

George Wickes
Ray Frazer

ERNEST HEMINGWAY

HEMINGWAY: *You go to the races?*
INTERVIEWER: *Yes, occasionally.*
HEMINGWAY: *Then you read the* Racing Form. . . . *There you have the true art of fiction.*
– Conversation in a Madrid café, May 1954

Ernest Hemingway writes in the bedroom of his house in the Havana suburb of San Francisco de Paula. He has a special work-room prepared for him in a square tower at the south-west corner of the house, but prefers to work in his bedroom, climbing to the tower room only when 'characters' drive him up there.

The bedroom is on the ground floor and connects with the main room of the house. The door between the two is kept ajar by a heavy volume listing and describing The World's Aircraft Engines. *The bedroom is large, sunny, the windows facing east and south letting in the day's light on white walls and a yellow-tinged tile floor.*

The room is divided into two alcoves by a pair of chest-high bookcases that stand out into the room at right angles from opposite walls. A large and low double bed dominates one section, oversized slippers and loafers neatly arranged at the foot, the two bedside tables at the head piled seven-high with books. In the other alcove stands a massive flat-top desk with a chair at either side, its surface an ordered clutter of papers and mementoes. Beyond it, at the far end of the room, is an armoire with a leopard skin draped across the top. The other walls are lined with white-painted bookcases from which books overflow to the floor, and are piled on top among old newspapers, bullfight journals, and stacks of letters bound together by rubber bands.

It is on the top of one of these cluttered bookcases – the one against the wall by the east window and three feet or so from his bed – that Hemingway has his 'work desk' – a square foot of cramped area hemmed in by books on one side and on the other by a newspaper-covered heap of papers, manuscripts and pamphlets. There is just enough space left on top of the bookcase for a typewriter, surmounted by a wooden reading board, five or six pencils and a chunk of copper ore to weight down papers when the wind blows in from the east window.

A working habit he has had from the beginning, Hemingway stands when he writes. He stands in a pair of his oversized loafers on the worn skin of a Lesser Kudu – the typewriter and the reading board chest-high opposite him.

When Hemingway starts on a project he always begins with a pencil, using the reading board to write on onionskin typewriter paper. He keeps a sheaf of the blank paper on a clipboard to the left of the typewriter, extracting the paper a sheet at a time from under a metal clip which reads 'These Must Be Paid.' He places the paper slantwise on the reading board, leans against the board with his left arm, steadying the paper with his hand, and fills the paper with handwriting which through the years has become larger, more boyish, with a paucity of punctuation, very few capitals, and often the period marked with an x. The page completed, he clips it face-down on another clipboard which he places off to the right of the typewriter.

Hemingway shifts to the typewriter, lifting off the reading board, only when the writing is going fast and well, or when the writing is, for him at least, simple: dialogue, for instance.

He keeps track of his daily progress – 'so as not to kid myself' – on a large chart made out of the side of a cardboard packing-case and set up against the wall under the nose of a mounted gazelle head. The numbers on the chart showing the daily output of words differ from 450, 575, 462, 1250, back to 512, the higher figures on days Hemingway puts in extra work so he won't feel guilty spending the following day fishing on the Gulf Stream.

A man of habit, Hemingway does not use the perfectly suitable desk in the other alcove. Though it allows more space for writing, it too has its miscellany: stacks of letters, a stuffed toy lion of the type sold in Broadway nighteries, a

small burlap bag full of carnivore teeth, shotgun shells, a
shoe-horn, wood carvings of lion, rhino, two zebras, and a
wart-hog – these last set in a neat row across the surface of
the desk – and, of course, books: piled on the desk, beside
tables, jamming the shelves in indiscriminate order – novels,
histories, collections of poetry, drama, essays. A look at their
titles shows their variety. On the shelf opposite Hemingway's
knee as he stands up to his 'work desk' are Virginia Woolf's
The Common Reader, *Ben Ames Williams's* House Divided,
The Partisan Reader, *Charles A. Beard's* The Republic,
Tarle's Napoleon's Invasion of Russia, How Young You
Look *by Peggy Wood, Alden Brooks's* Will Shakespeare and
the Dyer's Hand, *Baldwin's* African Hunting, *T. S. Eliot's*
Collected Poems, *and two books on General Custer's fall at*
the battle of the Little Big Horn.

The room, however, for all the disorder sensed at first
sight, indicates on inspection an owner who is basically neat
but cannot bear to throw anything away – especially if sen-
timental value is attached. One bookcase top has an odd as-
sortment of mementoes: a giraffe made of wood beads, a
little cast-iron turtle, tiny models of a locomotive, two jeeps
and a Venetian gondola, a toy bear with a key in its back, a
monkey carrying a pair of cymbals, a miniature guitar, and
a little tin model of a U.S. Navy biplane (one wheel missing)
resting awry on a circular straw place mat – the quality of
the collection that of the odds-and-ends which turn up in a
shoe-box at the back of a small boy's closet. It is evident,
though, that these tokens have their value, just as three
buffalo horns Hemingway keeps in his bedroom have a value
dependent not on size but because during the acquiring of
them things went badly in the bush which ultimately turned
out well. 'It cheers me up to look at them,' he says.

Hemingway may admit superstitions of this sort, but he
prefers not to talk about them, feeling that whatever value
they may have can be talked away. He has much the same
attitude about writing. Many times during the making of
this interview he stressed that the craft of writing should not
be tampered with by an excess of scrutiny – 'that though
there is one part of writing that is solid and you do it no

*harm by talking about it, the other is fragile, and if you talk
about it, the structure cracks and you have nothing.'*

*As a result, though a wonderful raconteur, a man of rich
humour, and possessed of an amazing fund of knowledge on
subjects which interest him, Hemingway finds it difficult to
talk about writing – not because he has few ideas on the subject, but rather that he feels so strongly that such ideas
should remain unexpressed, that to be asked questions on
them 'spooks' him (to use one of his favourite expressions) to
the point where he is almost inarticulate. Many of the replies
in this interview he preferred to work out on his reading
board. The occasional waspish tone of the answers is also
part of this strong feeling that writing is a private, lonely
occupation with no need for witnesses until the final work is
done.*

*This dedication to his art may suggest a personality
at odds with the rambunctious, carefree, world-wheeling
Hemingway-at-play of popular conception. The fact is that
Hemingway, while obviously enjoying life, brings an equivalent dedication to everything he does – an outlook that is
essentially serious, with a horror of the inaccurate, the
fraudulent, the deceptive, the half-baked.*

*Nowhere is the dedication he gives his art more evident
than in the yellow-tiled bedroom – where early in the morning Hemingway gets up to stand in absolute concentration
in front of his reading board, moving only to shift weight
from one foot to another, perspiring heavily when the work is
going well, excited as a boy, fretful, miserable when the
artistic touch momentarily vanishes – slave of a self-imposed
discipline which lasts until about noon when he takes a
knotted walking stick and leaves the house for the swimming
pool where he takes his daily half-mile swim.*

INTERVIEWER: Are these hours during the actual process of writing pleasurable?

HEMINGWAY: Very.

INTERVIEWER: Could you say something of this process?
When do you work? Do you keep to a strict schedule?

HEMINGWAY: When I am working on a book or a story

I write every morning as soon after first light as possible. There is no one to disturb you and it is cool or cold and you come to your work and warm as you write. You read what you have written and, as you always stop when you know what is going to happen next, you go on from there. You write until you come to a place where you still have your juice and know what will happen next and you stop and try to live through until the next day when you hit it again. You have started at six in the morning, say, and may go on until noon or be through before that. When you stop you are as empty, and at the same time never empty but filling, as when you have made love to someone you love. Nothing can hurt you, nothing can happen, nothing means anything until the next day when you do it again. It is the wait until the next day that is hard to get through.

INTERVIEWER: Can you dismiss from your mind whatever project you're on when you're away from the typewriter?

HEMINGWAY: Of course. But it takes discipline to do it and this discipline is acquired. It has to be.

INTERVIEWER: Do you do any rewriting as you read up to the place you left off the day before? Or does that come later, when the whole is finished?

HEMINGWAY: I always rewrite each day up to the point where I stopped. When it is all finished, naturally you go over it. You get another chance to correct and rewrite when someone else types it, and you see it clean in type. The last chance is in the proofs. You're grateful for these different chances.

INTERVIEWER: How much rewriting do you do?

HEMINGWAY: It depends. I rewrote the ending to *Farewell to Arms*, the last page of it, thirty-nine times before I was satisfied.

INTERVIEWER: Was there some technical problem there? What was it that had stumped you?

HEMINGWAY: Getting the words right.

INTERVIEWER: Is it the re-reading that gets the 'juice' up?

HEMINGWAY: Re-reading places you at the point where

it *has* to go on, knowing it is as good as you can get it up to there. There is always juice somewhere.

INTERVIEWER: But are there times when the inspiration isn't there at all?

HEMINGWAY: Naturally. But if you stopped when you knew what would happen next, you can go on. As long as you can start, you are all right. The juice will come.

INTERVIEWER: Thornton Wilder speaks of mnemonic devices that get the writer going on his day's work. He says you once told him you sharpened twenty pencils.

HEMINGWAY: I don't think I ever owned twenty pencils at one time. Wearing down seven number two pencils is a good day's work.

INTERVIEWER: Where are some of the places you have found most advantageous to work? The Ambos Mundos hotel must have been one, judging from the number of books you did there. Or do surroundings have little effect on the work?

HEMINGWAY: The Ambos Mundos in Havana was a very good place to work in. This Finca is a splendid place, or was. But I have worked well everywhere. I mean I have been able to work as well as I can under varied circumstances. The telephone and visitors are the work destroyers.

INTERVIEWER: Is emotional stability necessary to write well? You told me once that you could only write well when you were in love. Could you expound on that a bit more?

HEMINGWAY: What a question. But full marks for trying. You can write any time people will leave you alone and not interrupt you. Or rather you can if you will be ruthless enough about it. But the best writing is certainly when you are in love. If it is all the same to you I would rather not expound on that.

INTERVIEWER: How about financial security? Can that be a detriment to good writing?

HEMINGWAY: If it came early enough and you loved life as much as you loved your work it would take much character to resist the temptations. Once writing has become your major vice and greatest pleasure only death can stop it. Financial security then is a great help as it keeps you from worrying. Worry destroys the ability to write. Ill health is bad in the ratio that it produces worry which attacks your subconscious and destroys your reserves.

INTERVIEWER: Can you recall an exact moment when you decided to become a writer?

HEMINGWAY: No, I always wanted to be a writer.

INTERVIEWER: Philip Young in his book on you suggests that the traumatic shock of your severe 1918 mortar wound had a great influence on you as a writer. I remember in Madrid you talked briefly about his thesis, finding little in it, and going on to say that you thought the artist's equipment was not an acquired characteristic, but inherited, in the Mendelian sense.

HEMINGWAY: Evidently in Madrid that year my mind could not be called very sound. The only thing to recommend it would be that I spoke only briefly about Mr Young's book and his trauma theory of literature. Perhaps the two concussions and a skull fracture of that year had made me irresponsible in my statements. I do remember telling you that I believed imagination could be the result of inherited racial experience. It sounds all right in good jolly post-concussion talk, but I think that is more or less where it belongs. So until the next liberation trauma, let's leave it there. Do you agree? But thanks for leaving out the names of any relatives I might have implicated. The fun of talk is to explore, but much of it and all that is irresponsible should not be written. Once written you have to stand by it. You may have said it to see whether you believed it or not. On the question you raised, the effects of wounds vary greatly. Simple wounds which do not break bone are of little account. They sometimes give confidence. Wounds which do extensive bone and nerve damage are not good for writers, nor anybody else.

INTERVIEWER: What would you consider the best intellectual training for the would-be writer?

HEMINGWAY: Let's say that he should go out and hang himself because he finds that writing well is impossibly difficult. Then he should be cut down without mercy and forced by his own self to write as well as he can for the rest of his life. At least he will have the story of the hanging to commence with.

INTERVIEWER: How about people who've gone into the academic career? Do you think the large numbers of writers who hold teaching positions have compromised their literary careers?

HEMINGWAY: It depends on what you call compromise. Is the usage that of a woman who has been compromised? Or is it the compromise of the statesman? Or the compromise made with your grocer or your tailor that you will pay a little more but will pay it later? A writer who can both write and teach should be able to do both. Many competent writers have proved it could be done. I could not do it, I know, and I admire those who have been able to. I would think though that the academic life could put a period to outside experience which might possibly limit growth of knowledge of the world. Knowledge, however, demands more responsibility of a writer and makes writing more difficult. Trying to write something of permanent value is a full-time job even though only a few hours a day are spent on the actual writing. A writer can be compared to a well. There are as many kinds of wells as there are writers. The important thing is to have good water in the well and it is better to take a regular amount out than to pump the well dry and wait for it to refill. I see I am getting away from the question, but the question was not very interesting.

INTERVIEWER: Would you suggest newspaper work for the young writer? How helpful was the training you had with the *Kansas City Star*?

HEMINGWAY: On the *Star* you were forced to learn to write a simple declarative sentence. This is useful to anyone. Newspaper work will not harm a young writer and could help him if he gets out of it in time. This is one of the dustiest clichés there is and I apologize for it. But when you ask someone old tired questions you are apt to receive old tired answers.

INTERVIEWER: You once wrote in the *Transatlantic Review* that the only reason for writing journalism was to be well paid. You said: 'And when you destroy the valuable things you have by writing about them, you want to get big money for it.' Do you think of writing as a type of self-destruction?

HEMINGWAY: I do not remember even writing that. But it sounds silly and violent enough for me to have said it to avoid having to bite on the nail and make a sensible statement. I certainly do not think of writing as a type of self-destruction, though journalism, after a point has been reached, can be a daily self-destruction for a serious creative writer.

INTERVIEWER: Do you think the intellectual stimulus of the company of other writers is of any value to an author?

HEMINGWAY: Certainly.

INTERVIEWER: In the Paris of the 'twenties did you have any sense of 'group feeling' with other writers and artists?

HEMINGWAY: No. There was no group feeling. We had respect for each other. I respected a lot of painters, some of my own age, others older – Gris, Picasso, Braque, Monet, who was still alive then – and a few writers: Joyce, Ezra, the good of Stein ...

INTERVIEWER: When you're writing, do you ever find yourself influenced by what you're reading at the time?

HEMINGWAY: Not since Joyce was writing *Ulysses*. He was not a direct influence. But in those days when words we knew were barred to us, and we had to fight for a single word, the influence of his work was what changed everything, and made it possible for us to break away from the restrictions.

INTERVIEWER: Could you learn anything about writing from the writers? You were telling me yesterday that Joyce, for example, couldn't bear to talk about writing.

HEMINGWAY: In company with people of your own trade you ordinarily speak of other writers' books. The better the writers the less they will speak about what they have written themselves. Joyce was a very great writer and he would only explain what he was doing to jerks. Other writers that he respected were supposed to be able to know what he was doing by reading it.

INTERVIEWER: You seem to have avoided the company of writers in late years. Why?

HEMINGWAY: That is more complicated. The further you go in writing the more alone you are. Most of your best and oldest friends die. Others move away. You do not see them except rarely, but you write and have much the same contact with them as though you were together at the café in the old days. You exchange comic, sometimes cheerfully obscene and irresponsible letters, and it is almost as good as talking. But you are more alone because that is how you must work and the time to work is shorter all the time and if you waste it you feel you have committed a sin for which there is no forgiveness.

INTERVIEWER: What about the influence of some of these people – your contemporaries – on your work? What was Gertrude Stein's contribution, if any? Or Ezra Pound's? or Max Perkins'?

HEMINGWAY: I'm sorry but I am no good at these postmortems. There are coroners literary and non-literary provided to deal with such matters. Miss Stein wrote at some length and with considerable inaccuracy about her influence on my work. It was necessary for her to do this after she had learned to write dialogue from a book called *The Sun Also Rises*. I was very fond of her and thought it was splendid she had learned to write conversation. It was no new thing to me to learn from everyone I could, living or dead, and I had no idea it would affect Gertrude so violently. She already wrote very well in other ways. Ezra was extremely intelligent on the subjects he really knew. Doesn't this sort of talk bore you? This backyard literary gossip while washing out the dirty clothes of thirty-five years ago is disgusting to me. It would be different if one had tried to tell the whole truth. That would have some value. Here it is simpler and better to thank Gertrude for everything I learned from her about the abstract relationship of words, say how fond I was of her, reaffirm my loyalty to Ezra as a great poet and a loyal friend, and say that I cared so much for Max Perkins that I have never been able to accept that he is dead. He never asked me to change anything I wrote except to re-

move certain words which were not then publishable. Blanks
were left, and anyone who knew the words would know what
they were. For me he was not an editor. He was a wise
friend and a wonderful companion. I liked the way he wore
his hat and the strange way his lips moved.

INTERVIEWER: Who would you say are your literary
forebears – those you learned the most from?

HEMINGWAY: Mark Twain, Flaubert, Stendhal, Bach,
Turgenev, Tolstoi, Dostoevski, Chekhov, Andrew Marvell,
John Donne, Maupassant, the good Kipling, Thoreau, Captain Marryat, Shakespeare, Mozart, Quevedo. Dante, Vergil,
Tintoretto, Hieronymus Bosch, Brueghel, Patinir, Goya,
Giotto, Cézanne, Van Gogh, Gauguin, San Juan de la Cruz,
Góngora – it would take a day to remember everyone. Then
it would sound as though I were claiming erudition I did
not possess instead of trying to remember all the people who
have been an influence on my life and work. This isn't an
old dull question. It is a very good but a solemn question
and requires an examination of conscience. I put in painters,
or started to, because I learn as much from painters about
how to write as from writers. You ask how this is done? It
would take another day of explaining. I should think what
one learns from composers and from the study of harmony
and counterpoint would be obvious.

INTERVIEWER: Did you ever play a musical instrument?

HEMINGWAY: I used to play 'cello. My mother kept me
out of school a whole year to study music and counterpoint.
She thought I had ability, but I was absolutely without
talent. We played chamber music – someone came in to play
the violin; my sister played the viola, and Mother the piano.
That 'cello – I played it worse than anyone on earth. Of
course, that year I was out doing other things too.

INTERVIEWER: Do you reread the authors of your list?
Twain for instance?

HEMINGWAY: You have to wait two or three years with
Twain. You remember too well. I read some Shakespeare
every year, *Lear* always. Cheers you up if you read that.

INTERVIEWER: Reading, then, is a constant occupation
and pleasure.

HEMINGWAY: I'm always reading books – as many as there are. I ration myself on them so that I'll always be in supply.

INTERVIEWER: Do you ever read manuscripts?

HEMINGWAY: You can get into trouble doing that unless you know the author personally. Some years ago I was sued for plagiarism by a man who claimed that I'd lifted *For Whom the Bell Tolls* from an unpublished screen scenario he'd written. He'd read this scenario at some Hollywood party. I was there, he said, at least there was a fellow called 'Ernie' there listening to the reading, and that was enough for him to sue for a million dollars. At the same time he sued the producers of the motion pictures *North-west Mounted Police* and the *Cisco Kid*, claiming that these, as well, had been stolen from that same unpublished scenario. We went to court and, of course, won the case. The man turned out to be insolvent.

INTERVIEWER: Well, could we go back to that list and take one of the painters – Hieronymus Bosch, for instance? The nightmare symbolic quality of his work seems so far removed from your own.

HEMINGWAY: I have the nightmares and know about the ones other people have. But you do not have to write them down. Anything you can omit that you know you still have in the writing and its quality will show. When a writer omits things he does not know, they show like holes in his writing.

INTERVIEWER: Does that mean that a close knowledge of the works of the people on your list helps fill the 'well' you were speaking of a while back? Or were they consciously a help in developing the techniques of writing?

HEMINGWAY: They were a part of learning to see, to hear, to think, to feel and not feel, and to write. The well is where your 'juice' is. Nobody knows what it is made of, least of all yourself. What you know is if you have it, or you have to wait for it to come back.

INTERVIEWER: Would you admit to there being symbolism in your novels?

HEMINGWAY: I suppose there are symbols since critics keep finding them. If you do not mind I dislike talking about them and being questioned about them. It is hard enough to write books and stories without being asked to explain them as well. Also it deprives the explainers of work. If five or six or more good explainers can keep going why should I interfere with them? Read anything I write for the pleasure of reading it. Whatever else you find will be the measure of what you brought to the reading.

INTERVIEWER: Continuing with just one more question on this line: One of the advisory staff editors wonders about a parallel he feels he's found in *The Sun Also Rises* between the dramatis personae of the bull ring and the characters of the novel itself. He points out that the first sequence of the book tells us Robert Cohn is a boxer; later, during the *desencajonada*, the bull is described as using his horns like a boxer, hooking and jabbing. And just as the bull is attracted and pacified by the presence of a steer, Robert Cohn defers to Jake who is emasculated precisely as is a steer. He sees Mike as the picador, baiting Cohn repeatedly. The editor's thesis goes on, but he wondered if it was your conscious intention to inform the novel with the tragic structure of the bullfight ritual.

HEMINGWAY: It sounds as though the advisory staff editor was a little bit screwy. Who ever said Jake was 'emasculated precisely as is a steer'? Actually he had been wounded in quite a different way and his testicles were intact and not damaged. Thus he was capable of all normal feelings as a *man* but incapable of consummating them. The important distinction is that his wound was physical and not psychological and that he was not emasculated.

INTERVIEWER: These questions which inquire into craftsmanship really are an annoyance.

HEMINGWAY: A sensible question is neither a delight nor an annoyance. I still believe, though, that it is very bad for a writer to talk about how he writes. He writes to be read by the eye and no explanations or dissertations should be necessary. You can be sure that there is much more there than will be read by any first reading and having made this it is not the writer's province to explain it or to run guided tours through the difficult country of his work.

INTERVIEWER: In connection with this, I remember you have also written that it is dangerous for a writer to talk about a work-in-progress, that he can 'talk it out' so to speak. Why should this be so? I only ask because there are so many writers – Twain, Wilde, Thurber, Steffens come to mind – who would seem to have polished their material by testing it on listeners.

HEMINGWAY: I cannot believe Twain ever 'tested out' *Huckleberry Finn* on listeners. If he did they probably had him cut out good things and put in the bad parts. Wilde was said by people who knew him to have been a better talker than a writer. Steffens talked better than he wrote. Both his writing and his talking were sometimes hard to believe, and I heard many stories change as he grew older. If Thurber can talk as well as he writes he must be one of the greatest and least boring talkers. The man I know who talks best about his own trade and has the pleasantest and most wicked tongue is Juan Belmonte, the matador.

INTERVIEWER: Could you say how much thought-out effort went into the evolvement of your distinctive style?

HEMINGWAY: That is a long-term tiring question and if you spent a couple of days answering it you would be so self-conscious that you could not write. I might say that what amateurs call a style is usually only the unavoidable awkwardness in first trying to make something that has not heretofore been made. Almost no new classics resemble other previous classics. At first people can see only the awkwardness. Then they are not so perceptible. When they show so very awkwardly people think these awkwardnesses are the style and many copy them. This is regrettable.

INTERVIEWER: You once wrote me that the simple circumstances under which various pieces of fiction were written could be instructive. Could you apply this to 'The Killers' – you said that you had written it, 'Ten Indians', and 'Today Is Friday' in one day – and perhaps to your first novel *The Sun Also Rises*?

HEMINGWAY: Let's see. *The Sun Also Rises* I started in Valencia on my birthday, July twenty-first. Hadley, my wife, and I had gone to Valencia early to get good tickets for the

Feria there which started the twenty-fourth of July. Everybody my age had written a novel and I was still having a difficult time writing a paragraph. So I started the book on my birthday, wrote all through the Feria, in bed in the morning, went on to Madrid and wrote there. There was no Feria there, so we had a room with a table and I wrote in great luxury on the table and around the corner from the hotel in a beer palace in the Pasaje Alvarez where it was cool. It finally got too hot to write and we went to Hendaye. There was a small cheap hotel there on the big long lovely beach and I worked very well there and then went up to Paris and finished the first draft in the apartment over the sawmill at 113 rue Notre-Dame-des-Champs six weeks from the day I started it. I showed the first draft to Nathan Asch, the novelist, who then had quite a strong accent, and he said, 'Hem, vaht do you mean saying you wrote a novel? A novel huh. Hem you are riding a travhel büch.' I was not too discouraged by Nathan and rewrote the book keeping in the travel (that was the part about the fishing trip and Pamplona) at Schruns in the Vorarlberg at the Hotel Taube.

The stories you mention I wrote in one day in Madrid on May sixteenth when it snowed out the San Isidro bullfights. First I wrote 'The Killers', which I'd tried to write before and failed. Then after lunch I got in bed to keep warm and wrote 'Today Is Friday'. I had so much juice I thought maybe I was going crazy and I had about six other stories to write. So I got dressed and walked to Fornos, the old bullfighters' café, and drank coffee and then came back and wrote 'Ten Indians'. This made me very sad and I drank some brandy and went to sleep. I'd forgotten to eat and one of the waiters brought me up some *bacalao* and a small steak and fried potatoes and a bottle of Valdepeñas.

The woman who ran the Pension was always worried that I did not eat enough and she had sent the waiter. I remember sitting up in bed and eating and drinking the Valdepeñas. The waiter said he would bring up another bottle. He said the Señora wanted to know if I was going to write all night. I said no, I thought I would lay off for a while. Why don't you try to write just one more, the waiter asked. I'm only supposed to write one, I said. Nonsense, he said. You could write six. I'll try tomorrow, I said. Try it tonight, he said. What do you think the old woman sent the food up for?

I'm tired, I told him. Nonsense, he said (the word was not nonsense). You tired after three miserable little stories. Translate me one.

Leave me alone, I said. How am I going to write if you don't leave me alone? So I sat up in bed and drank the Valdepeñas and thought what a hell of a writer I was if the first story was as good as I'd hoped.

INTERVIEWER: How complete in your own mind is the conception of a short story? Does the theme, or the plot, or a character change as you go along?

HEMINGWAY: Sometimes you know the story. Sometimes you make it up as you go along and have no idea how it will come out. Everything changes as it moves. That is what makes the movement which makes the story. Sometimes the movement is so slow it does not seem to be moving. But there is always change and always movement.

INTERVIEWER: Is it the same with the novel, or do you work out the whole plan before you start and adhere to it rigorously?

HEMINGWAY: *For Whom the Bell Tolls* was a problem which I carried on each day. I knew what was going to happen in principle. But I invented what happened each day I wrote.

INTERVIEWER: Were *The Green Hills of Africa, To Have and Have Not,* and *Across the River and Into the Trees* all started as short stories and developed into novels? If so, are the two forms so similar that the writer can pass from one to the other without completely revamping his approach?

HEMINGWAY: No, that is not true. *The Green Hills of Africa* is not a novel but was written in an attempt to write an absolutely true book to see whether the shape of a country and the pattern of a month's action could, if truly presented, compete with a work of the imagination. After I had written it I wrote two short stories, 'The Snows of Kilimanjaro' and 'The Short Happy Life of Francis Macomber'. These were stories which I invented from the knowledge and experience acquired on the same long hunting trip one month of which I had tried to write a truthful account of in *The Green Hills*. *To Have and Have Not* and *Across the River and Into the Trees* were both started as short stories.

INTERVIEWER: Do you find it easy to shift from one literary project to another or do you continue through to finish what you start?

HEMINGWAY: The fact that I am interrupting serious work to answer these questions proves that I am so stupid that I should be penalized severely. I will be. Don't worry.

INTERVIEWER: Do you think of yourself in competition with other writers?

HEMINGWAY: Never. I used to try to write better than certain dead writers of whose value I was certain. For a long time now I have tried simply to write the best I can. Sometimes I have good luck and write better than I can.

INTERVIEWER: Do you think a writer's power diminishes as he grows older? In *The Green Hills of Africa* you mention that American writers at a certain age change into Old Mother Hubbards.

HEMINGWAY: I don't know about that. People who know what they are doing should last as long as their heads last. In that book you mention, if you look it up, you'll see I was sounding off about American literature with a humourless Austrian character who was forcing me to talk when I wanted to do something else. I wrote an account of the conversation. Not to make deathless pronouncements. A fair per cent of the pronouncements are good enough.

INTERVIEWER: We've not discussed character. Are the characters of your work taken without exception from real life?

HEMINGWAY: Of course they are not. *Some* come from real life. Mostly you invent people from a knowledge and understanding and experience of people.

INTERVIEWER: Could you say something about the process of turning a real-life character into a fictional one?

HEMINGWAY: If I explained how that is sometimes done, it would be a handbook for libel lawyers.

INTERVIEWER: Do you make a distinction – as E. M. Forster does – between 'flat' and 'round' characters?

HEMINGWAY: If you describe someone, it is flat, as a photograph is, and from my standpoint a failure. If you make him up from what you know, there should be all the dimensions.

INTERVIEWER: Which of your characters do you look back on with particular affection?

HEMINGWAY: That would make too long a list.

INTERVIEWER: Then you enjoy reading over your books – without feeling there are changes to make?

HEMINGWAY: I read them sometimes to cheer me up when it is hard to write and then I remember that it was always difficult and how nearly impossible it was sometimes.

INTERVIEWER: How do you name your characters?

HEMINGWAY: The best I can.

INTERVIEWER: Do the titles come to you while you're in the process of doing the story?

HEMINGWAY: No. I make a list of titles *after* I've finished the story or the book – sometimes as many as a hundred. Then I start eliminating them, sometimes all of them.

INTERVIEWER: And you do this even with a story whose title is supplied from the text – 'Hills Like White Elephants', for example?

HEMINGWAY: Yes. The title comes afterwards. I met a girl in Prunier where I'd gone to eat oysters before lunch. I knew she'd had an abortion. I went over and we talked, not about that, but on the way home I thought of the story, skipped lunch, and spent that afternoon writing it.

INTERVIEWER: So when you're not writing, you remain constantly the observer, looking for something which can be of use.

HEMINGWAY: Surely. If a writer stops observing he is finished. But he does not have to observe consciously nor think how it will be useful. Perhaps that would be true at the beginning. But later everything he sees goes into the great reserve of things he knows or has seen. If it is any use to know it, I always try to write on the principle of the iceberg. There is seven-eighths of it underwater for every part that shows. Anything you know you can eliminate and it only strengthens your iceberg. It is the part that doesn't show. If a writer omits something because he does not know it then there is a hole in the story.

The Old Man and the Sea could have been over a thousand pages long and had every character in the village in it and all the processes of how they made their living, were born educated, bore children, etc. That is done excellently and well by other writers. In writing you are limited by what has already been done satisfactorily. So I have tried to learn to do something else. First I have tried to eliminate everything unnecessary to conveying experience to the reader so that after he or she has read something it will become a part of his or her experience and seem actually to have happened. This is very hard to do and I've worked at it very hard.

Anyway, to skip how it is done, I had unbelievable luck this time and could convey the experience completely and have it be one that no one had ever conveyed. The luck was that I had a good man and a good boy and lately writers have forgotten there still are such things. Then the ocean is worth writing about just as man is. So I was lucky there. I've seen the marlin mate and know about that. So I leave that out. I've seen a school (or pod) of more than fifty sperm whales in that same stretch of water and once harpooned one nearly sixty feet in length and lost him. So I left that out. All the stories I know from the fishing village I leave out. But the knowledge is what makes the underwater part of the iceberg.

INTERVIEWER: Archibald MacLeish has spoken of a method of conveying experience to a reader which he said you developed while covering baseball games back in those *Kansas City Star* days. It was simply that experience is communicated by small details, intimately preserved, which have the effect of indicating the whole by making the reader conscious of what he had been aware of only subconsciously . . .

HEMINGWAY: The anecdote is apocryphal. I never wrote baseball for the *Star*. What Archie was trying to remember was how I was trying to learn in Chicago in around 1920 and was searching for the unnoticed things that made emotions, such as the way an outfielder tossed his glove without looking back to where it fell, the squeak of resin on canvas under a fighter's flat-soled gym shoes, the grey colour of Jack Blackburn's skin when he had just come out of stir, and other things I noted as a painter sketches. You saw Blackburn's strange colour and the old razor cuts and the way he spun a man before you knew his history. These were the things which moved you before you knew the story.

INTERVIEWER: Have you ever described any type of situation of which you had no personal knowledge?

HEMINGWAY: That is a strange question. By personal knowledge you mean carnal knowledge? In that case the answer is positive. A writer, if he is any good, does not describe. He invents or *makes* out of knowledge personal and impersonal and sometimes he seems to have unexplained knowledge which could come from forgotten racial or family experience. Who teaches the homing pigeon to fly as he does; where does a fighting bull get his bravery, or a hunting dog his nose? This is an elaboration or a condensation on that stuff we were talking about in Madrid that time when my head was not to be trusted.

INTERVIEWER: How detached must you be from an experience before you can write about it in fictional terms? The African air crashes you were involved in, for instance?

HEMINGWAY: It depends on the experience. One part of you sees it with complete detachment from the start. Another part is very involved. I think there is no rule about how soon one should write about it. It would depend on how well adjusted the individual was and on his or her recuperative powers. Certainly it is valuable to a trained writer to crash in an aircraft which burns. He learns several important things very quickly. Whether they will be of use to him is conditioned by survival. Survival, with honour, that outmoded and all-important word, is as difficult as ever and as all-important to a writer. Those who do not last are always more beloved since no one has to see them in their long dull, unrelenting, no-quarter-given-and-no-quarter-received, fights that they make to do something as they believe it should be done before they die. Those who die or quit early and easy and with every good reason are preferred because they are understandable and human. Failure and well-disguised cowardice are more human and more beloved.

INTERVIEWER: Could I ask you to what extent you think the writer should concern himself with the socio-political problems of his times?

HEMINGWAY: Everyone has his own conscience, and there should be no rules about how a conscience should function. All you can be sure about in a political-minded writer is that if his work should last you will have to skip the politics when you read it. Many of the so-called politically enlisted writers change their politics frequently. This is very exciting to them and to their political-literary reviews. Sometimes they even have to rewrite their viewpoints ... and in a hurry. Perhaps it can be respected as a form of the pursuit of happiness.

INTERVIEWER: Has the political influence of Ezra Pound on the segregationalist Kasper had any effect on your belief that the poet ought to be released from St Elizabeth's Hospital?*

HEMINGWAY: No. None at all. I believe Ezra should be released and allowed to write poetry in Italy on an undertaking by him to abstain from any politics. I would be happy to see Kasper jailed as soon as posible. Great poets are not necessarily girl guides nor scoutmasters nor splendid influences on youth. To name a few: Verlaine, Rimbaud, Shelley, Byron, Baudelaire, Proust, Gide should not have been confined to prevent them from being aped in their thinking, their manners or their morals by local Kaspers. I am sure that it will take a footnote to this paragraph in ten years to explain who Kasper was.

INTERVIEWER: Would you say, ever, that there is any didactic intention in your work?

HEMINGWAY: Didactic is a word that has been misused

* In 1958 a Federal court in Washington, D.C., dismissed all charges against Pound, clearing the way for his release from St Elizabeth's.

and has spoiled. *Death in the Afternoon* is an instructive book.

INTERVIEWER: It has been said that a writer only deals with one or two ideas throughout his work. Would you say your work reflects one or two ideas?

HEMINGWAY: Who said that? It sounds much too simple. The man who said it possibly *had* only one or two ideas.

INTERVIEWER: Well, perhaps it would be better put this way: Graham Greene said that a ruling passion gives to a shelf of novels the unity of a system. You yourself have said, I believe, that great writing comes out of a sense of injustice. Do you consider it important that a novelist be dominated in this way – by some such compelling sense?

HEMINGWAY: Mr Greene has a facility for making statements that I do not possess. It would be impossible for me to make generalizations about a shelf of novels or a wisp of snipe or a gaggle of geese. I'll try a generalization though. A writer without a sense of justice and injustice would be better off editing the Year Book of a school for exceptional children than writing novels. Another generalization. You see; they are not so difficult when they are sufficiently obvious. The most essential gift for a good writer is a built-in, shock-proof shit detector. This is the writer's radar and all great writers have had it.

INTERVIEWER: Finally, a fundamental question: namely, as a creative writer what do you think is the function of your art? Why a representation of fact, rather than fact itself?

HEMINGWAY: Why be puzzled by that? From things that have happened and from things as they exist and from all things that you know and all those you cannot know, you make something through your invention that is not a representation but a whole new thing truer than anything true and alive, and you make it alive, and if you make it well enough, you give it immortality. That is why you write and for no other reason that you know of. But what about all the reasons that no one knows?

George Plimpton

EVELYN WAUGH

The interview which follows is the result of two meetings on successive days at the Hyde Park Hotel, London, during April 1962.

I had written to Mr Waugh earlier asking permission to interview him and in this letter I had promised that I should not bring a tape recorder with me. I imagined, from what he had written in the early part of The Ordeal of Gilbert Pinfold, *that he was particularly averse to them.*

We met in the hall of the hotel at three in the afternoon. Mr Waugh was dressed in a dark-blue suit with a heavy overcoat and a black Homburg hat. Apart from a neatly tied small brown paper parcel, he was unencumbered. After we had shaken hands and he had explained that the interview would take place in his own room, the first thing he said was, 'Where is your machine?'

I explained that I hadn't brought one.

'Have you sold it?' he continued as we got into the lift. I was somewhat nonplussed. In fact I had at one time owned a tape recorder and I had indeed sold it three years earlier, before going to live abroad. None of this seemed very relevant. As we ascended slowly, Mr Waugh continued his cross-questioning about the machine. How much had I bought it for? How much had I sold it for? Whom did I sell it to?

'Do you have shorthand, then?' he asked as we left the lift. I explained that I did not.

'Then it was very foolhardy of you to sell your machine, wasn't it?'

He showed me into a comfortable, soberly furnished room, with a fine view over the trees across Hyde Park. As he moved about the room he repeated twice under his breath, 'The horrors of London life! The horrors of London life!'

'I hope you won't mind if I go to bed,' he said, going through into the bathroom. From there he gave me a number of comments and directions.

'*Go and look out of the window. This is the only hotel with a civilized view left in London. . . . Do you see a brown paper parcel? Open it, please.*'

I did so.

'*What do you find?*'

'*A box of cigars.*'

'*Do you smoke?*'

'*Yes. I am smoking a cigarette now.*'

'*I think cigarettes are rather squalid in the bedroom. Wouldn't you rather smoke a cigar?*'

He re-entered, wearing a pair of white pyjamas and metal-rimmed spectacles. He took a cigar, lit it, and got into bed.

I sat down in an armchair at the foot of the bed, juggling notebook, pen, and enormous cigar between hands and knees.

'*I shan't be able to hear you there. Bring up that chair.*' *He indicated one by the window, so I rearranged my paraphernalia as we talked of mutual friends. Quite soon he said, 'When is the inquisition to begin?*'

I had prepared a number of lengthy questions – the reader will no doubt detect the shadows of them in what follows – but I soon discovered that they did not, as I had hoped, elicit long or ruminative replies. Perhaps what was most striking about Mr Waugh's conversation was his command of language: his spoken sentences were as graceful, precise, and rounded as his written sentences. He never faltered, nor once gave the impression of searching for a word. The answers he gave to my questions came without hesitation or qualification, and any attempt I made to induce him to expand a reply generally resulted in a rephrasing of what he had said before.

I am well aware that the result on the following pages is unlike the majority of Paris Review interviews; first it is very much shorter and secondly it is not 'an interview in depth'. Personally, I believe that Mr Waugh did not lend himself, either as a writer or as a man, to the forms of delicate psychological probing and self-analysis which are characteristic of many of the other interviews. He would consider impertinent an attempt publicly to relate his life and his art, as was demonstrated conclusively when he appeared on an English television programme, 'Face to Face', some time ago and parried all such probing with brief, flat, and, wherever possible, monosyllabic replies.

However, I should like to do something to dismiss the mythical image of Evelyn Waugh as an ogre of arrogance and reaction. Although he carefully avoided taking part in the market place of literary life, of conferences, prize-giving, and reputation-building, he was, nonetheless, both well informed and decided in his opinions about his contemporaries and juniors. Throughout the three hours I spent with him he was consistently helpful, attentive, and courteous, allowing himself only minor flights of ironic exasperation if he considered my questions irrelevant or ill-phrased.

INTERVIEWER: Were there attempts at other novels before *Decline and Fall*?

WAUGH: I wrote my first piece of fiction at seven. *The Curse of the Horse Race*. It was vivid and full of action. Then, let's see, there was *The World to Come*, written in the metre of 'Hiawatha'. When I was at school I wrote a five-thousand-word novel about modern school life. It was intolerably bad.

INTERVIEWER: Did you write a novel at Oxford?

WAUGH: No. I did sketches and that sort of thing for the *Cherwell*, and for a paper Harold Acton edited – *Broom* it was called. The *Isis* was the official undergraduate magazine: it was boring and hearty, written for beer drinkers and rugger players. The *Cherwell* was a little more frivolous.

INTERVIEWER: Did you write your life of Rossetti at that time?

WAUGH: No. I came down from Oxford without a degree, wanting to be a painter. My father settled my debts and I tried to become a painter. I failed as I had neither the talent nor the application – I didn't have the moral qualities.

INTERVIEWER: Then what?

WAUGH: I became a prep-school master. It was very jolly

and I enjoyed it very much. I taught at two private schools for a period of nearly two years and during this I started an Oxford novel which was of no interest. After I had been expelled from the second school for drunkenness I returned penniless to my father. I went to see my friend Anthony Powell, who was working with Duckworths, the publishers, at the time, and said, 'I'm starving.' (This wasn't true: my father fed me.) The director of the firm agreed to pay me fifty pounds for a brief life of Rossetti. I was delighted, as fifty pounds was quite a lot then. I dashed off and dashed it off. The result was hurried and bad. I haven't let them reprint it again. Then I wrote *Decline and Fall*. It was in a sense based on my experiences as a schoolmaster, yet I had a much nicer time than the hero.

INTERVIEWER: Did *Vile Bodies* follow on immediately?

WAUGH: I went through a form of marriage and travelled about Europe for some months with this consort. I wrote accounts of these travels which were bundled together into books and paid for the journeys, but left nothing over. I was in the middle of *Vile Bodies* when she left me. It was a bad book, I think, not so carefully constructed as the first. Separate scenes tended to go on for too long – the conversation in the train between those two women, the film shows of the dotty father.

INTERVIEWER: I think most of your readers would group these two novels closely together. I don't think that most of us would recognize that the second was the more weakly constructed.

WAUGH [*briskly*]: It was. It was secondhand too. I cribbed much of the scene at the customs from Firbank. I popularized a fashionable language, like the beatnik writers today, and the book caught on.

INTERVIEWER: Have you found that the inspiration or starting point of each of your novels has been different? Do you sometimes start with a character, sometimes with an event or circumstance? Did you, for example, think of the ramifications of an aristocratic divorce as the centre of *A Handful of Dust*, or was it the character of Tony and his ultimate fate which you started from?

WAUGH: I wrote a story called *The Man Who Liked Dickens*, which is identical to the final part of the book. About two years after I had written it, I became interested in the circumstances which might have produced this character; in his delirium there were hints of what he might have been like in his former life, so I followed them up.

INTERVIEWER: Did you return again and again to the story in the intervening two years?

WAUGH: I wasn't haunted by it, if that's what you mean. Just curious. You can find the original story in a collection got together by Alfred Hitchcock.

INTERVIEWER: Did you write these early novels with ease or –

WAUGH: Six weeks' work.

INTERVIEWER: Including revisions?

WAUGH: Yes.

INTERVIEWER: Do you write with the same speed and ease today?

WAUGH: I've got slower as I grow older. *Men at Arms* took a year. One's memory gets so much worse. I used to be able to hold the whole of a book in my head. Now if I take a walk whilst I am writing, I have to hurry back and make a correction, before I forget it.

INTERVIEWER: Do you mean you worked a bit every day over a year, or that you worked in concentrated periods?

WAUGH: Concentrated periods. Two thousand words is a good day's work.

INTERVIEWER: E. M. Forster has spoken of 'flat characters and round characters'; if you recognize this distinction, would you agree that you created no 'round' characters until *A Handful of Dust*?

WAUGH: All fictional characters are flat. A writer can give an illusion of depth by giving an apparently stereoscopic view of a character – seeing him from two vantage points; all a writer can do is give more or less information about a character, not information of a different order.

INTERVIEWER: Then do you make no radical distinction between characters as differently conceived as Mr Prendergast and Sebastian Flyte?

WAUGH: Yes, I do. There are the protagonists and there are characters who are furniture. One gives only one aspect of the furniture. Sebastian Flyte was a protagonist.

INTERVIEWER: Would you say, then, that Charles Ryder was the character about whom you gave most information?

WAUGH: No, Guy Crouchback. [*A little restlessly*] But look, I think that your questions are dealing too much with the creation of character and not enough with the technique of writing. I regard writing not as investigation of character, but as an exercise in the use of language, and with this I am obsessed. I have no technical psychological interest. It is drama, speech, and events that interest me.

INTERVIEWER: Does this mean that you continually refine and experiment?

WAUGH: Experiment? God forbid! Look at the results of experiment in the case of a writer like Joyce. He started off writing very well, then you can watch him going mad with vanity. He ends up a lunatic.

INTERVIEWER: I gather from what you said earlier that you don't find the act of writing difficult.

WAUGH: I don't find it easy. You see, there are always words going round in my head; some people think in pictures, some in ideas. I think entirely in words. By the time I come to stick my pen in my inkpot these words have reached a stage of order which is fairly presentable.

INTERVIEWER: Perhaps that explains why Gilbert Pinfold was haunted by voices – by disembodied words.

WAUGH: Yes, that's true – the word made manifest.

INTERVIEWER: Can you say something about the direct influences on your style? Were any of the nineteenth-century writers an influence on you? Samuel Butler, for example?

WAUGH: They were the basis of my education, and as such of course I was affected by reading them. P. G. Wodehouse affected my style directly. Then there was a little book by E. M. Forster called *Pharos and Pharillon* – sketches of the history of Alexandria. I think that Hemingway made real discoveries about the use of language in his first novel,

The Sun Also Rises. I admired the way he made drunk people talk.

INTERVIEWER: What about Ronald Firbank?

WAUGH: I enjoyed him very much when I was young. I can't read him now.

INTERVIEWER: Why?

WAUGH: I think there would be something wrong with an elderly man who could enjoy Firbank.

INTERVIEWER: Whom do you read for pleasure?

WAUGH: Anthony Powell. Ronald Knox, both for pleasure and moral edification. Erle Stanley Gardner.

INTERVIEWER: And Raymond Chandler!

WAUGH: No. I'm bored by all those slugs of whisky. I don't care for all the violence either.

INTERVIEWER: But isn't there a lot of violence in Gardner?

WAUGH: Not of the extraneous lubricious sort you find in other American crime writers.

INTERVIEWER: What do you think of other American writers, of Scott Fitzgerald or William Faulkner, for example?

WAUGH: I enjoyed the first part of *Tender Is the Night.* I find Faulkner intolerably bad.

INTERVIEWER: It is evident that you reverence the authority of established institutions – the Catholic Church and the army. Would you agree that on one level both *Brideshead Revisited* and the army trilogy were celebrations of this reverence?

WAUGH: No, certainly not. I reverence the Catholic Church because it is true, not because it is established or an institution. *Men at Arms* was a kind of uncelebration, a history of Guy Crouchback's disillusion with the army. Guy has old-fashioned ideas of honour and illusions of chivalry; we see these being used up and destroyed by his encounters with the realities of army life.

INTERVIEWER: Would you say that there was any direct moral to the army trilogy?

WAUGH: Yes, I imply that there is a moral purpose, a chance of salvation, in every human life. Do you know the old Protestant hymn which goes: 'Once to every man and nation/Comes the moment to decide'? Guy is offered this chance by making himself responsible for the upbringing of Trimmer's child, to see that he is not brought up by his dissolute mother. He is essentially an unselfish character.

INTERVIEWER: Can you say something about the conception of the trilogy? Did you carry out a plan which you had made at the start?

WAUGH: It changed a lot in the writing. Originally I had intended the second volume, *Officers and Gentlemen*, to be two volumes. Then I decided to lump them together and finish it off. There's a very bad transitional passage on board the troop ship. The third volume really arose from the fact that Ludovic needed explaining. As it turned out, each volume had a common form because there was an irrelevant figure in each to make the running.

INTERVIEWER: Even if, as you say, the whole conception of the trilogy was not clearly worked out before you started to write, were there not some things which you saw from the beginning?

WAUGH: Yes, both the sword in the Italian church and the sword of Stalingrad were, as you put it, there from the beginning.

INTERVIEWER: Can you say something about the germination of *Brideshead Revisited*?

WAUGH: It is very much a child of its time. Had it not been written when it was, at a very bad time in the war when there was nothing to eat, it would have been a different book. The fact that it is rich in evocative description – in gluttonous writing – is a direct result of the privations and austerity of the times.

INTERVIEWER: Have you found any professional criticism of your work illuminating or helpful? Edmund Wilson, for example?

WAUGH: Is he an American?

INTERVIEWER: Yes.

WAUGH: I don't think what they have to say is of much interest, do you? I think the general state of reviewing in England is contemptible – both slovenly and ostentatious. I used to have a rule when I reviewed books as a young man never to give an unfavourable notice to a book I hadn't read. I find even this simple rule is flagrantly broken now. Naturally I abhor the Cambridge movement of criticism, with its horror of elegance and its members mutually encouraging uncouth writing. Otherwise, I am pleased if my friends like my books.

INTERVIEWER: Do you think it just to describe you as a reactionary?

WAUGH: An artist must be a reactionary. He has to stand out against the tenor of the age and not go flopping along; he must offer some little opposition. Even the great Victorian artists were all anti-Victorian, despite the pressures to conform.

INTERVIEWER: But what about Dickens? Although he preached social reform he also sought a public image.

WAUGH: Oh, that's quite different. He liked adulation and he liked showing off. But he was still deeply antagonistic to Victorianism.

INTERVIEWER: Is there any particular historical period, other than this one, in which you would like to have lived?

WAUGH: The seventeenth century. I think it was the time of the greatest drama and romance. I think I might have been happy in the thirteenth century, too.

INTERVIEWER: Despite the great variety of the characters you have created in your novels, it is very noticeable that you have never given a sympathetic or even a full-scale portrait of a working-class character. Is there any reason for this?

WAUGH: I don't know them, and I'm not interested in them. No writer before the middle of the nineteenth century wrote about the working classes other than as grotesques or as pastoral decorations. Then when they were given the vote certain writers started to suck up to them.

INTERVIEWER: What about Pistol ... or much later, Moll Flanders and –

WAUGH: Ah, the criminal classes. That's rather different. They have always had a certain fascination.

INTERVIEWER: May I ask you what you are writing at the moment?

WAUGH: An autobiography.

INTERVIEWER: Will it be conventional in form?

WAUGH: Extremely.

INTERVIEWER: Are there any books which you would like to have written and have found impossible?

WAUGH: I have done all I could. I have done my best.

Julian Jebb

SAUL BELLOW

The interview 'took place' over a period of several weeks. Beginning with some exploratory discussions during May of 1965, it was shelved during the summer, and actually accomplished during September and October. Two recording sessions were held, totalling about an hour and a half, but this was only a small part of the effort Mr Bellow gave to this interview. A series of meetings, for over five weeks, was devoted to the most careful revision of the original material. Recognizing at the outset the effort he would make for such an interview, he had real reluctance about beginning it at all. Once his decision had been reached, however, he gave a remarkable amount of his time freely to the task – up to two hours a day, at least twice and often three times a week throughout the entire five-week period. It had become an opportunity, as he put it, to say some things which were important but which weren't being said.

Certain types of questions were ruled out in early discussions. Mr Bellow was not interested in responding to criticisms of his work which he found trivial or stupid. He quoted the Jewish proverb that a fool can throw a stone into the water which ten wise men cannot recover. Nor did he wish to discuss what he considered his personal writing habits, whether he used a pen or typewriter, how hard he pressed on the page. For the artist to give such loving attention to his own shoelaces was dangerous, even immoral. Finally, there were certain questions that led into too 'wide spaces' for this interview, subjects for fuller treatment on other occasions.

The two tapes were made in Bellow's University of Chicago office on the fifth floor of the Social Sciences Building. The office, though large, is fairly typical of those on the main quadrangles: much of it rather dark with one brightly lighted area, occupied by his desk, immediately before a set of three dormer windows; dark-green metal *bookcases line the walls, casually used as storage for a miscellany of books, magazines, and correspondence. A set of* The Complete Works of Rudyard Kipling *('it was given to me') shares space with examination copies of new novels and with a few of Bellow's own books, including recent French and Italian translations of* Herzog. *A table, a couple of typing stands, and various decrepit and mismatched chairs are scattered in apparently haphazard fashion throughout the room. A wall rack just inside the door holds his jaunty black felt hat and his walking cane. There is a general sense of disarray, with stacks of papers, books, and letters lying everywhere. When one comes to the door, Bellow is frequently at his typing stand, rapidly pounding out on a portable machine responses to some of the many letters he gets daily. Occasionally a secretary enters and proceeds to type away on some project at the far end of the room.*

During the two sessions with the tape recorder, Bellow sat at his desk, between the eaves which project prominently into the room, backlighted by the dormer windows which let in the bright afternoon sun from the south. Four storeys below lie Fifty-ninth Street and Chicago's Midway, their automobile and human noises continually penetrating the office. As the questions were asked, Bellow listened carefully and often developed an answer slowly, pausing frequently to think out the exact phrase he sought. His answers were serious, but full of his special quality of humour. He took obvious pleasure in the amusing turns of thought with which he often concluded an answer. Throughout, he was at great pains to make his ideas transparent to the interviewer, asking repeatedly if this was clear or if he should say more on the subject. His concentration during these sessions was intense enough to be tiring, and both tapes were brought to a close with his confessing to some exhaustion.

Following each taping session, a typescript of his remarks was prepared. Bellow worked over these typed sheets extensively with pen and ink, taking as many as three separate meetings to do a complete revision. Then another typescript was made, and the process started over. This work was done when the interviewer could be present, and again the changes were frequently tested on him. Generally these sessions occurred at Bellow's office or at his apartment, over-looking the Outer Drive and Lake Michigan. Once, how-ever, revisions were made while he and the interviewer sat on a Jackson Park bench on a fine October afternoon, and one typescript was worked on along with beer and ham-burgers at a local bar.

Revisions were of various sorts. Frequently there were slight changes in meaning: 'That's what I really meant to say.' Other alterations tightened up his language or were in the nature of stylistic improvements. Any sections which he judged to be excursions from the main topic were de-leted. Most regretted by the interviewer were prunings that eliminated certain samples of the characteristic Bellow wit: in a few places he came to feel he was simply 'exhibiting' himself, and these were scratched out. On the other hand, whenever he could substitute for conventional literary dic-tion an unexpected colloquial turn of phrase – which often proved humorous in context – he did so.

INTERVIEWER: Some critics have felt that your work falls within the tradition of American naturalism, possibly because of some things you've said about Dreiser. I was won-dering if you saw yourself in a particular literary tradition?

BELLOW: Well, I think that the development of realism in the nineteenth century is still the major event of modern literature. Dreiser, a realist of course, had elements of genius. He was clumsy, cumbersome, and in some respects a poor thinker. But he was rich in a kind of feeling which has been ruled off the grounds by many contemporary writers – the kind of feeling that every human being intuitively recog-nizes as primary. Dreiser has more open access to primary feelings than any American writer of the twentieth century. It makes a good many people uncomfortable that his emo-tion has not found a more developed literary form. It's true his art may be too 'natural'. He sometimes conveys his un-derstanding by masses of words, verbal approximations. He blunders, but generally in the direction of truth. The result is that we are moved in an unmediated way by his characters, as by life, and then we say that his novels are simply torn from the side of life, and therefore not novels. But we can't escape reading them. He somehow conveys, without much refinement, depths of feeling that we usually associate with Balzac or Shakespeare.

INTERVIEWER: This realism, then, is a particular kind of sensibility, rather than a technique?

BELLOW: Realism specializes in *apparently* unmediated experiences. What stirred Dreiser was simply the idea that you could bring unmediated feeling to the novel. He took it up naïvely without going to the trouble of mastering an art. We don't see this because he makes so many familiar 'art' gestures, borrowed from the art-fashions of his day, and even from the slick magazines, but he is really a natural, a primitive. I have great respect for his simplicities and I think they are worth more than much that has been praised as high art in the American novel.

INTERVIEWER: Could you give me an example of what you mean?

BELLOW: In a book like *Jennie Gerhardt* the delicacy with which Jennie allows Lester Kane to pursue his conventional life while she herself lives unrecognized with her illegitimate daughter, the depth of her understanding, and the depth of her sympathy and of her truthfulness impress me. She is not a sentimental figure. She has a natural sort of honour.

INTERVIEWER: Has recent American fiction pretty much followed this direction?

BELLOW: Well, among his heirs there are those who believe that clumsiness and truthfulness go together. But cumbersomeness does not necessarily imply a sincere heart. Most of the 'Dreiserians' lack talent. On the other hand, people who put Dreiser down, adhering to a 'high art' standard for the novel, miss the point.

INTERVIEWER: Aside from Dreiser, what other American writers do you find particularly of interest?

BELLOW: I like Hemingway, Faulkner, and Fitzgerald. I think of Hemingway as a man who developed a significant manner as an artist, a life-style which is important. For his generation, his language created a life-style, one which pathetic old gentlemen are still found clinging to. I don't think of Hemingway as a great novelist. I like Fitzgerald's novels better, but I often feel about Fitzgerald that he couldn't distinguish between innocence and social climbing. I am thinking of *The Great Gatsby*.

INTERVIEWER: If we go outside American literature, you've mentioned that you read the nineteenth-century Russian writers with a good deal of interest. Is there anything particular about them that attracts you?

BELLOW: Well, the Russians have an immediate charismatic appeal – excuse the Max Weberism. Their conventions allow them to express freely their feelings about nature and human beings. We have inherited a more restricted and imprisoning attitude towards the emotions. We have to work around puritanical and stoical restraints. We lack the Russian openness. Our path is narrower.

INTERVIEWER: In what other writers do you take special interest?

BELLOW: I have a special interest in Joyce; I have a special interest in Lawrence. I read certain poets over and over again. I can't say where they belong in my theoretical scheme; I only know that I have an attachment to them. Yeats is one such poet. Hart Crane is another. Hardy and Walter de la Mare. I don't know what these have in common – probably nothing. I know that I am drawn repeatedly to these men.

INTERVIEWER: It's been said that one can't like *both* Lawrence and Joyce, that one has to choose between them. You don't feel this way?

BELLOW: No. Because I really don't take Lawrence's sexual theories very seriously. I take his art seriously, not his doctrine. But he himself warned us repeatedly not to trust the artist. He said trust the work itself. So I have little use for the Lawrence who wrote *The Plumed Serpent* and great admiration for the Lawrence who wrote *The Lost Girl*.

INTERVIEWER: Does Lawrence at all share the special feeling you find attractive in Dreiser?

BELLOW: A certain openness to experience, yes. And a willingness to trust one's instinct, to follow it freely – that Lawrence has.

INTERVIEWER: You mentioned before the interview that you would prefer not to talk about your early novels, that you feel you are a different person now from what you were then. I wonder if this is all you want to say, or if you can say something about how you have changed.

BELLOW: I think that when I wrote those early books I was timid. I still felt the incredible effrontery of announcing myself to the world (in part I mean the W.A.S.P. world) as a writer and an artist. I had to touch a great many bases, demonstrate my abilities, pay my respects to formal requirements. In short, I was afraid to let myself go.

INTERVIEWER: When do you find a significant change occurring?

BELLOW: When I began to write *Augie March*. I took off many of these restraints. I think I took off too many, and went too far, but I was feeling the excitement of discovery. I had just increased my freedom, and like any emancipated plebeian I abused it at once.

INTERVIEWER: What were these restraints that you took off in *Augie March*?

BELLOW: My first two books are well made. I wrote the first quickly but took great pains with it. I laboured with the second and tried to make it letter-perfect. In writing *The Victim* I accepted a Flaubertian standard. Not a bad standard to be sure, but one which, in the end, I found repressive – repressive because of the circumstances of my life and because of my upbringing in Chicago as the son of immigrants. I could not, with such an instrument as I developed in the first two books, express a variety of things I knew intimately. Those books, though useful, did not give me a form in which I felt comfortable. A writer should be able to express himself easily, naturally, copiously in a form which frees his mind, his energies. Why should he hobble himself with formalities? With a borrowed sensibility? With the desire to be 'correct'? Why should I force myself to write like an Englishman or a contributor to *The New Yorker*?

I soon saw that it was simply not in me to be a mandarin. I should add that for a young man in my position there were social inhibitions, too. I had good reason to fear that I would be put down as a foreigner, an interloper. It was made clear to me when I studied literature in the university that as a Jew and the son of Russian Jews I would probably never have the right *feeling* for Anglo-Saxon traditions, for English words. I realized even in college that the people who told me this were not necessarily disinterested friends. But they had an effect on me, nevertheless. This was something from which I had to free myself. I fought free because I had to.

INTERVIEWER: Are these social inhibitors as powerful today as they were when you wrote *Dangling Man*?

BELLOW: I think I was lucky to have grown up in the Middle West, where such influences are less strong. If I'd grown up in the East and attended an Ivy League university, I might have been damaged more badly. Puritan and Protestant America carries less weight in Illinois than in Massachusetts. But I don't bother much with such things now.

INTERVIEWER: Did another change in your writing occur between *Augie March* and *Herzog*? You've mentioned writing *Augie March* with a great sense of freedom, but I take it that *Herzog* was a very difficult book to write.

BELLOW: It was. I had to tame and restrain the style I developed in *Augie March* in order to write *Henderson* and *Herzog*. I think both those books reflect that change in style. I wouldn't really know how to describe it. I don't care to trouble my mind to find an exact description for it, but it has something to do with a kind of readiness to record impressions arising from a source of which we know little. I suppose that all of us have a primitive prompter or commentator within, who from earliest years has been advising us, telling us what the real world is. There is such a commentator in me. I have to prepare the ground for him. From this source come words, phrases, syllables; sometimes only sounds, which I try to interpret, sometimes whole paragraphs, fully punctuated. When E. M. Forster said, 'How do I know what I think until I see what I say?' he was perhaps referring to his own prompter. There is that observing instrument in us – in childhood at any rate. At the sight of a man's face, his shoes, the colour of light, a woman's mouth or perhaps her ear, one receives a word, a phrase, at times nothing but a nonsense syllable from the primitive commentator.

INTERVIEWER: So this change in your writing –

BELLOW: – was an attempt to get nearer to that primitive commentator.

INTERVIEWER: How do you go about getting nearer to him, preparing the way for him?

BELLOW: When I say the commentator is primitive, I don't mean that he's crude; God knows he's often fastidious. But he won't talk until the situation's right. And if you prepare the ground for him with too many difficulties underfoot, he won't say anything. I must be terribly given to fraud and deceit because I sometimes have great difficulty preparing a suitable ground. This is why I've had so much trouble with my last two novels. I appealed directly to my prompter. The prompter, however, has to find the occasion perfect – that is to say, truthful, and necessary. If there is any superfluity or inner falsehood in the preparations, he is aware of it. I have to stop. Often I have to begin again, with the first word. I can't remember how many times I wrote *Herzog*. But at last I did find the acceptable ground for it.

INTERVIEWER: Do these preparations include your coming to some general conception of the work?

BELLOW: Well, I don't know exactly how it's done. I let it alone a good deal. I try to avoid common forms of strain and distortion. For a long time, perhaps from the middle of the nineteenth century, writers have not been satisfied to regard themselves simply as writers. They have required also a theoretical framework. Most often they have been their own theoreticians, have created their own ground as artists, and have provided an exegesis for their own works. They have found it necessary to take a position, not merely to write novels. In bed last night I was reading a collection of articles by Stendhal. One of them amused me very much, touched me. Stendhal was saying how lucky writers were in the age of Louis XIV not to have anyone take them very seriously. Their obscurity was very valuable. Corneille had been dead for several days before anyone at court considered the fact important enough to mention. In the nineteenth century, says Stendhal, there would have been several public orations, Corneille's funeral covered by all the papers. There are great advantages in not being taken *too* seriously. Some writers are excessively serious about themselves. They accept the ideas of the 'cultivated public'. There is such a thing as overcapitalizing the A in artist. Certain writers and musicians understand this. Stravinsky says the composer should practice his trade exactly as a shoemaker does. Mozart and Haydn accepted commissions – wrote to order. In the nineteenth century, the artist loftily waited for Inspiration. Once you elevate yourself to the rank of a cultural institution, you're in for a lot of trouble.

Then there is a minor modern disorder – the disease of people who live by an image of themselves created by papers, television, Broadway, Sardi's, gossip, or the public need for celebrities. Even buffoons, prize fighters, and movie stars have caught the bug. I avoid these 'images'. I have a longing, not for downright obscurity – I'm too egotistical for that – but for peace, and freedom from meddling.

INTERVIEWER: In line with this, the enthusiastic response to *Herzog* must have affected your life considerably. Do you have any thoughts as to why this book became and remained the bestseller it did?

BELLOW: I don't like to agree with the going view that if you write a bestseller it's because you betrayed an important principle or sold your soul. I know that sophisticated opinion believes this. And although I don't take much stock in sophisticated opinion, I have examined my conscience. I've tried to find out whether I had unwittingly done wrong. But I haven't yet discovered the sin. I do think that a book like *Herzog*, which ought to have been an obscure book with a total sale of eight thousand, has such a reception because it appeals to the unconscious sympathies of many people. I know from the mail I've received that the book described a common predicament. *Herzog* appealed to Jewish readers, to those who have been divorced, to those who talk to themselves, to college graduates, readers of paperbacks, autodidacts, to those who yet hope to live awhile, etc.

INTERVIEWER: Do you feel there were deliberate attempts at lionizing by the literary tastemakers? I was thinking that the recent deaths of Faulkner and Hemingway have been seen as creating a vacuum in American letters, which we all know is abhorrent.

BELLOW: Well, I don't know whether I would say a vacuum. Perhaps a pigeonhole. I agree that there is a need to keep the pigeonholes filled and that people are uneasy when there are vacancies. Also the mass media demand material – grist – and literary journalists have to create a major-league atmosphere in literature. The writers don't offer to fill the pigeonholes. It's the critics who want figures in the Pantheon. But there are many people who assume that every writer must be bucking for the niche. Why should writers wish to be rated – seeded – like tennis players? Handicapped like racehorses? What an epitaph for a novelist: 'He won all the polls'!

INTERVIEWER: How much are you conscious of the reader when you write? Is there an ideal audience that you write for?

BELLOW: I have in mind another human being who will understand me. I count on this. Not on perfect understanding, which is Cartesian, but on approximate understanding, which is Jewish. And on a meeting of sympathies, which is human. But I have no ideal reader in my head, no. Let me just say this, too. I seem to have the blind self-acceptance of the eccentric who can't conceive that his eccentricities are not clearly understood.

INTERVIEWER: So there isn't a great deal of calculation about rhetoric?

BELLOW: These are things that can't really be contrived. People who talk about contrivance must think that a novelist is a man capable of building a skyscraper to conceal a dead mouse. Skyscrapers are not raised simply to conceal mice.

INTERVIEWER: It's been said that contemporary fiction

sees man as a victim. You gave this title to one of your early novels, yet there seems to be very strong opposition in your fiction to seeing man as simply determined or futile. Do you see any truth to this claim about contemporary fiction?

BELLOW: Oh, I think that realistic literature from the first has been a victim literature. Pit any ordinary individual – and realistic literature concerns itself with ordinary individuals – against the external world and the external world will conquer him, of course. Everything that people believed in the nineteenth century about man's place in nature, about the power of productive forces in society, made it inevitable that the hero of the realistic novel should not be a hero but a sufferer who is eventually overcome. So I was doing nothing very original by writing another realistic novel about a common man and calling it *The Victim*. I suppose I was discovering independently the essence of much of modern realism. In my innocence, I put my finger on it. Serious realism also contrasts the common man with aristocratic greatness. He is overborne by fate, just as the great are in Shakespeare or Sophocles. But this contrast, inherent in literary tradition, always damages him. In the end the force of tradition carries realism into parody, satire, mock-epic – Leopold Bloom.

INTERVIEWER: Haven't you yourself moved away from the suggestion of plebian tragedy toward a treatment of the sufferer that has greater comic elements? Although the concerns and difficulties are still fundamentally serious, the comic elements in *Henderson*, in *Herzog*, even in *Seize the Day* seem much more prominent than in *Dangling Man* or *The Victim*.

BELLOW: Yes, because I got very tired of the solemnity of complaint, altogether impatient with complaint. Obliged to choose between complaint and comedy, I choose comedy, as more energetic, wiser and manlier. This is really one reason why I dislike my own early novels. I find them plaintive, sometimes querulous. *Herzog* makes comic use of complaint.

INTERVIEWER: When you say you are obliged to choose

between complaint and comedy, does it mean this is the only choice – that you are limited to choosing between just these two alternatives?

BELLOW: I'm not inclined to predict what will happen. I may feel drawn to comedy again, I may not. But modern literature was dominated by a tone of elegy from the 'twenties to the 'fifties, the atmosphere of Eliot in 'The Waste Land' and that of Joyce in *A Portrait of the Artist as a Young Man*. Sensibility absorbed this sadness, this view of the artist as the only contemporary link with an age of gold, forced to watch the sewage flowing in the Thames, every aspect of modern civilization doing violence to his (artist-patrician) feelings. This went much farther than it should have been allowed to go. It descended to absurdities, of which I think we have had enough.

INTERVIEWER: I wonder if you could say something about how important the environments are in your works. I take it that for the realist tradition the context in which the action occurs is of vital importance. You set your novels in Chicago, New York, as far away as Africa. How important are these settings for the fiction?

BELLOW: Well, you present me with a problem to which I think no one has the answer. People write realistically but at the same time they want to create environments which are somehow desirable, which are surrounded by atmospheres in which behaviour becomes significant, which display the charm of life. What is literature without these things? Dickens's London is gloomy, but also cozy. And yet realism has always offered to annihilate precisely such qualities. That is to say, if you want to be ultimately realistic you bring artistic space itself in danger. In Dickens, there is no void beyond the fog. The environment is human, at all times. Do you follow me?

INTERVIEWER: I'm not sure I do.

BELLOW: The realistic tendency is to challenge the human significance of things. The more realistic you are the more you threaten the grounds of your own art. Realism has always both accepted and rejected the circumstances of ordinary life. It accepted the task of writing about ordinary life and tried to meet it in some extraordinary fashion. As Flaubert did. The subject might be common, low, degrading; all this was to be redeemed by art. I really do see those Chicago environments as I represent them. They suggest their own style of presentation. I elaborate it.

INTERVIEWER: Then you aren't especially disturbed by readers of *Henderson*, for example, who say that Africa really isn't like that? One sort of realist would require a writer to spend several years on location before daring to place his characters there. You're not troubled by him, I take it?

BELLOW: Perhaps you should say 'factualist' rather than 'realist'. Years ago, I studied African ethnography with the late Professor Herskovits. Later he scolded me for writing a book like *Henderson*. He said the subject was much too serious for such fooling. I felt that my fooling was fairly serious. Literalism, factualism, will smother the imagination altogether.

INTERVIEWER: You have on occasion divided recent American fiction into what you call the 'cleans' and the 'dirties'. The former, I gather, tend to be conservative and easily optimistic, the latter the eternal nay-sayers, rebels, iconoclasts. Do you feel this is still pretty much the picture of American fiction today?

BELLOW: I feel that both choices are rudimentary and pitiful, and though I know the uselessness of advocating any given path to other novelists, I am still inclined to say, Leave both these extremes. They are useless, childish. No wonder the really powerful men in our society, whether politicians or scientists, hold writers and poets in contempt. They do it because they get no evidence from modern literature that anybody is thinking about any significant question. What does the radicalism of radical writers nowadays amount to? Most of it is hand-me-down bohemianism, sentimental populism, D. H. Lawrence-and-water, or imitation Sartre. For American writers radicalism is a question of honour. They must be radicals for the sake of their dignity. They see it as their function, and a noble function, to say Nay, and to bite not only the hand that feeds them (and feeds them with comic abundance, I might add) but almost any other hand held out to them. Their radicalism, however, is contentless. A genuine radicalism, which truly challenges authority, we need desperately. But a radicalism of posture is easy and banal. Radical criticism requires knowledge, not posture, not slogans, not rant. People who maintain their dignity as artists, in a small way, by being mischievous on television, simply delight the networks and the public. True radicalism requires homework – thought. Of the cleans, on the other hand, there isn't much to say. They seem faded.

INTERVIEWER: Your context is essentially that of the modern city, isn't it? Is there a reason for this beyond the fact that you come out of an urban experience?

BELLOW: Well, I don't know how I could possibly separate my knowledge of life, such as it is, from the city. I could no more tell you how deeply it's gotten into my bones than the lady who paints radium dials in the clock factory can tell you.

INTERVIEWER: You've mentioned the distractive character of modern life. Would this be most intense in the city?

BELLOW: The volume of judgements one is called upon to make depends upon the receptivity of the observer, and if one is very receptive, one has a terrifying number of opinions to render – 'What do you think about this, about that, about Viet Nam, about city planning, about expressways, or garbage disposal, or democracy, or Plato, or pop art, or welfare states, or literacy in a "mass society"?' I wonder whether there will ever be enough tranquillity under modern circumstances to allow our contemporary Wordsworth to recollect anything. I feel that art has something to do with the achievement of stillness in the midst of chaos. A stillness which characterizes prayer, too, and the eye of the storm. I think that art has something to do with an arrest of attention in the midst of distraction.

INTERVIEWER: I believe you once said that it is the novel which must deal particularly with this kind of chaos, and that as a consequence certain forms appropriate to poetry or to music are not available to the novelist.

BELLOW: I'm no longer sure of that. I think the novelist can avail himself of similar privileges. It's just that he can't act with the same purity or economy of means as the poet. He has to traverse a very muddy and noisy territory before he can arrive at a pure conclusion. He's more exposed to the details of life.

INTERVIEWER: Is there anything peculiar about the *kind* of distractions you see the novelist having to confront today? Is it just that there are more details, or is their quality different today from what it used to be?

BELLOW: The modern masterpiece of confusion is Joyce's *Ulysses*. There the mind is unable to resist experience. Experience in all its diversity, its pleasure and horror, passes through Bloom's head like an ocean through a sponge. The sponge can't resist; it has to accept whatever the waters bring. It also notes every micro-organism that passes through it. This is what I mean. How much of this must the spirit suffer, in what detail is it obliged to receive this ocean with its human plankton? Sometimes it looks as if the power of the mind has been nullified by the volume of experiences. But of course this is assuming the degree of passivity that Joyce assumes in *Ulysses*. Stronger, more purposeful minds can demand order, impose order, select, disregard, but there is still the threat of disintegration under the particulars. A Faustian artist is unwilling to surrender to the mass of particulars.

INTERVIEWER: Some people have felt your protagonists are seeking the answer to a question that might be phrased, How is it possible today for a good man to live? I wonder if you feel there is any single recurring question like this in the novels?

BELLOW: I don't think that I've represented any really good men; no one is thoroughly admirable in any of my novels. Realism has restrained me too much for that. I should *like* to represent good men. I long to know who and what they are and what their condition might be. I often represent men who desire such qualities but seem unable to achieve them on any significant scale. I criticize this in myself. I find it a limitation.

INTERVIEWER: I'm sorry; what exactly is this limitation?

BELLOW: The fact that I have not discerned those qualities or that I have not shown them in action. Herzog wants very much to have effective virtues. But that's a source of comedy in the book. I think I am far more concerned with another matter, and I don't approach this as a problem with a ready answer. I see it rather as a piece of research, having to do with human characteristics or qualities which have no need of justification. It's an odd thing to do, it shouldn't be necessary to 'justify' certain things. But there are many sceptical, rebellious, or simply nervous writers all around us, who, having existed a full twenty or thirty years in this universe, denounce or reject life because it fails to meet their standards as philosophical intellectuals. It seems to me that they can't know enough about it for confident denial. The mystery is too great. So when they knock at the door of mystery with the knuckles of cognition it is quite right that the door should open and some mysterious power should squirt them in the eye. I think a good deal of *Herzog* can be explained simply by the implicit assumption that existence, quite apart from any of our judgements, has value, that existence is worth-ful. Here it is possible, however, that the desire to go on with his creaturely career vulgarly betrays Herzog. He wants to live? What of it! The clay that frames him contains this common want. Simple *aviditas vitae*. Does a man deserve any credit for this?

INTERVIEWER: Would this help to explain, then, why many of the difficulties which Herzog's mind throws up for him throughout the novel don't ever seem to be *intellectually* resolved?

BELLOW: The book is not anti-intellectual, as some have said. It simply points to the comic impossibility of arriving at a synthesis that can satisfy modern demands. That is to say, full awareness of all major problems, together with the necessary knowledge of history, science and philosophy. That's why Herzog paraphrases Thomas Marshall, Woodrow Wilson's Vice-President, who said what this country needs is a good five-cent cigar. (I think it was Bugs Baer who said it first.) Herzog's version: what this country needs is a good five-cent synthesis.

INTERVIEWER: Do you find many contemporary writers attempting to develop such syntheses or insisting that significant fiction provide them?

BELLOW: Well, I don't know that too many American novelists, young or old, are tormenting their minds with these problems. Europeans do. I don't know that they can ever reach satisfactory results on the grounds they have chosen. At any rate, they write few good novels. But that leads us into some very wide spaces.

INTERVIEWER: Do the ideas in *Herzog* have any other major roles to play? The 'anti-intellectual' charge seems to come from people who don't feel the ideas are essential either in motivating the action, the decisions Herzog makes, or in helping him to come through at the end.

BELLOW: To begin with, I suppose I should say something about the difference in the role ideas play in American literature. European literature – I speak now of the Continent – is intellectual in a different sense from ours. The intellectual hero of a French or a German novel is likely to be a philosophical intellectual, an ideological intellectual. We here, intellectuals – or the educated public – know that in our liberal democracy ideas become effective within an entirely different tradition. The lines are less clearly drawn. We do not expect thought to have results, say, in the moral sphere, or in the political, in quite the way a Frenchman would. To be an intellectual in the United States sometimes means to be immured in a private life in which one thinks, but thinks with some humiliating sense of how little thought can accomplish. To call therefore for a dramatic resolution in terms of ideas in an American novel is to demand something for which there is scarcely any precedent. My novel deals with the humiliating sense that results from the American mixture of private concerns and intellectual interests. This is something which most readers of the book seem utterly to have missed. Some, fortunately, have caught it. But in part *Herzog* is intended to bring to an end, under blinding light, a certain course of development. Many people feel a 'private life' to be an affliction. In some sense it is a genuine affliction; it cuts one off from a common life. To me, a significant theme of *Herzog* is the imprisonment of the individual in a shameful and impotent privacy. He feels humiliated by it; he struggles comically with it; and he comes to realize at last that what he considered his intellectual 'privilege' has proved to be another form of bondage. Anyone who misses this misses the point of the book. So that to say that Herzog is not motivated in his acts by ideas is entirely false. Any *Bildungsroman*—and *Herzog* is, to use that heavy German term, a *Bildungsroman*—concludes with the first step. The first *real* step. Any man who has rid himself of superfluous ideas in order to take that first step has done something significant. When people complain of a lack of ideas in novels, they may mean that they do not find familiar ideas, fashionable ideas. Ideas outside the 'canon' they don't recognize. So, if what they mean is ideas à la Sartre or ideas à la Camus, they are quite right: there are few such in *Herzog*. Perhaps they mean that the thoughts of a man fighting for sanity and life are not suitable for framing.

INTERVIEWER: Herzog rejects certain of these fashionable ideas, doesn't he – the ideas à la Sartre or à la Camus?

BELLOW: I think he tests them first upon his own sense of life and against his own desperate need for clarity. With him these thoughts are not a game. Though he may laugh as he thinks them, his survival depends upon them. I didn't have him engage in full combat with figures like Sartre. If he had chosen to debate with Sartre in typical Herzogian fashion he would perhaps have begun with Sartre's proposition that Jews exist only because of anti-Semitism, that the Jew has to choose between authentic and inauthentic existence, that authentic existence can never be detached from this anti-Semitism which determines it. Herzog might have remembered that for Sartre, the Jew exists because he is hated, not because he has a history, not because he has origins of his own – but simply because he is designated,

created, in his Jewishness by an outrageous evil. Sartre offers
a remedy for those Jews who are prepared to make the authentic choice: he extends to them the invitation to become
Frenchmen. If this great prince of contemporary European
philosophy offers Herzog ideas such as this to embrace (or
dispute), who can blame him for his scepticism towards what
is called, so respectfully, Thought, towards contemporary intellectual fare? Often Herzog deals with ideas in negative
fashion. He needs to dismiss a great mass of irrelevancy and
nonsense in order to survive. Perhaps this was what I meant
earlier when I said that we were called upon to make innumerable judgements. We can be consumed simply by the
necessity to discriminate between multitudes of propositions.
We have to dismiss a great number of thoughts if we are to
have any creaturely or human life at all. It seems at times
that we are on trial seven days a week answering the questions, giving a clear account of ourselves. But when does one
live? How does one live if it is necessary to render ceaseless
judgements?

INTERVIEWER: Herzog's rejection of certain ideas has
been widely recognized, but –

BELLOW: – why he rejects them is not at all clear. Herzog's scepticism toward ideas is very deep. Though Jews are
often accused of being 'rootless' rationalists, a man like Herzog knows very well that habit, custom, tendency, temperament, inheritance, and the power to recognize real and
human facts have equal weight with ideas.

INTERVIEWER: You've spoken also of the disabling
effects of basing a novel on ideas. Does this mean structur-
ing a novel according to a philosophical conception?

BELLOW: No, I have no objection to that, nor do I have
any objection to basing novels on philosophical conceptions
or anything else that works. But let us look at one of the
dominant ideas of the century, accepted by many modern
artists – the idea that humankind has reached a terminal
point. We find this terminal assumption in writers like Joyce,
Céline, Thomas Mann. In *Doktor Faustus* politics and art
are joined in the destruction of civilization. Now here is an
idea, found in some of the greatest novelists of the twentieth

century. How good is this idea? Frightful things have happened, but is the apocalyptic interpretation true? The terminations did not fully terminate. Civilization is still here. The prophecies have not been borne out. Novelists are wrong to put an interpretation of history at the base of artistic creation – to speak 'the last word'. It is better that the novelist should trust his own sense of life. Less ambitious. More likely to tell the truth.

INTERVIEWER: Frequently in your fiction the hero strives to avoid being swallowed up by other people's ideas or versions of reality. On occasion you seen to present him with something like the whole range of contemporary alternatives – say, in *Augie March* or *Herzog*. Was this one of your intentions?

BELLOW: All these matters are really so complicated. Of course these books are somewhat concerned with free choice. I don't think that they pose the question successfully – the terms are not broad enough. I think I have let myself off easily. I seem to have asked in my books, How can one resist the controls of this vast society *without* turning into a nihilist, avoiding the absurdity of empty rebellion? I have asked, Are there other, more good-natured forms of resistance and free choice? And I suppose that, like most Americans, I have involuntarily favoured the more comforting or melioristic side of the question. I don't mean that I ought to have been more 'pessimistic', because I have found 'pessimism' to be in most of its forms nearly as empty as 'optimism'. But I am obliged to admit that I have not followed these questions to the necessary depth. I can't blame myself for not having been a stern moralist; I can always use the excuse that I'm after all nothing but a writer of fiction. But I don't feel satisfied with what I have done to date, except in the comic form. There is, however, this to be added – that our French friends invariably see the answers to such questions, and all questions of truth, to be overwhelmingly formidable, uncongenial, hostile to us. It may be, however, that truth is not always so punitive. I've tried to suggest this in my books. There may be truths on the side of life. I am quite prepared to admit that being habitual liars and selfdeluders, we have good cause to fear the truth, but I'm not at all ready to stop hoping. There may be some truths which are, after all, our friends in the universe.

Gordon Lloyd Harper

NORMAN MAILER

The interview took place on the afternoon of Saturday, July 6, 1963. The setting was Norman Mailer's Brooklyn Heights apartment, whose living room commands a panoramic view of lower Manhattan, the East River, and the New York harbour. The living room is fitted out with nautical or maritime furnishings and decorations, and Mailer, his curls unshorn, seemed at odd moments during the afternoon the novelist-as-ship-captain, though less Ahab than Captain Vere, and less both than Captain Shotover in ripe middle age. Mailer had recently stopped smoking, and the absence of nicotine had caused him to put on weight, which he carries gracefully and with vigour; the new amplitude of flesh seems to have influenced his spirit in the direction of benignity.

Shortly after the interviewer arrived, Mailer excused himself for a few moments. He wanted to change, he said, into his writer's costume. He emerged wearing faded dungarees and an open-necked sport shirt. His sharp blue eyes sparkled as he suggested that the interviewer keep this fashion note in mind. Lunch was then prepared and served by Mailer in what must be called lordly fashion. In general, he conducts himself without affectation as a kind of secular prince. The interviewer was repeatedly struck during the course of a long afternoon's work by Mailer's manners, which were exquisite. The role of novelist-being-interviewed suits him very well.

INTERVIEWER: Do you need any particular environment in which to write?

MAILER: I like a room with a view, preferably a long view. I dislike looking out on gardens. I prefer looking at the sea, or ships, or anything which has a vista to it. Oddly enough, I've never worked in the mountains.

INTERVIEWER: Do you need seclusion?

MAILER: I don't know if I need seclusion, but I do like to be alone in a room.

INTERVIEWER: When did you first think of becoming a writer?

MAILER: That's hard to answer. I did a lot of writing when I was young.

INTERVIEWER: How young?

MAILER: Seven.

INTERVIEWER: A real novel?

MAILER: Well, it was a science-fiction novel about people on Earth taking a rocket ship to Mars. The hero had a name which sounded like Buck Rogers. His assistant was called Dr Hoor.

INTERVIEWER: Doctor...?

MAILER: Dr Hoor. *Whore*, pronounced *H-o-o-r*. That's the way we used to pronounce 'whore' in Brooklyn. He was patterned directly after Dr Huer in Buck Rogers, who was then appearing on radio. This novel filled two and a half paper notebooks. You know the type, about seven by ten. They had soft shiny blue covers and they were, oh, only ten cents in those days, or a nickel. They ran to perhaps a hundred pages each, and I used to write on both sides. My writing was remarkable for the way I hyphenated words. I loved hyphenating, so I would hyphenate 'the' and make it th-e if it came at the end of the line. Or 'they' would become the-y. Then I didn't write again for a long time. I didn't even try out for the high-school literary magazine. I had friends who wrote short stories, and their short stories were far better than the ones I would write for assignments in high-school English, and I felt no desire to write. When I got to college I started again. The jump from Boys' High School in Brooklyn to Harvard came as a shock. I started reading some decent novels for the first time.

INTERVIEWER: You mentioned in *Advertisements for Myself* that reading *Studs Lonigan* made you want to be a writer.

MAILER: Yes. It was the best single literary experience I had had because the background of *Studs* was similar to mine. I grew up in Brooklyn, not Chicago, but the atmosphere had the same flatness of affect. Until then I had never considered my life or the life of the people around me as even remotely worthy of – well, I didn't believe they could be treated as subjects for fiction. It had never occurred to me. Suddenly I realized you could write about your own life.

INTERVIEWER: When did you feel that you were started as a writer?

MAILER: When I first began to write again at Harvard. I wasn't very good. I was doing short stories all the time, but I wasn't good. If there were fifty people in the class, let's say I was somewhere in the top ten. My teachers thought I was fair, but I don't believe they ever thought for a moment that I was really talented. Then in the middle of my sophomore year I started getting better. I got on the *Harvard Advocate*, and that gave me confidence, and about this time I did a couple of fairly good short stories for English A-1, one of which won *Story* magazine's college contest for that year. I must say that Robert Gorham Davies, who was my instructor then, picked the story to submit for the contest and was confident it would win.

INTERVIEWER: Was that the story about Al Groot?

MAILER: Yes. And when I found out it had won – which was at the beginning of the summer after my sophomore year (1941) – well, that fortified me, and I sat down and wrote a novel. It was a very bad novel. I wrote it in two months. It was called *No Percentage*. It was just terrible. But I never questioned any longer whether I was *started* as a writer.

INTERVIEWER: What do you think were some of the early influences in your life? What reading, as a boy, do you recall as important?

MAILER: *The Amateur Gentleman* and *The Broad Highway* were glorious works. So was *Captain Blood*. I think I read every one of Farnol's books and there must be twenty of them. And every one of Sabatini's.

INTERVIEWER: Did you ever read any of them again?

MAILER: No, now I have no real idea of their merit. But I never enjoyed a novel more than *Captain Blood*. Nor a movie. Do you remember Errol Flynn as Captain Blood?

Some years ago I was asked by a magazine what were the ten most important books in my development. The book I listed first was *Captain Blood*. Then came *Das Kapital*. Then *The Amateur Gentleman*.

INTERVIEWER: You wouldn't say that *Das Kapital* was boyhood reading?

MAILER: Oh, no, I read that many years later. But it had its mild influence.

INTERVIEWER: It's been said often that novelists are largely nostalgic for their boyhood, and in fact most novelists draw on their youthful experiences a great deal. In your novels, however, the evocation of scenes from boyhood is rare or almost absent.

MAILER: It is difficult to write about childhood. I never felt I understood it in any novel way. I never felt other authors did either. Not particularly. I think the portrait of childhood which is given by most writers is rarely true to anything more than the logic of their novel. Childhood is so protean.

INTERVIEWER: What about Twain, or Hemingway – who drew on their boyhoods successfully?

MAILER: I must admit they created some of the psychological reality of my own childhood. I wanted, for instance, to be like Tom Sawyer.

INTERVIEWER: Not Huck Finn?

MAILER: The magic of Huck Finn seems to have passed me by, I don't know quite why. *Tom Sawyer* was the book of Twain's I always preferred. I remember when I got to college I was startled to find that *Huckleberry Finn* was the classic. Of course I haven't looked at either novel in thirty years.

INTERVIEWER: Can you say something about your methods of working?

MAILER: They vary with each book. I wrote *The Naked and the Dead* on the typewriter. I used to write four days a week: Mondays, Tuesdays, Thursdays, and Fridays.

INTERVIEWER: Definite hours?

MAILER: Yes, very definite hours. I'd get up about eight or eight-thirty and I'd be at work by ten. And I'd work till twelve-thirty; then I'd have lunch. I'd get back to work about two-thirty or three, and work for another two hours. In the afternoon I usually needed a can of beer to prime me. But I'd write for about five hours a day. And I wrote a great deal. The average I tried to keep was seven type-written pages a day, twenty-eight pages a week. The first draft took seven months, the second draft – which really was only half a draft – took four months. The part about the platoon went well from the beginning, but the Lieutenant and the General in the first draft were stock characters. If it had been published at that point the book would have been considered an interesting war novel with some good scenes, no more. The second draft was the bonus. Cummings and Hearn were done in the second draft. If you look at the book you can see that the style shifts, that the parts about Cummings and Hearn are written in a somewhat more developed vein. Less forceful but more articulated. And you can see something of the turn my later writing would take in the scenes between Cummings and Hearn.

INTERVIEWER: What methods did you pursue in your next books?

MAILER: Well, with *Barbary Shore*, I began to run into trouble. I started it in Paris about six months after I finished *The Naked and the Dead*, and did about fifty pages. It was then called *Mrs Guinevere* and was influenced by Sally Bowles in Isherwood's *Berlin Stories*. *Mrs Guinevere* never went anywhere. It stopped, just ground down after those first fifty pages. My novelistic tanks ran out of gas. I dropped it completely, thought I'd never pick it up again, and started to work on another novel. Did all the research, went to Indiana to do research.

INTERVIEWER: On what?

MAILER: On a labour novel. There was a union in Evansville with which I had connections. So I stayed for a few days in Indiana, and then went to Jamaica, Vermont, to write the novel. I spent four to six weeks getting ready to begin. I made a great push on the beginning, worked for two weeks, and quit cold. I didn't have the book. I didn't know a damned thing about labour unions. In desperation (I was full of second-novel panic) I picked up *Mrs Guinevere* and looked at it. And found something there I could go on with. So I worked on it all through the spring of 1949, and then I moved out to Hollywood for the summer. I finished the second half in Hollywood. *Barbary Shore* is really a Hollywood novel. I think it reflected the impact of Hollywood on me in some subterranean fashion. Certainly the first draft is the wildest draft of the three; it's almost insane, and the most indigestible portions were written in the first couple of months I was in Hollywood. I never knew where the book was going, I had no idea where it was going to move from day to day. I'd wake up and push the typewriter in great dread, in literal terror, wondering when this curious and doubtful inspiration was going to stop. It never did. It ground along at the rate of three pages, three difficult pages, a day. But I'd get it out. I got a first draft done, and was quite unhappy with it; it was a very bad book at that point. When I rewrote it later, in Provincetown, a summer later, again it went at the rate of three pages a day. This revision was different from the first draft, and I think much better. But working on *Barbary Shore* I always felt as if I were not writing the book myself, but rather as if I were serving as a subject for some intelligence which had decided to use me to write the book. It had nothing to do with whether the work was good or bad. It just had to do with the fact that I had absolutely no conscious control of it; if I hadn't heard about the unconscious I would have had to postulate one to explain this phenomenon. For the first time I became powerfully aware of the fact that I had an unconscious which seemed to have little to do with me.

INTERVIEWER: What about *The Deer Park*?

MAILER: For *The Deer Park* I didn't have much of a method. It was agony; it was far and away the most difficult of my three novels to write. The first and second drafts were written with the idea that they were only the first part of an eight-part novel. I think I used that enormous scheme as a pretext to get into the work. Apparently I just couldn't sit down and write a nice modest Hollywood novel. I had to have something grandiose in conception, anyway. I started *The Deer Park* with 'The Man Who Studied Yoga'. That was supposed to be a prologue to all eight novels. It went along nicely and was done in a few weeks. And then I got into *The Deer Park*, and I forget what my methods were exactly; I think they varied. In the revisions of *Barbary Shore* I had started working in longhand; as soon as I found myself blocked on the typewriter I'd shift to longhand. By the time I got to *The Deer Park* I was writing in longhand all the time. I'd write in longhand in the morning and type up what I'd written in the afternoon. I was averaging about four-five pages a day, I think, three days a week; about fifteen pages a week. But I found it an unendurable book to write because I'd finish each day in the most profound depression; as I found out later it was even a physical depression. I was gutting my liver.

INTERVIEWER: It wasn't alcohol?

MAILER: No, I wasn't much of a drinker in those days. The liver, you see, is not unlike a car battery, and I was draining mine. I was writing with such anxiety and such fear and such distaste, and such gloom and such dissatisfaction that ...

INTERVIEWER: Dissatisfaction with what?

MAILER: Oh, everything. My work, my life, myself. The early draft of *The Deer Park* was terrible. It had a few good things in it, but it was slow to emerge, it took years, and was stubborn. It still emerges. I mean, I could sit down today and rewrite *The Deer Park*. Of course, what was happening was that this work, such as it was, was continuing to move in a direction which was completely against the grain of my intellect – insofar as my intellect was developed, and had standards and tastes and attitudes towards the novel. I was working towards a novel utterly outrageous to my notion of things.

INTERVIEWER: Say it again?

MAILER: Well, I was a socialist after all, and I believed in large literary works which were filled with characters, and were programmatic, and had large theses, and were developed, let's say, like the Tolstoyan novel. It's as if, all proportion naturally being kept, as if Tolstoy had sat down with the intention of writing *Anna Karenina* and instead came out with *Crime and Punishment*. Obviously, it would have been intolerable for him, and he would have disliked *Crime and Punishment* very much. That was what was going on with me at a much lower level.

INTERVIEWER: How does the idea of a novel come to you?

MAILER: I don't know that it comes. A more appropriate image for me might be that I start with the idea of constructing a treehouse and end with a skyscraper made of wood.

INTERVIEWER: Well, how did the idea of *The Naked and the Dead* come to you?

MAILER: I wanted to write a short novel about a long patrol. All during the war I kept thinking about this patrol. I even had the idea before I went overseas. Probably it was stimulated by a few war books I had read: John Hersey's *Into the Valley*, Harry Brown's *A Walk in the Sun*, and a couple of others I no longer remember. Out of these books came the idea to do a novel about a long patrol. And I began to create my characters. All the while I was overseas a part of me was working on this long patrol. I even ended up in a reconnaissance outfit which I had asked to get into. A reconnaissance outfit, after all, tends to take long patrols. Art kept traducing life. At any rate, when I started writing *The Naked and the Dead* I thought it might be a good idea to have a preliminary chapter or two in which to give the reader a chance to meet my characters before they went on patrol. But the next six mouths and the first five hundred pages went into that, and I remember in the early days I was annoyed at how long it was taking me to get to the patrol.

INTERVIEWER: Do you keep notes, or a journal, or diaries, or write scenarios? What's your preparatory material?

MAILER: That also varies with each of the books. For *The Naked and the Dead* I had a file full of notes, and a long dossier on each man. Many of these details never got into the novel, but the added knowledge made me feel more comfortable with each character. Indeed I even had charts to show which characters had not yet had scenes with other characters. For a book which seems spontaneous on its surface, *The Naked and the Dead* was written mechanically. I studied engineering at Harvard, and I suppose it was the book of a young engineer. The structure is sturdy, but there's no fine filigree to the joints. Just spot-welding and riveting. And the working plan was very simple. I devised some preliminary actions for the platoon in order to give the reader an opportunity to get to know the men, but this beginning, as I said, took over two-thirds of the book. The patrol itself is also simple, but I did give more thought to working it out ahead of time.

INTERVIEWER: People have commented on the pleasure you seem to take in the military detail of *The Naked and the Dead*.

MAILER: Compared to someone like James Jones, I'm an amateur at military detail. But at that time I did like all those details. I even used to enjoy patrols, or at least I did when I wasn't sick with jungle rot and viruses or atabrine poisoning. I was one of the few men in the platoon who could read a map. I was the only enlisted man I know who really cared about reading a map and once I gave myself away. We used to have classes after a campaign was over; we'd come back to garrison – one of those tent cities out in a rice paddy – and they would teach us all over again how to read maps and read compasses, or they would drill us on the nomenclature of the machine gun for the eighth time. One day, very bored, I was daydreaming, and the instructor pointed to a part of the map and said, 'Mailer, what are these coordinates?' If I had had a moment to think I would never have answered, it was bad form to be bright in my outfit, but I didn't think: he caught me in a daze, and I looked up and said, '320.017 dash 146.814' and everyone's mouth dropped. It was the first time anybody ever answered such a question thus briskly in the history of infantry map reading. At any rate, that was the fun for me, the part about the patrol. I suppose it had something to do with *Captain Blood* and *The Amateur Gentleman*.

INTERVIEWER: How much of a plan did you have for *Barbary Shore*?

MAILER: None. As I indicated earlier, *Barbary Shore* just

birthed itself slowly. The book came out sentence by sentence. I literally never knew where the next day's work was coming from.

INTERVIEWER: You don't mention (in your description of writing *Barbary Shore*) any relationship to politics. Wasn't your *engagement* at the time a considerable part of the plan?

MAILER: I think it was the unspoken drama in the working-up of the book. I started *Barbary Shore* as some sort of fellow-traveller and finished with a political position which was a far-flung mutation of Trotskyism. And the drafts of the book reflected these ideological changes so drastically that the last draft of *Barbary Shore* is a different novel altogether and has almost nothing in common with the first draft but the names.

INTERVIEWER: Did Jean Malaquais (to whom the book is dedicated) have much to do with this?

MAILER: Yes. He had an enormous influence on me. He's the only man I know who can combine a powerfully dogmatic mind with the keenest sense of nuance, and he has a formidable culture which seems to live in his veins and capillaries. Since he also had a most detailed vision of the Russian Revolution – he was steeped in it the way certain American families are imbued with the records of their clan – I spent a year living more closely in the history of Russia from 1917 to 1937 than in the events of my own life. I doubt if I would even have gone back to rewrite *Barbary Shore* if I didn't know Malaquais. Certainly I could never have conceived McLeod. Malaquais, of course, bears no superficial resemblance whatsoever to McLeod – indeed Malaquais was never even a communist, he started as an anti-Stalinist, but he had a quality when I first met him which was pure Old Bolshevik. One knew that if he had been born in Russia, a contemporary of Lenin's, he would have been one of the leaders of the Revolution and would doubtless have been executed in the trials. So his personality – as it filtered through the contradictory themes of my unconscious – inhabits *Barbary Shore*.

INTERVIEWER: Would you care to discuss what you mean by the 'contradictory themes' of your unconscious? Is that related to what you said a little while ago about becoming aware of your unconscious while writing *Barbary Shore*?

MAILER: *Barbary Shore* was built on the division which existed then in my mind. My conscious intelligence, as I've indicated, became obsessed by the Russian Revolution. But my unconscious was much more interested in other matters: murder, suicide, orgy, psychosis, all the themes I discuss in *Advertisements*. Since the gulf between these conscious and unconscious themes was vast and quite resistant to any quick literary coupling, the tension to get a bridge across resulted in the peculiar feverish hothouse atmosphere of the book. My unconscious felt one kind of dread, my conscious mind another, and *Barbary Shore* lives somewhere between. That's why its focus is so unearthly. And of course this difficulty kept haunting me from then on in all the work I did afterwards. But it was a book written without any plan.

INTERVIEWER: And *The Deer Park*?

MAILER: That was different. There I had an idea of what I was going to do. I knew it was going to be a story about a most unhappy love. The problem was getting to the affair: I could hardly wait to reach it, especially because the early parts of the novel were so difficult to write. It is truly difficult to trap Hollywood in a novel. Only in the last draft did I finally get the setting the way I wanted it. I think now the setting is probably the best part. In fact I would judge that the first fifty pages of *The Deer Park* are the best writing I have ever done in fiction. But they were the hardest fifty pages of the book to write and certainly took the longest time.

INTERVIEWER: Do you have any superstitions about your methods of work?

MAILER: I wouldn't call them superstitions exactly. I just think it's bad to talk about one's present work, for it spoils something at the root of the creative act. It discharges the tension.

INTERVIEWER: What writers have you learned the most from, technically?

MAILER: E. M. Forster, I suppose. I wouldn't say he is necessarily one of the novelists I admire most. But I have learned a lot from him. You remember in *The Longest Journey* somewhere about the fourth chapter, you turn the page and read, 'Gerald was killed that day. He was beaten to death in a football game.' It was quite extraordinary. Gerald had been very important through the beginning of the book. But now that he was suddenly and abruptly dead, everyone else's character began to shift. It taught me that personality was more fluid, more dramatic and startling, more inexact than I had thought. I was brought up on the idea that when you wrote a novel you tried to build a character who could be handled and walked around like a piece of sculpture. Suddenly character seemed related more closely to the paintings of the new realists. For instance, I saw one recently which had a painted girl reclining on a painted bed, and there was a television set next to her in the canvas, a real one which you could turn on. Turning on the literal factual set changes the girl and the painting both. Well, Forster gives you something of that sensation in his novels. I played with such a concept a great deal in *Barbary Shore* and I began to play with it in *The Deer Park* in an altogether different way. I suppose the concept was parallel to the 'Alexandria Quartet' in its preoccupations. When you tell the same story through the eyes of different characters, you have not only a different novel but a different reality. I think I could sit down today and write *The Deer Park* through Charles Francis Eitel's eyes, and if I changed the names and the place, no one might know the new book had anything to do with *The Deer Park*. I suppose what I realized, after reading Forster, was that a novel written in the third person was now impossible for me for many years.

INTERVIEWER: Forster has never written a novel in the first person.

MAILER: I know he hasn't, but in some funny way Forster gave my notion of personality a sufficient shock that I could not manage to write in the third person. Forster, after all, had a developed view of the world; I did not. I think I must have felt at that time as if I would never be able to write in the third person until I developed a coherent view of life. I don't know that I've been able to altogether.

INTERVIEWER: You know, Thackeray says at one point that the novelist knows everything. He is like God, and this may be why he could write in the third person.

MAILER: God can write in the third person only so long as He understands His world. But if the world becames contradictory or incomprehensible to Him, then God begins to grow concerned with his own nature. It's either that, or borrow notions from other Gods.

INTERVIEWER: Have you ever cribbed anything from other writers?

MAILER: Oh, you know, I have such a – what shall I say? – such a stuffy view of myself that I could never *conceive* of cribbing. But I have been *influenced* by – well, Farrell to begin with. Dos Passos, Steinbeck (I am trying to do it chronologically), Hemingway, and later Fitzgerald – much, much later. And Thomas Wolfe, of course.

INTERVIEWER: But back to cribbing. Shakespeare cribs, for example. He never invented a plot.

MAILER: No, but my plots are always rudimentary. Whatever I've accomplished certainly does not depend on my virtuosity with plot. Generally I don't even have a plot. What happens is that my characters engage in an action, and out of that action little bits of plot sometimes adhere to the narrative. I never have to worry about lifting a plot, because I don't conceive of a book that way.

INTERVIEWER: In connection with plot, when did the idea of using a hornet's nest to thwart the climbers in *The Naked and the Dead* come to you?

MAILER: That idea was there before I wrote the first sentence of the book. Actually that incident happened to my reconnaissance platoon on the most ambitious patrol I ever took with them. They sent out thirty of us to locate and destroy one hundred Japanese marines who had gotten behind our lines. Well, we never found the marines, but we did get stuck climbing one hell of an enormous hill with a mean slimy trail, and when we were almost up to the ridge, somebody kicked over a hornet's nest. Half the platoon went tearing up the hill, and the machine-gun squad went flying down to the valley. We never did find each other again that day. We just slunk back to our bivouac.

INTERVIEWER: Apart from the fact that it happened, do you think in fact it was a satisfactory device? It seems to have bothered some people.

MAILER: I think I'd do it the same way again. War is disproportions, and the hornet's nest seemed a perfect disproportion to me. We were ready to lose our lives but we weren't up to getting stung by a hornet.

INTERVIEWER: Would you say something about style, prose style, in relation to the novel?

MAILER: A really good style comes only when a man has become as good as he can be. Style is character. A good style cannot come from a bad, undisciplined character. Now a man may be evil, but I believe that people can be evil in their essential natures and still have good characters. Good in the sense of being well-tuned. They can have characters which are flexible, supple, adaptable, principled in relation to their own good or their own evil – even an evil man can have principles – he can be true to his own evil, which is not always so easy, either. I think good style is a matter of rendering out of oneself all the cupidities, all the cripplings, all the velleities. And then I think one has to develop one's physical grace. Writers who are possessed of some physical grace may tend to write better than writers who are physically clumsy. It's my impression this is so. I don't know that I'd care to attempt to prove it.

INTERVIEWER: Well, how would you describe your own style? I ask this question because certain critics have pointed to deficiencies in it, or what they think of as deficiencies. Didn't Diana Trilling, for instance, criticize certain flatnesses in your style?

MAILER: I think that flatness comes out of certain flatnesses in me. And in trying to overcome that flatness I may push too hard in the other direction. Alfred Kazin once said something very funny about the way I write: 'Mailer is as fond of his style as an Italian tenor is of his vocal cords.'

INTERVIEWER: Have you ever written to merely improve your writing, practised your writing as an athlete would work out?

MAILER: No. I don't think it's a proper activity. That's too much like doing a setting-up exercise; any workout which does not involve a certain minimum of danger or responsibility does not improve the body – it just wears it out.

INTERVIEWER: In writing your novels, has any particular formal problem given you trouble – let's say a problem of joining two parts of a narrative together, getting people from point A to point B?

MAILER: You mean like getting them out of a room? I think formal problems exist in inverse proportion to one's honesty. You get to the problem of getting someone out of the room when there's something false about the scene.

INTERVIEWER: Do you do any research or special reading to prepare for writing a novel, or while you're writing a novel?

MAILER: Occasionally I have to look something up. But I'm always unhappy about that and mistrust the writing which comes out of it. I feel in a way that one's ignorance is part of one's creation, too. I don't know quite how to put it, but for instance if I, as a Jew, am writing about other Jews, and if my knowledge of Jewish culture is exceptionally spotty, as indeed it is, I am not so sure that that isn't an advantage in creating a modern American Jew. Because *his* knowledge of Jewish culture is also extremely spotty, and the way in which his personality is composed may be more in accordance with my ignorance than with a cultivated Jew's immersion in the culture. So in certain limited ways one's ignorance can help to buttress the validity of a novel.

INTERVIEWER: Have you ever written about a situation of which you have had no personal experience or knowledge?

MAILER: I don't know. Let's see ... *Barbary Shore*, for example, is the most imaginative of my novels. But I did live in a rooming house for a short period while I was writing *The Naked and the Dead*. I certainly didn't live in it the way Lovett lived in it. I never met an F.B.I. agent – at least I had no sense of having met one at the time I was

writing *Barbary Shore*. I am sure I have met a great many
since. They didn't necessarily introduce themselves to me. I
had never met an Old Bolshevik, either, although ironically,
writing about F.B.I. agents and Old Bolsheviks in *Barbary
Shore*, the greatest single difficulty with the book was that
my common sense thought it was impossible to have all
these agents and impossible heroes congregating in a rooming house in Brooklyn Heights. Yet a couple of years later I
was working in a studio on Fulton Street at the end of
Brooklyn Heights, a studio I have had for some years. It
was a fine old studio building and they're tearing it down
now to make room for a twenty-storey building which will
look like a Kleenex box. At any rate, on the floor below me,
worked one Colonel Rudolph Abel, who was the most important spy for the Russians in this country for a period of
about eight or ten years, and I am sure we used to be in the
elevator together many times. I think he literally had the
room beneath me. I have always been overcome with that.
It made me decide there's no clear boundary between experience and imagination. Who knows what glimpses of
reality we pick up unconsciously, telepathically.

INTERVIEWER: To what extent are your characters
modelled on real people?

MAILER: I think half of them might have a point of departure from somebody real. Up to now I've not liked writing about people who are close to me, because they're too
difficult to do. Their private reality obviously interferes with
the reality one is trying to create. They become alive not as
creatures in your imagination but as actors in your life. And
so they seem real while you work but you're not working
their reality into your book. For example, it's not a good
idea to try to put your wife into a novel. Not your latest
wife, anyway. In practice, I prefer to draw a character from
someone I hardly know. Hollingsworth came from someone
I met in Paris, a vapid young American who inveigled me
to have a cup of coffee with him in a café and asked a lot of
dull questions. *The Naked and the Dead* had just come out
and I think he was impressed with that. Yet, there was
something sinister about him. I had met him at the Sor-

bonne a week or two before and I saw him again just for this afternoon for no more than an hour, but he stayed in my memory and became Leroy Hollingsworth in *Barbary Shore*.

INTERVIEWER: How do you name your characters?

MAILER: I try to let the name emerge, because I've found out that the names of my characters usually have roots in the book. I try to avoid quick or cheap symbolisms. Although I contradict myself, for much is made in *The Deer Park* of the way the name 'Eitel' is pronounced Eye-tell.

INTERVIEWER: *I*-tell?

MAILER: Eye-tell. But I became aware of that, believe it or not, only when the book was half done. The original title of *The Deer Park* was *The Idol and the Octopus*. The book was going to be about Charles Francis Eitel, the Director, and Herman Teppis, the Producer, and the underlying theme was the war between those who wished to make an idol out of art, the artists, and the patron who used art for power, the octopus.

INTERVIEWER: You also called him 'Idell'.

MAILER: Frankie Idell in 'The Man Who Studied Yoga', yes, but there again, I was obviously getting ready for some, shall we say, hanky-panky, in the eight novels.

INTERVIEWER: Can you describe how you turn a real person into a fictional one?

MAILER: I try to put the model in situations which have very little to do with his real situations in life. Very quickly the model disappears. His private reality can't hold up. For instance, I might take somebody who is a professional football player, a man, let's say, whom I know slightly, and make him a movie star. In a transposition of this sort, everything which relates particularly to the professional football player quickly disappears, and what is left, curiously, is what is *exportable* in his character. But this process, while interesting in the early stages, is not as exciting as the more creative act of allowing your characters to grow once they're separated from the model. It's when they become almost as complex as one's own personality that the fine excitement begins. Because then they are not really characters any

longer – they're beings, which is a distinction I like to make.
A character is someone you can grasp as a whole, you can
have a clear idea of him, but a being is someone whose
nature keeps shifting. Like a character of Forster's. In *The
Deer Park* Lulu Myers is a being rather than a character. If
you study her closely you will see that she is a different person in every scene. Just a little different. I don't know
whether initially I did this by accident or purposefully, but
at a certain point I made the conscious decision *not* to try to
straighten her out, she seemed right in her changeableness.

INTERVIEWER: Is Marion Faye a character or a –

MAILER: No, he's a being. Everybody in *The Deer Park*
is a being except the minor characters like Herman Teppis.

INTERVIEWER: Do specific characters reappear in different guises as the novels appear?

MAILER: To a mild degree. Actually it's easier for me to
create a new character than to drag along one of the old
ones. No, I think it's more that certain themes reappear in
my novels, but I'd rather not get into this just yet.

INTERVIEWER: How did Marion Faye emerge?

MAILER: The book needed something which wasn't in
the first draft, some sort of evil genius. One felt a dark pressure there in the inner horizon of the book. But even as I
say this I know it's not true to the grain of my writing experience. I violate that experience by talking in these terms.
I am not sure it's possible to describe the experience of novel-
writing authentically. It may be that it is not an experience.

INTERVIEWER: What is it, then?

MAILER: It may be more like a relation, if you will – a
continuing relation between a man and his wife. You can't
necessarily speak of that as an experience because it may
consist of several experiences which are braided together; or
it may consist of many experiences which are all more or less
similar; or indeed it may consist of two kinds of experiences
which are antagonistic to one another. Throughout all of
this I've spoken of characters' *emerging*. Quite often they
don't emerge; they fail to emerge. And what one's left with
is the dull compromise which derives from two kinds of
experiences' warring with one another within oneself. A

character who should have been brilliant is dull. Or even if a character does prove to be first-rate, it's possible you should have done twice as much with him, three times as much.

INTERVIEWER: You speak of character as emerging, and I gather by that that you mean emerging from yourself and emerging from your idea?

MAILER: They are also emerging from the book. A book takes on its own life in the writing. It has its laws, it becomes a creature to you after a while. One feels a bit like a master who's got a fine animal. Very often I'll feel a certain shame for what I've done with a novel. I won't say it's the novel that's bad; I'll say it's I who was bad. Almost as if the novel did not really belong to me, as if it was something raised by me like a child. I know what's potentially beautiful in my novel, you see. Very often after I've done the novel I realize that the beauty which I recognize in it is not going to be recognized by the reader. I didn't succeed in bringing it out. It's very odd – it's as though I had let the novel down, owed it a duty which I didn't fulfill.

INTERVIEWER: Would you say that there was any secret or hidden pattern being worked out in your novels?

MAILER: I'd rather leave that to others. If I answer the question badly, nothing is accomplished. If I answer too well, it's going to discourage critics. I can imagine nothing more distressing to a critic than to have a writer see accurately into his own work. But I will say one thing, which is that I have some obsession with how God exists. Is He an essential god or an existential god; is He all-powerful or is He, too, an embattled existential creature who may succeed or fail in His vision? I think this theme may become more apparent as the novels go on.

INTERVIEWER: When did this obsession begin?

MAILER: I think it began to show itself while I was doing the last draft of *The Deer Park*. Then it continued to grow as a private theme during all the years I was smoking marijuana.

INTERVIEWER: You have spoken so often of the existential view. What reading or individuals brought you to this?

MAILER: The experience came first. One's condition on

marijuana is always existential. One can feel the importance of each moment and how it is changing one. One feels one's being, one becomes aware of the enormous apparatus of nothingness – the hum of a hi-fi set, the emptiness of a point-less interruption, one becomes aware of the war between each of us, how the nothingness in each of us seeks to attack the being of others, how our being in turn is attacked by the nothingness in others. I'm not speaking now of violence or the active conflict between one being and another. That still belongs to drama. But the war between being and nothing-ness is the underlying illness of the twentieth century. Bore-dom slays more of existence than war.

INTERVIEWER: Then you didn't come to existentialism because it was a literary influence?

MAILER: No. I'd hardly read anything by Sartre at this time, and nothing by Heidegger. I've read a bit since, and have to admire their formidable powers, but I suspect they are no closer to the buried continent of existentialism than were mediaeval cartographers near to a useful map of the world. The new continent which shows on our psychic maps as intimations of eternity is still to be discovered.

INTERVIEWER: What do you feel about the other kinds of writing you have done and are doing? How do they stand in relation to your work as a novelist?

MAILER: The essays?

INTERVIEWER: Yes: journalism, essays.

MAILER: Well, you know, there was a time when I wanted very much to belong to the literary world. I wanted to be respected the way someone like Katherine Anne Porter used to be respected.

INTERVIEWER: How do you think she was respected?

MAILER: The way a cardinal is respected – weak people get to their knees when the cardinal goes by.

INTERVIEWER: As a master of the craft, do you mean?

MAILER: As a master of the craft, yes. Her name is in-voked in an argument. 'Well, Katherine Anne Porter would not do it *that* way.' But by now I'm a bit cynical about craft. I think there's a natural mystique in the novel which is more important than craft. One is trying, after all, to capture

reality, and that is extraordinarily and exceptionally difficult. I think craft is merely a series of way stations. I think
of craft as being like a Saint Bernard dog with that little
bottle of brandy under his neck. Whenever you get into *real*
trouble the thing that can save you as a novelist is to have
enough craft to be able to keep warm long enough to be
rescued. Of course this is exactly what keeps good novelists
from becoming great novelists. Robert Penn Warren might
have written a major novel if he hadn't had just that little
extra bit of craft to get him out of all the trouble in *All the
King's Men.* If Penn Warren hadn't known anything about
Elizabethan literature, the true Elizabethan in him might
have emerged. I mean, he might have written a fantastic
novel. As it was, he knew enough about craft to –

INTERVIEWER: – to use it as an escape hatch?

MAILER: Yes. And his plot degenerated into a slam-bang
of exits and entrances, confrontations, tragedies, quick wits,
and woe. But he was really forcing an escape from the
problem.

INTERVIEWER: Which was?

MAILER: Oh, the terror of confronting a reality which
might open into more and more anxiety and so present a
deeper view of the abyss. Craft protects one from facing
those endless expanding realities of deterioration and responsibility.

INTERVIEWER: Deterioration in what sense?

MAILER: The terror, let's say, of being reborn as something much less noble or something much more ignoble. I
think this sort of terror depresses us profoundly. Which may
by why we throw up our enormous evasions – such as craft.
Indeed, I think this adoration of craft, this specific respect
for craft makes a church of literature for that vast number
of writers who are somewhere on the spectrum between
mediocrity and talent. But I think it's fatal for somebody
who has a large ambition and a chance of becoming a great
writer. I know, for myself, if I am going to make this attempt
– that the only way to do it is to keep in shape in a peculiar
way.

INTERVIEWER: Can you explain what you mean by that?

MAILER: It's hard to talk about. Harry Greb, for example, was a fighter who used to keep in shape. He was completely a fighter, the way one might wish to be completely a writer. He always did the things which were necessary to him as a fighter. Now, some of these things were extremely irrational, that is, extremely irrational from a prize-fight manager's point of view. That is, before he had a fight he would go to a brothel, and he would have two prostitutes, not one, taking the two of them into the same bed. And this apparently left him feeling like a wild animal. Don't ask me why. Perhaps he picked the two meanest whores in the joint and so absorbed into his system all the small, nasty, concentrated evils which had accumulated from carloads of men. Greb was known as the dirtiest fighter of his time. He didn't have much of a punch but he could spoil other fighters and punish them, he know more dirty tricks than anyone around. This was one of his training methods and he did it over and over again until he died at a relatively early age of a heart attack, on an operating table. I think he died before he was thirty-eight or so. They operated on him, and bang, he went. Nothing could be done. But the point I make is that he stayed in training by the way he lived his life. The element which was paramount in it was to keep in shape. If he were drinking, you see, the point was to keep in shape *while* drinking. I'm being a touch imprecise about this.

INTERVIEWER: Well . . . what?

MAILER: He would not just drink to release his tension. Rather, what went on was that there was tension in him which was insupportable, so he had to drink. But reasoning as a professional, he felt that if he had to drink, he might as well use that too. In the sense that the actor uses everything which happens to him, so Greb as a fighter used everything which happened to him. As he drank he would notice the way his body moved. One of the best reasons one drinks is to become aware of the way his mind and body move.

INTERVIEWER: Well, how do you keep in shape?

MAILER: Look, before we go on, I want to say a little more about craft. It is a grab bag of procedures, tricks, lore, formal gymnastics, symbolic superstructures – methodology, in short. It's the compendium of what you've acquired from others. And since great writers communicate a vision of existence, one can't usually borrow their methods. The method is married to the vision. No, one acquires craft more from good writers and mediocre writers with a flair. Craft, after all, is what you can take out whole from their work. But keeping in shape is something else. For example, you can do journalism, and it can be terrible for your style. Or it can temper your style ... in other words, you can become a *better* writer by doing a lot of different kinds of writing. Or you can deteriorate. There's a book came out a few years ago which was a sociological study of some Princeton men – I forget the name of it. One of them said something which I thought was extraordinary. He said he wanted to perform the sexual act under every variety of condition, emotion, and mood available to him. I was struck with this not because I ever wanted necessarily to have that kind of sexual life, but because it seemed to me that was what I was trying to do with my writing. I try to go over my work in every conceivable mood. I edit on a spectrum which runs from the high clear manic impressions of a drunk which has made one electrically alert all the way down to the soberest reaches of depression where I can hardly bear my words. By the time I'm done with writing I care about I usually have worked on it through the full gamut of my consciousness. If you keep yourself in this peculiar kind of shape, the craft will take care of itself. Craft is very little finally. But if you're continually worrying about whether you're growing or deteriorating as a man, whether your integrity is turning soft or firming itself, why then it's in that slow war, that slow rear-guard battle you fight against diminishing talent that you stay in shape as a writer and have a consciousness. You develop a consciousness as you grow older which enables you to write about anything, in effect, and write about it well. That is, provided you keep your consciousness in shape and don't relax into the flabby styles of thought which surround one everywhere. The moment you borrow other writers' styles of thought, you need craft to shore up the walls. But if what you write is a reflection of your own consciousness, then even journalism can become interesting. One wouldn't want to spend one's life at it, and I wouldn't want ever to be caught justifying journalism as a major activity (it's obviously less interesting than to write a novel), but it's better, I think, to see journalism as a venture of one's ability to keep in shape than to see it as an essential betrayal of the chalice of your literary art. Temples are for women.

INTERVIEWER: Temples are for women?

MAILER: Temples are for women.

INTERVIEWER: Well, Faulkner once said that nothing can injure a man's writing if he's a first-rate writer.

MAILER: Faulkner said more asinine things than any other major American writer. I can't remember a single interesting remark Faulkner ever made.

INTERVIEWER: He once called Henry James a 'nice old lady'.

MAILER: Faulkner had a mean small Southern streak in him, and most of his pronunciamentos reflect that meanness. He's a great writer, but he's not at all interesting in most of his passing remarks.

INTERVIEWER: Well, then, what can ruin a first-rate writer?

MAILER: Booze, pot, too much sex, too much failure in one's private life, too much attrition, too much recognition, too little recognition, frustration. Nearly everything in the scheme of things works to dull a first-rate talent. But the worst probably is cowardice – as one gets older, one becomes aware of one's cowardice, the desire to be bold which once was a joy gets heavy with caution and duty. And finally there's apathy. About the time it doesn't seem to be important any more to be a great writer you know you've slipped far enough to be doing your work now on the comeback trail.

INTERVIEWER: Would you say that is where you are now?

MAILER: Let others say it. I don't know that I choose to. The hardest thing for a writer to decide is whether he's burned out or merely lying fallow. I was ready to think I was burned out before I even started *The Naked and the Dead*.

INTERVIEWER: What kind of an audience do you keep in mind when you write?

MAILER: I suppose it's that audience which has no tradition by which to measure their experience but the intensity and clarity of their inner lives. That's the audience I'd like to be good enough to write for.

INTERVIEWER: Do you feel under any obligation to them?

MAILER: Yes. I have a consciousness now which I think is of use to them. I've got to be able to get it out and do it well, to transmit it in such a way that their experience can rise to a higher level. It's exactly ... I mean, one doesn't want one's children to make one's own mistakes. Let them make better mistakes, more exceptional mistakes.

INTERVIEWER: What projects do you have for the future?

MAILER: I've got a very long novel I want to do. And beyond that I haven't looked. Some time ahead I'd like to be free of responsibilities so I could spend a year just taking on interesting assignments – cover the World Series, go to report a war. I can't do that now. I have a feeling I've got to come to grips with myself, with my talent, with what I've made of it and what I've spoiled of it. I've got to find out whether I really can write a large novel or not.

INTERVIEWER: What have you spoiled?

MAILER: All sorts of potentialities. I've burned them out – squandered them, wasted them. I think everybody does. It's a question of whether I've spoiled more than my share.

INTERVIEWER: You once said that you wished to become consecutively more disruptive, more dangerous, and more powerful, and you felt this sentence was a description of your function as a novelist. I wonder if you still think that?

MAILER: I might take out 'disruptive'. It's an unhappy word to use. It implies a love of disruption for the sake of disruption. Actually, I have a fondness for order.

INTERVIEWER: Do you enjoy writing, or is such a term irrelevant to your experience?

MAILER: Oh, no. No, no. You set me thinking of something Jean Malaquais once said. He always had a terrible time writing. He once complained with great anguish about the unspeakable difficulties he was having with a novel. And I asked him, 'Why do you do it? You can do many other things well. Why do you bother with it?' I really meant this. Because he suffered when writing like no one I know. He looked up in surprise and said, 'Oh, but this is the only way one can ever find the truth. The only time I know that something is true is at the moment I discover it in the act of writing.' I think it's that. I think it's this moment when one knows it's true. One may not have written it well enough for others to know, but you're in love with the truth when you discover it at the point of a pencil. That, in and by itself, is one of the few rare pleasures in life.

INTERVIEWER: How do you feel when you aren't working?

MAILER: Edgy. I get into trouble. I would say I'm wasting my substance completely when I'm not writing.

INTERVIEWER: And to be writing ... to be a writer?

MAILER: Well, at best you affect the consciousness of your time, and so indirectly you affect the history of the time which succeeds you. Of course, you need patience. It takes a long time for sentiments to collect into an action and often they never do. Which is why I was once so ready to conceive of running for Mayor of New York. I wanted to make actions rather than effect sentiments. But I've come to the middle-aged conclusion that I'm probably better as a writer than a man of action. Too bad. Still it's no little matter to be a writer. There's that godawful *Time*-magazine world out there, and one can make raids on it. There are palaces and prisons to attack. One can even succeed now and again in blowing holes in the line of the world's communications. Sometimes I feel as if there's a vast guerrilla war going on for the mind of man, communist against communist, capitalist against capitalist, artist against artist. And the stakes are huge. Will we spoil the best secrets of life or will we help to free a new kind of man? It's intoxicating to think of that. There's something rich waiting if one of us is brave enough and good enough to get there.

Steven Marcus

ALLEN GINSBERG

Allen Ginsberg was elected King of the May by Czech students in Prague on May Day 1965. Soon afterwards he was expelled by the Czech government. He had been travelling for several months – in Cuba, Russia, and Poland – and from Prague he flew to London to negotiate the English publication of his poems. I didn't know he was in the country, but one night in Bristol before a poetry reading I saw him in a bar. He read that night; I hadn't heard him read before and was struck that evening by the way he seemed to enter each of his poems emotionally while reading them, the performance as much a discovery for him as for his audience.

Ginsberg and I left Bristol the day after the reading, and hitch-hiked to Wells Cathedral and then to Glastonbury, where he picked a flower from King Arthur's grave to send, he said, to Peter Orlovsky. He studied carefully the exhibit of tools and weapons under the huge conical chimney of the ancient kings' kitchen, as later in Cambridge he was to study the Fitzwilliam Museum's store of Blake manuscripts; Ginsberg's idea of a Jerusalemic Britain occurring now in the day of long hair and new music meant equally the fulfilment of Blake's predictions of Albion. As we came out of a teashop in Glastonbury (where customers had glanced cautiously at the bearded, prophetic – and unfazed – stranger), Allen spoke of Life's simulacrum of a report of his Oxford encounter with Dame Edith Sitwell. ('Dope makes me come out all over in spots,' she's supposed to have said.)

Leaving the town, we were caught in a rainstorm, and took a bus to Bath. Then, hitchhiking towards London, we were unsuccessful until Ginsberg tried using Buddhist hand signals instead of thumbing; half a minute later a car stopped. Riding through Somerset he talked about notation, the mode he says he learned from Kerouac and has used in composing his enormous journals; he read from an

*account he'd made of a recent meeting with the poets Yev-
tushenko and Vosnessensky in Moscow, and then, looking
up at a knot in a withered oak by the road, said, 'The tree
has cancer of the breast ... that's what I mean ...'*

*Two weeks later he was in Cambridge for a reading, and
I asked him to submit to this interview. He was still busy
with Blake, and roaming and musing around the university
and countryside in his spare moments; it took two days to
get him to sit still long enough to turn on the tape-recorder.
He spoke slowly and thoughtfully, tiring after two hours.
We stopped for a meal when guests came – when Ginsberg
learned one of them was a biochemist he questioned him
about viruses and D.N.A. for an hour – then we returned
to record the other half of the tape. The words that follow
are his, with little alteration save the omission of repetitive
matter in half a dozen places.*

INTERVIEWER: I think Diana Trilling, speaking about
your reading at Columbia, remarked that your poetry, like
all poetry in English when dealing with a serious subject,
naturally takes on the iambic pentameter rhythm. Do you
agree?

GINSBERG: Well, it really isn't an accurate thing, I don't
think. I've never actually sat down and made a technical
analysis of the rhythms that I write. They're probably more
near choriambic – Greek metres, dithyrambic metres – and
tending toward de DA de de DA de de ... what is that?
Tending towards dactylic, probably. Williams once remarked that American speech tends towards dactylic. But
it's more complicated than dactyl because dactyl is a three,
three units, a foot consisting of three parts, whereas the
actual rhythm is probably a rhythm which consists of five,
six, or seven, like DA de de DA de de DA de de DA DA.
Which is more toward the line of Greek dance rhythms –
that's why they call them choriambic. So actually, probably
it's not really technically correct, what she said. But – and
that applies to certain poems, like certain passages of 'Howl'
and certain passages of 'Kaddish' – there are definite
rhythms which could be analyzed as corresponding to clas-

sical rhythms, though not necessarily *English* classical rhythms; they might correspond to Greek classical rhythms, or Sanskrit prosody. But probably most of the other poetry, like 'Aether' or 'Laughing Gas' or a lot of those poems, they simply don't fit into that. I think she felt very comfy, to think that that would be so. I really felt quite hurt about that, because it seemed to me that she ignored the main prosodic technical achievements that I had proffered forth to the academy, and they didn't even recognize it. I mean not that I want to stick her with being the academy.

INTERVIEWER: And in 'Howl' and 'Kaddish' you were working with a kind of classical unit? Is that an accurate description?

GINSBERG: Yeah, but it doesn't do very much good, because I wasn't really working with my own neural impulses and writing impulses. See, the difference is between someone sitting down to write a poem *in* a definite preconceived metrical pattern and filling in that pattern, and someone working with his physiological movements and *arriving* at a pattern, and perhaps even arriving at a pattern which might even have a name, or might even have a classical usage, but arriving at it organically rather than synthetically. Nobody's got any objection to even iambic pentameter if it comes from a source deeper than the mind – that is to say, if it comes from the breathing and the belly and the lungs.

INTERVIEWER: American poets have been able to break away from a kind of English specified rhythm earlier than English poets have been able to do. Do you think this has anything to do with a peculiarity in English spoken tradition?

GINSBERG: No, I don't really think so, because the English don't speak in iambic pentameter either; they don't speak in the recognizable pattern that they write in. The dimness of their speech and the lack of emotional variation is parallel to the kind of dim diction and literary usage in the poetry now. But you can hear all sorts of Liverpudlian or Geordian – that's Newcastle – you can hear all sorts of variants aside from an upper-tone accent, a high-class accent, that don't fit into the tone of poetry being written right now. It's not being used like in America – I think it's just that British poets are more cowardly.

INTERVIEWER: Do you find any exception to this?

GINSBERG: It's pretty general, even the supposedly avant-garde poets. They write, you know, in a very toned-down manner.

INTERVIEWER: How about a poet like Basil Bunting?

GINSBERG: Well, he was working with a whole bunch of wild men from an earlier era, who were all breaking through I guess. And so he had that experience – also he knew Persian, he knew Persian prosody. He was better educated than most English poets.

INTERVIEWER: The kind of organization you use in 'Howl', a recurrent kind of syntax – you don't think this is relevant any longer to what you want to do?

GINSBERG: No, but it was relevant to what I wanted to do then, it wasn't even a conscious decision.

INTERVIEWER: Was this related in any way to a kind of music or jazz that you were interested in at the time?

GINSBERG: Mmm ... the myth of Lester Young as described by Kerouac, blowing eighty-nine choruses of 'Lady Be Good', say, in one night, or my own hearing of Illinois Jacquet's *Jazz at the Philharmonic*, Volume 2; I think: Can't Get Started' was the title.

INTERVIEWER: And you've also mentioned poets like Christopher Smart, for instance, as providing an analogy – is this something you discovered later on?

GINSBERG: When I looked into it, yeah. Actually, I keep reading, or earlier I kept reading, that I was influenced by Kenneth Fearing and Carl Sandburg, whereas actually I was more conscious of Christopher Smart, and Blake's Prophetic Books, and Whitman and some aspects of Biblical rhetoric. And a lot of specific prose things, like Genet, Genet's *Our Lady of the Flowers* and the rhetoric in that, and Céline; Kerouac, most of all, was the biggest influence I think – Kerouac's prose.

INTERVIEWER: When did you come onto Burroughs's work?

GINSBERG: Let's see ... Well, first thing of Burroughs's

I ever read was 1946 ... which was a skit later published
and integrated in some other work of his, called *So Proudly
We Hail*, describing the sinking of the *Titanic* and an
orchestra playing 'The Star Spangled Banner' while everybody rushed out to the lifeboats and the captain got up in
woman's dress and rushed into the purser's office and shot
the purser and stole all the money, and a spastic paretic
jumped into a lifeboat with a machete and began chopping
off people's fingers that were trying to climb into the boat,
saying, 'Out of the way, you foolth ... dirty thunthufbithes.'
That was a thing he had written up at Harvard with a friend
named Kells Elvins. Which is really the whole key of all his
work, like the sinking of America, and everybody like frightened rats trying to get out, or that was his vision of the
time.

Then he and Kerouac later in 1945 – forty-five or forty-six
– wrote a big detective book together, alternating chapters.
I don't know where that book is now – Kerouac has his
chapters and Burroughs's are somewhere in his papers. So
I think in a sense it was Kerouac that encouraged Burroughs
to write really, because Kerouac was so enthusiastic about
prose, about writing, about lyricism, about the honour of
writing ... the Thomas Wolfe-ian delights of it. So anyway
he turned Burroughs on in a *sense*, because Burroughs
found a companion who could write really interestingly, and
Burroughs admired Kerouac's perceptions. Kerouac could
imitate Dashiell Hammett as well as Bill, which was Bill's
natural style: dry, bony, factual. At that time Burroughs
was reading John O'Hara, simply for facts, not for any sublime stylistic thing, just because he was a hard-nosed
reporter.

Then in Mexico around 1951 he started writing *Junkie*.
I've forgotten what relation I had to that – I think I wound
up as the agent for it, taking it around New York trying to
get it published. I think he sent me portions of it at the time
– I've forgotten how it worked out now. This was around
1949 or 1950. He was going through a personal crisis, his wife
had died. It was in Mexico or South America ... but it was
a very generous thing of him to do, to start writing all of a

sudden. Burroughs was always a very *tender* sort of person, but very dignified and shy and withdrawn, and for him to *commit* himself to a big autobiographical thing like that was ... at the time, struck me as like a piece of eternity is in love with the ... what is it, 'Eternity is in love with the productions of Time'? So he was making a production of Time then.

Then I started taking that around. I've forgotten who I took that to but I think maybe to Louis Simpson who was then working at Bobbs-Merrill. I'm not sure whether I took it to him – I remember taking it to Jason Epstein who was then working at Doubleday I think. Epstein at the time was not as experienced as he is now. And his reaction to it, I remember when I went back to his office to pick it up, was, well this is all very interesting, but it isn't really interesting, on account of if it were an autobiography of a junkie written by Winston *Churchill* then it'd be interesting, but written by somebody he'd never heard of, well then it's *not* interesting. And anyway I said what about the *prose*, the prose is interesting, and he says, oh, a difference of opinion on that. Finally I wound up taking it to Carl Solomon who was then a reader for A. A. Wynn Company, which was his uncle; and they finally got it through there. But it was finally published as a cheap paperback. With a whole bunch of frightened footnotes; like Burroughs said that marijauna was nonhabit-forming, which is now accepted as a fact, there'd be a footnote by the editor, 'Reliable, er, responsible medical opinion does not confirm this.' Then they also had a little introduction ... literally they were afraid of the book being censored or *seized* at the time, is what they said. I've forgotten what the terms of censorship or seizure were that they were worried about. This was about 1952. They *said* that they were afraid to publish it straight for fear there would be a Congressional investigation or something, I don't know what. I think there was some noise about narcotics at the time. Newspaper noise ... I've forgotten exactly what the arguments were. But anyway they had to write a preface which hedged on the book a lot.

INTERVIEWER: Has there been a time when fear of

censorship or similar trouble has made your own expression difficult?

GINSBERG: This is so complicated a matter. The beginning of the fear with me was, you know, what would my father say to something that I would write. At the time, writing 'Howl' – for instance, like I assumed when writing it that it was something that *could* not be published because I wouldn't want my daddy to see what was in there. About my sex life, being fucked in the ass, imagine your father reading a thing like that, was what I thought. Though that disappeared as soon as the thing was real, or as soon as I manifested my ... you know, it didn't make that much importance finally. That was sort of a help for writing, because I assumed that it wouldn't be published, therefore I could say anything that I wanted. So literally just for myself or anybody that I knew personally well, writers who would be willing to appreciate it with a breadth of tolerance – in a piece of work like 'Howl' – who wouldn't be judging from a moralistic viewpoint but looking for evidences of humanity or secret thought or just actual truthfulness.

Then there's later the problem of publication – we had a lot. The English printer refused at first I think, we were afraid of customs; the first edition we had to print with asterisks on some of the dirty words, and then the *Evergreen Review* in reprinting it used asterisks, and various people reprinting it later always wanted to use the *Evergreen* version rather than the corrected legal City Lights version – like I think there's an anthology of Jewish writers, I forgot who edited that, but a couple of the high-class intellectuals from Columbia. I had written asking them specifically to use the later City Lights version, but they went ahead and printed an asterisked version. I forget what was the name of that – something like *New Generation of Jewish Writing*, Philip Roth, et cetera.

INTERVIEWER: Do you take difficulties like these as social problems, problems of communication simply, or do you feel they also block your own ability to express yourself for yourself?

GINSBERG: The problem is, where it gets to literature, is

this. We all talk among ourselves and we have common understandings, and we say anything we want to say, and we talk about our assholes, and we talk about our cocks, and we talk about who we fucked last night, or who we're gonna fuck tomorrow, or what kind of love affair we have, or when we got drunk, or when we stuck a broom in our ass in the Hotel Ambassador in Prague – anybody tells one's friends about that. So then – what happens if you make a distinction between what you tell your friends and what you tell your Muse? The problem is to break down that distinction: when you approach the Muse to talk as frankly as you would talk with yourself or with your friends. So I began finding, in conversations with Burroughs and Kerouac and Gregory Corso, in conversations with people whom I knew well, whose souls I respected, that the things we were telling each other for real were totally different from what was already in literature. And that was Kerouac's great discovery in *On the Road*. The kinds of things that he and Neal Cassady were talking about, he finally discovered were *the* subject matter for what he wanted to write down. That meant, at that minute, a complete reversion of what literature was supposed to be, in *his* mind, and actually in the minds of the people that first read the book. Certainly in the minds of the critics, who had at first attacked it as not being ... proper structure, or something. In other words, a gang of friends running around in an automobile. Which obviously is like a great picaresque literary device, and a classical one. And was *not* recognized, at the time, as suitable literary subject matter.

INTERVIEWER: So it's not just a matter of themes – sex, or any other one –

GINSBERG: It's the ability to commit to writing, to *write*, the same way that you ... are! Anyway! You have many writers who have preconceived ideas about what literature is supposed to be, and their ideas seem to exclude that which makes them most charming in private conversation. Their faggishness, or their campiness, or their neurasthenia, or their solitude, or their goofiness, or their – even – masculinity, at times. Because they think that they're gonna write something that sounds like something else that they've read before, instead of sounds like them. Or comes from their own life. In other words, there's no distinction, there should be no distinction between what we write down, and what we really know, to begin with. As we know it every day, with each other. And the hypocrisy of literature has been – you know like there's supposed to be formal literature, which is supposed to be different from ... in subject, in diction, and even in organization, from our quotidian inspired lives.

It's also like in Whitman, 'I find no fat sweeter than that which sticks to my own bones' – that is to say the self-confidence of someone who knows that he's really alive, and that his existence is just as good as any other subject matter.

INTERVIEWER: Is physiology a part of this too – like the difference between your long breath line, and William Carlos Williams's shorter unit.

GINSBERG: Analytically, ex post facto, it all begins with fucking around and intuition and without any idea of *what* you're doing, I think. Later, I have a tendency to explain it, 'Well, I got a longer breath than Williams, or I'm Jewish, or I study yoga, or I sing long lines. ...' But anyway, what it boils down to is this, it's my *movement*, my feeling is for a big long clanky statement – partly that's something that I share, or maybe that I even got from Kerouac's long prose line; which is really, like he once remarked, an extended poem. Like one long sentence page of his *Doctor Sax* or *Railroad Earth* or occasionally *On the Road* – if you examine them phrase by phrase they usually have the density of poetry, and the beauty of poetry, but most of all the single elastic rhythm running from beginning to end of the line and ending 'mop!'

INTERVIEWER: Have you ever wanted to extend this rhythmic feeling as far as, say, Artaud or now Michael McClure have taken it – to a line that is actually animal noise?

GINSBERG: The rhythm of the long line is also an animal cry.

INTERVIEWER: So you're following that feeling and not a thought or visual image?

GINSBERG: It's simultaneous. The poetry generally is

like a rhythmic articulation of feeling. The feeling is like
an impulse that rises within – just like sexual impulses, say;
it's almost as definite as that. It's a feeling that begins somewhere in the pit of the stomach and rises up forward in the
breast and then comes out through the mouth and ears, and
comes forth a croon or a groan or a sigh. Which, if you put
words to it by looking around and seeing and trying to describe what's making you sigh – and sigh in words – you
simply articulate what you're feeling. As simple as that. Or
actually what happens is, at best what happens, is there's a
definite body rhythm that has no definite words, or may
have one or two words attached to it, one or two key words
attached to it. And then, in writing it down, it's simply a
process of association that I find what the rest of the statement is – what can be collected around that word, what that
word is connected to. Partly by simple association, the first
thing that comes into my mind like 'Moloch is' or 'Moloch
who', and then whatever comes out. But that also goes along
with a definite rhythmic impulse, like DA de de DA de de
DA de de DA DA. '*M*oloch whose eyes are a *thou*sand
blind *windows*.' And before I wrote 'Moloch whose eyes are
a thousand blind windows', I had the word, 'Moloch,
Moloch, Moloch', and I also had the feeling DA de de DA
de de DA de de DA DA. So it was just a question of looking up and seeing a lot of windows, and saying, Oh, windows, of course, but what kind of windows? But not even
that – 'Moloch whose eyes.' 'Moloch whose *eyes*' – which is
beautiful in itself – but what about it, Moloch whose eyes are
what? So Moloch whose eyes – then probably the next thing
I thought was 'thousands'. O.K., and then thousands *what*?
'Thousands blind.' And I had to finish it somehow. So I
hadda say 'windows'. It looked good *afterward*.

Usually during the composition, step by step, word by
word and adjective by adjective, if it's at all spontaneous, I
don't know whether it even makes sense, sometimes. Sometimes I do know it makes complete sense, and I start cry-
ing. Because I realize I'm hitting some area which is absolutely true. And in that sense applicable universally, or
understandable universally. In that sense able to survive

through time – in that sense to be read by somebody and wept to, maybe, centuries later. In that sense prophecy, because it touches a common key ... what prophecy actually is is not that you actually know that the bomb will fall in 1942. It's that you know and feel something which somebody knows and feels in a hundred years. And maybe articulate it in a hint – concrete way that they can pick up on in a hundred years.

INTERVIEWER: You once mentioned something you had found in Cézanne – a remark about the reconstitution of the *petites sensations* of experience, in his own painting – and you compared this with the method of your poetry.

GINSBERG: I got all hung up on Cézanne around 1949 in my last year at Columbia, studying with Meyer Schapiro. I don't know how it led into it – I think it was about the same time that I was having these Blake visions. So. The thing I understood from Blake was that it was possible to transmit a message through time which could reach the enlightened, that poetry had a definite effect, it wasn't just pretty, or just beautiful, as I had understood pretty beauty before – it was something basic to human existence, or it reached something, it reached the bottom of human existence. But anyway the impression I got was that it was like a kind of time machine through which he could transmit, Blake could transmit, his basic consciousness and communicate it to somebody else after he was dead – in other words, build a time machine.

Now just about that time I was looking at Cézanne and I suddenly got a strange shuddering impression looking at his canvases, partly the effect when someone pulls a Venetian blind, reverses the Venetian – there's a sudden shift, a flashing that you see in Cézanne canvases. Partly it's when the canvas opens up into three dimensions and looks like wooden objects, like solid-space objects, in three dimensions rather than flat. Partly it's the enormous spaces which open up in Cézanne landscapes. And it's partly that mysterious quality around his figures, like of his wife or the cardplayers or the postman or whoever, the local Aix characters. They look like great huge 3-D wooden dolls, sometimes.

Very *uncanny* thing, like a very mysterious thing – in other words, there's a strange sensation that one gets, looking at his canvases, which I began to associate with the extraordinary sensation – cosmic sensation, in fact – that I had experienced catalyzed by Blake's 'Sun-flower' and 'Sick Rose' and a few other poems. So I began studiously investigating Cézanne's intentions and method, and looking at all the canvases of his that I could find in New York, and all the reproductions I could find, and I was writing at the time a paper on him, for Schapiro at Columbia in the fine-arts course.

And the whole thing opened up, two ways: first I read a book on Cézanne's composition by Earl Loran, who showed photographs, analyses and photographs of the original motifs, side by side with the actual canvases – and years later I actually went to Aix, with all the postcards, and stood in the spots, and tried to find the places where he painted Mont-Sainte-Victoire from, and got in his studio and saw some of the motifs he used, like his big black hat and his cloak. Well, first of all, I began to see that Cézanne had all sorts of literary symbolism in him, on and off. I was preoccupied with Plotinian terminology, of time and eternity, and I saw it in Cézanne paintings, an early painting of a clock on a shelf which I associated with time and eternity, and I began to think he was a big secret mystic. And I saw a photograph of his studio in Loran's book and it was like an alchemist's studio, because he had a skull, and he had a long black coat, and he had this big black hat. So I began thinking of him as, you know, like a magic character. Like the original version I had thought of him was like this austere dullard from Aix. So I began getting really interested in him as a hermetic type, and then I symbolically read into his canvases things that probably weren't there, like there's a painting of a winding road which turns off, and I saw that as the mystical path: it turns off into a village and the end of the path is hidden. Something he painted I guess when he went out painting with Bernard. Then there was an account of a very fantastic conversation that he had had. It's quoted in Loran's book: there's a long long long paragraph where he says, 'By means of squares, cubes, triangles I try to reconstitute the impression that I have from nature: the means that I use to reconstitute the impression of solidity that I think-feel-see when I am looking at a motif like Victoire is to reduce it to some kind of pictorial language, so I use these squares, cubes, and triangles, but I try to build them together so interknit [*and here in the conversation he held his hands together with his fingers interknit*] so that *no light gets through.*' And I was mystified by that, but it seemed to make sense in terms of the grid of paint strokes that he had on his canvas, so that he produced a solid two-dimensional surface which when you looked *in*to it, maybe from a slight distance with your eyes unfocused or your eyelids lowered slightly, you could see a great three-dimensional opening, mysterious, stereoscopic, like going into a stereopticon. And I began discovering in 'The Cardplayers' all sorts of sinister symbols, like there's one guy leaning against the wall with a stolid expression on his face, that he doesn't want to get involved; and then there's two guys who are peasants, who are looking as if they've just been dealt *Death* cards; and then the *dealer* you look at and he turns out to be a city slicker with a big blue cloak and almost rouge doll-like cheeks and a fat-faced Kafkian-agent impression about him, like he's a cardsharp, he's a cosmic cardsharp dealing out Fate to all these people. This looks like a great big hermetic Rembrandtian portrait in Aix! That's why it has that funny monumentality – aside from the quote plastic values unquote.

Then, I smoked a lot of marijuana and went to the basement of the Museum of Modern Art in New York and looked at his water colours and that's where I began really turning on to space in Cézanne and the way he built it up. Particularly there's one of rocks, I guess 'Rocks at Garonne', and you look at them for a while, and after a while they seem like they're rocks, just the rock parts, you don't know where they are, whether they're on the ground or in the air or on top of a cliff, but then they seem to be floating in space like clouds, and then they seem to be also a bit like they're amorphous, like kneecaps or cockheads or faces without eyes. And it has a very mysterious impression. Well, that may have been the result of the pot. But it's a definite thing that I got from that. Then he did some very odd studies after classical statues, Renaissance statues, and they're great gigantesque herculean figures with little tiny pinheads ... so that apparently was his comment on them!

And then ... the things were endless to find in Cézanne. Finally I was reading his letters and I discovered this phrase again, *mes petites sensations* – 'I'm an old man and my passions are not, my senses are not coarsened by passions like some *other* old men I know, and I have worked for years trying to,' I guess it was the phrase, '*reconstitute* the *petites sensations* that I get from nature, and I could stand on a hill and merely by moving my head half an inch the composition of the landscape was totally changed.' So apparently he'd refined his optical perception to such a point where it's a real contemplation of optical phenomena in an almost yogic way, where he's standing there, from a specific point studying the optical field, the depth in the optical field, looking, actually looking at his own eyeballs in a sense. The attempting to reconstitute the sensation in his own eyeballs. And what does he say finally – in a very weird statement which one would not expect of the austere old workman – he said, 'And this *petite sensation* is nothing other than *pater omnipotens aeterna deus*.'

So that was, I felt the key to Cézanne's hermetic method ... everybody knows his workman-like, artisan-like, petrified-like painting method which is so great, but the really ro-*man*ticistic motif behind it is absolutely marvellous, so you realize that he's really a saint! Working on his form of yoga, all that time, in obvious saintly circumstances of retirement in a small village, leading a relatively nonsociable life, going through the motions of going to church or not, but really containing in his skull these supernatural phenomena and observations ... you know, and it's very humble actually, because he didn't know if he was crazy or not – that is a flash of the physical, miracle dimensions of existence, trying to do it in such a way as it would look – if the observer looked at it long enough – it would look like as much three dimension as the actual *world* of optical phenomena when

one looks through one's eyes. Actually he's *re*constituted
the whole fucking universe in his canvases – it's like a fantastic thing! – or at least the appearance of the universe.

So. I used a lot of this material in the references in the
last part of the first section of 'Howl': 'sensation of Pater
Omnipotens Aeterna Deus.' The last part of 'Howl' was
really an homage to art but also in specific terms an homage
to Cézanne's method, in a sense I adapted what I could to
writing; but that's a very complicated matter to explain. Except, putting it very simply, that just as Cézanne doesn't use
perspective lines to create space, but it's a juxtaposition of
one colour against another colour (that's one element of
space), so, I had the idea, perhaps overrefined, that by the
unnexplainable, unexplained nonperspective line, that is,
juxtaposition of one *word* against another, a *gap* between
the two words – like the space gap in the canvas – there'd
be a gap between the two words which the mind would fill in
with the sensation of existence. In other words when I say,
oh ... when Shakespeare says, 'In the dread vast and middle
of the night,' something happens between 'dread vast' and
'middle'. That creates like a whole space of, spaciness of
black night. How it gets that is very odd, those words put
together. Or in the haiku, you have two distinct images, set
side by side without drawing a connection, without drawing a logical connection between them: the *mind* fills in this
... this space. Like

> O ant
> crawl up Mount Fujiyama,
> but slowly, slowly.

Now you have the small ant and you have Mount Fuji-
yama and you have the slowly, slowly, and what happens is
that you feel almost like ... a cock in your mouth! You
feel this enormous space-universe, it's almost a tactile thing.
Well, anyway, it's a phenomenon-sensation, phenomenon
hyphen sensation, that's created by this little haiku of Issa,
for instance.

So I was trying to do similar things with juxtapositions
like 'hydrogen jukebox'. Or ... 'winter midnight smalltown

streetlight rain'. Instead of cubes and squares and triangles. Cézanne is reconstituting by means of triangles, cubes, and colours – I have to reconstitute by means of words, rhythms of course, and all that – but say it's words, phrasings. So. The problem is then to reach the different parts of the mind, which are existing simultaneously, the different associations which are going on simultaneously, choosing elements from both, like: jazz, jukebox, and all that, and we have the jukebox from that; politics, hydrogen bomb, and we have the hydrogen from that, you see 'hydrogen jukebox'. And that actually compresses in one instant like a whole series of things. Or the end of 'Sun-flower' with 'cunts of wheelbarrows', whatever that all meant, or 'rubber dollar bills' – 'skin of machinery'; see, and actually in the moment of composition I don't necessarily *know* what it means, but it comes to mean something later, after a year or two, I realize that it meant something clear, unconsciously. Which takes on meaning in time, like a photograph developing slowly. Because we're not really always conscious of the entire depth of our minds – in other words, we just know a lot more than we're able to be aware of, normally – though at moments we're completely aware, I guess.

There's some other element of Cézanne that was interesting ... oh, his patience, of course. In recording the optical phenomena. Has something to do with Blake: *with* not *through* the eye – 'You're led to believe a lie when you see with not through the eye.' He's seeing through his eye. One can see *through* his canvas to God, really, is the way it boils down. Or to Pater Omnipotens Aeterna Deus. I could imagine someone not prepared, in a peculiar chemical-physiological state, peculiar mental state, psychic state, someone not prepared who had no experience of eternal ecstacy, passing in front of a Cézanne canvas, distracted and without noticing it, his eye travelling in, to, through the canvas into the space and suddenly stopping with his hair standing on end, dead in his tracks, *see*ing a whole universe. And I think that's what Cézanne really does, to a lot of people.

Where were we now? Yeah, the idea that I had was that

gaps in space and time through images juxtaposed, just as in the haiku you get two images which the mind connects in a flash, and so that *flash* is the *petite sensation*; or the *satori*, perhaps, that the Zen haikuists would speak of – if they speak of it like that. So, the poetic experience that Housman talks about, the hair-standing-on-end or the hackles-rising, whatever it is, visceral thing. The interesting thing would be to know if certain combinations of words and rhythms actually had an electrochemical reaction on the body, which could catalyze specific states of consciousness. I think that's what probably happened to me with Blake. I'm *sure* it's what happens on a perhaps lower level with Poe's 'Bells' or 'Raven', or even Vachel Lindsay's 'Congo': that there is a hypnotic rhythm there, which when you introduce it into your nervous system, causes all sorts of electronic changes – permanently alters it. There's a statement by Artaud on that subject, that certain music when introduced into the nervous system changes the molecular composition of the nerve cells or something like that, it permanently alters the being that has experience of this. Well, anyway, this is certainly true. In other words, any experience we have is recorded in the brain and goes through neural patterns and whatnot: so I suppose brain recordings are done by means of shifting around of little electrons – so there is actually an electrochemical effect caused by art.

So ... the problem is what is the maximum electrochemical effect in the desired direction. That is what I was taking Blake as having done to me. And what I take as one of the optimal possibilities of art. But this is all putting it in a kind of bullshit abstract way. But it's an interesting – toy. To play with. That idea.

INTERVIEWER: In the last five or six months you've been in Cuba, Czechoslovakia, Russia, and Poland. Has this helped to clarify your sense of the current world situation?

GINSBERG: Yeah, I no longer feel – I didn't ever feel that there was any answer in dogmatic Leninism-Marxism – but I feel very definitely now that there's no answer to my desires there. Nor do most of the people in those countries

– in Russia or Poland or Cuba – really feel that either. It's
sort of like a religious theory imposed from above and
usually used to beat people on the head with. Nobody takes
it seriously because it doesn't mean anything, it means different things in different countries anyway. The general idea
of revolution against American idiocy is good, it's still
sympathetic, and I guess it's a good thing like in Cuba, and
obviously Viet Nam. But what's gonna follow – the dogmatism that follows is a big drag. And everybody apologizes
for the dogmatism by saying, well, it's an inevitable consequence of the struggle against American repression. And
that may be true too.

But there's one thing I feel certain of, and that's that
there's no human answer in communism or capitalism as
it's practised outside of the U.S. in any case. In other words,
by hindsight, the interior of America is not bad, at least
for me, though it might be bad for a spade, but not too bad,
creepy, but it's not impossible. But travelling in countries
like Cuba and Viet Nam I realize that the people that get
the real evil side effects of America are there – in other
words, it really is like imperialism, in that sense. People in
the United States all got money, they got cars, and everybody else *starves* on account of American foreign policy.
Or in being bombed out, torn apart, and bleeding on the
street, they get all their teeth bashed in, tear gassed, or hot
pokers up their ass, things that would be, you know, considered terrible in the United States. Except for Negroes.

So I don't know. I don't see any particular answer, and
this month it seemed to me like actually an atomic war was
inevitable on account of both sides were so dogmatic and
frightened and had nowhere to go and didn't know what to
do with themselves anymore except fight. Everybody too
intransigent. Everybody too mean. I don't suppose it'll take
place, but . . . Somebody has got to sit in the British Museum
again like Marx and figure out a new system; a new blueprint. Another century has gone, technology has changed
everything completely, so it's time for a new utopian system.
Burroughs is almost working on it.

But one thing that's impressive is Blake's idea of Jerusalem, Jerusalemic Britain, which I think is *now* more and more valid. He, I guess, defined it. I'm still confused about Blake, I still haven't read him all through enough to understand what direction he was really pointing to. It seems to be the *naked human form divine*, seems to be Energy, it seems to be sexualization, or sexual liberation, which are the directions we all believe in. He also seems, however, to have some idea of imagination which I don't fully understand yet. That is, it's something outside of the body, with a rejection of the body, and I don't quite understand that. A life after death even. Which I still haven't comprehended. There's a letter in the Fitzwilliam Museum, written several months before he died. He says, 'My body is in turmoil and stress and decaying, *but* my ideas, my power of ideas and my imagination, are stronger than ever.' And I find it hard to conceive of that. I think if I were lying in bed dying, with my body pained, I would just give up. I mean, you know, because I don't think I could *exist* outside my body. But he apparently was able to. Williams didn't seem to be able to. In other words Williams's universe was tied up with his body. Blake's universe didn't seem to be tied up with his body. Real mysterious, like far other worlds and other seas, so to speak. Been puzzling over that today.

The Jerusalemic world of Blake seems to be Mercy-Pity-Peace. Which has human form. Mercy has a human face. So that's all clear.

INTERVIEWER: How about Blake's statement about the senses being the chief inlets of the soul in this age – I don't know what 'this age' means; is there another one?

GINSBERG: What he says is interesting because there's the same thing in Hindu mythology, they speak of This Age as the Kali Yuga, the age of destruction, or an age so sunk in materialism. You'd find a similar formulation in Vico, like what is it, the Age of Gold running on to the Iron and then Stone, again. Well, the Hindus say that *this* is the Kali Age or Kali Yuga or Kali Cycle, and we are also so sunk in matter, the five senses are matter, sense, that they say there is absolutely no way out by intellect, by thought, by discipline, by practice, by sadhana, by jnanayoga, nor

karma yoga – that is, doing good works – no way out through
our own will or our own effort. The *only* way out that they
generally now prescribe, generally in India at the moment,
is through bhakti yoga, which is Faith-Hope-Adoration-
Worship, or like probably the equivalent of the Christian
Sacred Heart, which I find a very lovely doctrine – that is
to say, pure delight, the only way you can be saved is to
sing. In other words, the only way to drag up, from the
depths of this depression, to drag up your soul to its proper
bliss, and understanding, is to give yourself, completely, to
your heart's desire. The image will be determined by the
heart's compass, by the compass of what the heart moves
towards and desires. And then you get on your knees or on
your lap or on your head and you sing and chant prayers
and mantras, till you reach a state of ecstasy and understanding, and the bliss overflows out of your body. They say
intellect, like Saint Thomas Aquinas, will never do it, because it's just like me getting all hung up on whether I
could remember what happened before I was born – I
mean you could get lost there very easily, and it has no
relevance *anyway*, to the existent flower. Blake says something similar, like Energy, and Excess ... leads to the
palace of wisdom. The Hindu bhakti is like excess of devotion; you just, you know, give yourself all out to devotion.

Very oddly a lady saint Shri Matakrishnaji in Brindaban,
whom I consulted about my spiritual problems, told me to
take Blake for my guru. There's all kinds of different gurus,
there can be living and nonliving gurus – apparently whoever
initiates you, and I apparently was intiated by Blake in
terms of at least having an ecstatic experience from him. So
that when I got here to Cambridge I had to rush over to
the Fitzwilliam Museum to find his misspellings in *Songs
of Innocence*.

INTERVIEWER: What was the Blake experience you
speak of?

GINSBERG: About 1945 I got interested in Supreme Reality with a capital S and R, and I wrote big long poems
about a last voyage looking for Supreme Reality. Which was
like a Dostoevskian or Thomas Wolfeian idealization or like

Rimbaud – what was Rimbaud's term, new vision, was that it? Or Kerouac was talking about a new vision, verbally, and intuitively out of longing, but also out of a funny kind of tolerance of this universe. In 1948 in East Harlem in the summer I was living – this is like the Ancient Mariner, I've said this so many times: 'stoppeth one of three./ "By thy long grey beard ..."' Hang an albatross around your neck... The one thing I felt at the time was that it would be a terrible horror, that in one or two decades I would be trying to explain to people that one day something like this happened to me! I even wrote a long poem saying, 'I will grow old, a grey and groaning man,/ and with each hour the same thought, and with each thought the same denial./ Will I spend my life in praise of the *idea* of God?/ Time leaves no hope. We creep and wait. We wait and go alone.' Psalm II – which I never published. So anyway – there I was in my bed in Harlem ... jacking off. With my pants open, lying around on a bed by the window sill, looking out into the cornices of Harlem and the sky above. And I had just come. And had perhaps hardly even wiped the come off my thighs, my trousers, or whatever it was. As I often do, I had been jacking off while reading – I think it's probably a common phenomenon to be noticed among adolescents. Though I was a little older than an adolescent at the time. About twenty-two. There's a kind of interesting thing about, you know, distracting your attention while you jack off – that is, you know, reading a book or looking out of a window, or doing something else with the conscious mind which kind of makes it sexier.

So anyway, what I had been doing that week – I'd been in a very lonely solitary state, dark night of the soul sort of, reading Saint John of the Cross, maybe on account of that everybody'd gone away that I knew, Burroughs was in Mexico, Jack was out in Long Island and relatively isolated, we didn't see each other, and I had been very close with them for several years. Huncke I think was in jail, or something. Anyway, there was nobody I knew. Mainly the thing was that I'd been making it with N.C., and finally I think I got a letter from him saying it was all off, no more, we shouldn't consider ourselves lovers any more on account of it just wouldn't work out. But previously we'd had an understanding that we – Neal Cassady, I said 'N.C.' but I suppose you can use his name – we'd had a big tender lovers' understanding. But I guess it got too much for him, partly because he was three thousand miles away and he had six thousand girl friends on the other side of the continent, who were keeping him busy, and then here was my lone cry of despair from New York. So. I got a letter from him saying, Now, Allen, we gotta move on to *new* territory. So I felt this is like a great mortal blow to all of my tenderest hopes. And I figured I'd never find any sort of psychospiritual sexo-cock jewel fulfilment in my existence! So, I went into ... like I felt cut off from what I'd idealized romantically. And I was also graduating from school and had nowhere to go and the difficulty of getting a job. So finally there was nothing for me to do except to eat vegetables and live in Harlem. In an apartment I'd rented from someone. Sublet.

So, in that state therefore, of hopelessness, or dead end, change of phase, you know – growing up – and in an equilibrium in any case, a psychic, a mental equilibrium of a kind, like of having no New Vision and no Supreme Reality and nothing but the world in front of me, and of not knowing what to do with *that* ... there was a funny balance of tension, in every direction. And just after I came, on this occasion, with a Blake book on my lap – I wasn't even reading, my eye was idling over the page of 'Ah, Sun-flower', and it suddenly appeared – the poem I'd read a lot of times before, overfamiliar to the point where it didn't make any particular meaning except some sweet thing about flowers – and suddenly I realized that the poem was talking about *me*. 'Ah, Sun-flower! weary of time,/ Who countest the steps of the sun;/ Seeking after that sweet golden clime,/ Where the traveller's journey is done.' Now, I began understanding it, the poem while looking at it, and suddenly, simultaneously with understanding it, heard a very deep earthen grave voice in the room, which I immediately assumed, I didn't think twice, was Blake's voice; it wasn't any voice that I knew, though I had previously had a conception of a voice of rock, in a poem, some image like that – or maybe that came after this experience.

And my eye on the page, simultaneously the auditory hallucination, or whatever terminology here used, the apparitional voice, in the room, woke me further deep in my understanding of the poem, because the voice was so completely tender and beautifully ... ancient. Like the voice of the Ancient of Days. But the peculiar quality of the voice was something unforgettable because it was like God had a human voice, with all the infinite tenderness and anciency and mortal gravity of a living Creator speaking to his son. 'Where the Youth pined away with desire,/ And the pale Virgin shrouded in snow,/ Arise from their graves, and aspire/ Where my Sun-flower wishes to go.' Meaning that there *was* a *place*, there was a sweet golden clime, and the *sweet golden*, what was that ... and simultaneous to the voice there was also an emotion, risen in my soul in response to the voice, and a sudden *visual* realization of the same awesome phenomena. That is to say, looking out at the window, through the window at the sky, suddenly it seemed that I saw into the depths of the universe, by looking simply into the ancient sky. The sky suddenly seemed very *ancient*. And this was the very ancient place that he was talking about, the sweet golden clime, I suddenly realized that *this* existence was *it*! And, that I was born in order to experience up to this very moment that I was having this experience, to realize what this was all about – in other words that this was the moment that I was born for. This initiation. Or this vision or this consciousness, of being alive unto myself, alive myself unto the Creator. As the son of the Creator – who loved me, I realized, or who responded to my desire, say. It was the same desire both ways.

Anyway, my first thought was this was what I was born for, and second thought, never forget – never forget, never renege, never deny. Never deny the voice – no, never *forget* it, don't get lost mentally wandering in other spirit worlds or American or job worlds or advertising worlds or war worlds or earth worlds. But the spirit of the universe was what I was born to realize. What I was speaking about visually was, immediately, that the cornices in the old tenement building in Harlem across the back-yard court had been carved very finely in 1890 or 1910. And were like the solidification of a great deal of intelligence and care and love also. So that I began noticing in every corner where I looked evidences of a living hand, even in the bricks, in the arrangement of each brick. Some hand placed them there – that some hand had placed the whole universe in front of me. That some hand had placed the sky. No, that's exaggerating – not that some hand had placed the sky but that the sky was the living blue hand itself. Or that God was in front of my eyes – existence itself was God. Well, the formulations are like that – I didn't formulate it in exactly those terms; what I was seeing was a visionary thing, it was a lightness in my body ... my body suddenly felt *light*, and a sense of cosmic consciousness, vibrations, understanding, awe, and wonder and surprise. And it was a sudden awakening into a totally deeper real universe than I'd been existing in. So, I'm trying to avoid generalizations about that sudden deeper real universe and keep it strictly to observations of phenomenal data, or a voice with a certain sound, the appearance of cornices, the appearance of the sky, say, of the great blue hand, the living hand – to keep to images.

But anyway – the same ... *petite sensation* recurred several minutes later, with the same voice, while reading the poem 'The Sick Rose'. This time it was a slightly different sense-depth mystic impression. Because 'The Sick Rose' – you know I can't interpret the poem now, but it had a meaning – I mean I can interpret it on a verbal level, the sick rose is my self, or self, or the living body, sick because the mind, which is the worm 'That flies in the night,/ In the howling storm', or Urizen, reason; Blake's character might be the one that's entered the body and is destroying it, or let us say death, the worm as being death, the natural process of death, some kind of mystical being of its own trying to come in and devour the body, the rose. Blake's drawing for it is complicated, it's a big drooping rose, drooping because it's dying, and there's a worm in it, and the worm is wrapped around a little sprite that's trying to get out of the mouth of the rose.

But anyway, I experienced 'The Sick Rose', with the voice of Blake reading it, as something that applied to the whole universe, like hearing the doom of the whole universe, and at the same time the inevitable beauty of doom. I can't remember now, except it was very beautiful and very awesome. But a little of it slightly scary, having to do with the knowledge of death – my death and also the death of being itself, and that was the great pain. So, like a prophecy, not only in human terms but a prophecy as if Blake had penetrated the very secret core of the *entire* universe and had come forth with some little magic formula statement in rhyme and rhythm that, if properly heard in the inner inner ear, would deliver you beyond the universe.

So then, the other poem that brought this on in the same day was 'The Little Girl Lost', where there was a repeated refrain,

> '*Do father, mother*, weep?
> *Where can Lyca* sleep?
>
> '*How can Lyca* sleep
> *If her mother* weep?
>
> '*If her heart does* ache
> *Then let Lyca* wake;
> *If my mother* sleep,
> *Lyca shall not* weep.'

It's that hypnotic thing – and I suddenly realized that Lyca was me, or Lyca was the self; father, mother seeking Lyca, was God seeking, Father, the Creator; and 'If her heart does ache/ Then let Lyca wake' – wake to what? *Wake* meaning wake to the same awakeness I was just talking about – of existence in the entire universe. The total consciousness then, of the complete universe. Which is what Blake was talking about. In other words a break-through from ordinary habitual quotidian consciousness into consciousness that was really seeing all of heaven in a flower. Or what was it – eternity in a flower ... heaven in a grain

of sand? As I was seeing heaven in the cornice of the building. By heaven here I mean this imprint or concretization
or living form, of an intelligent hand – the work of an
intelligent hand, which still had the intelligence moulded
into it. The gargoyles on the Harlem cornices. What was interesting about the cornice was that there's cornices like that
on every building, but I never noticed them before. And I
never realized that they meant spiritual labour, to anyone
– that somebody had laboured to make a curve in a piece
of tin – to make a cornucopia out of a piece of industrial
tin. Not only that man, the workman, the artisan, but the
architect had thought of it, the builder had paid for it, the
smelter had *smelt* it, the miner had dug it up out of the
earth, the earth had gone through aeons preparing it. So
the little molecules had slumbered for ... for Kalpas. So
out of *all* of these Kalpas it all got together in a great succession of impulses, to be frozen finally in that one form of
a cornucopia cornice on the building front. And God knows
how many people made the moon. Or what spirits laboured
... to set fire to the sun. As Blake says, 'When I look in the
sun I don't see the rising sun, I see a band of angels singing
holy, holy, holy.' Well, his perception of the field of the
sun is different from that of a man who just sees the sun
sun, without any emotional relationship to it.

   But then, there was a point later in the week when the
intermittent flashes of the same ... bliss – because the experience was quite blissful – came back. In a sense all this
is described in 'The Lion for Real' by anecdotes of different
experiences – actually it was a very difficult time, which I
won't go into here. Because suddenly I thought, also simultaneously, Ooh, I'm going *mad*! That's described in the
line in 'Howl', 'who thought they were *only* mad when Balti-
more gleamed in supernatural ecstasy' – 'who thought they
were *only* mad. ...' If it were only that easy! In other words
it'd be a lot easier if you just were crazy, instead of – then
you could chalk it up, 'Well, I'm nutty' – but on the other
hand what if it's all true and you're *born* into this great
cosmic universe in which you're a spirit angel – terrible
fucking situation to be confronted with. It's like being

woken up one morning by Joseph K's captors. Actually what I think I did was there was a couple of girls living next door and I crawled out on the fire escape and tapped on their window and said, 'I've seen God!' and they *banged* the window shut. Oh, what tales I could have told them if they'd let me in! Because I was in a very exalted state of mind and the consciousness was still with me – I remember I immediately rushed to Plato and read some great image in the *Phaedrus* about horses flying through the sky, and rushed over to Saint John and started reading fragments of *con un no saber sabiendo ... que me quede balbuciendo*, and rushed to the other part of the bookshelf and picked up Plotinus about The Alone – the Plotinus I found more difficult to interpret.

But I *immediately* doubled my thinking process, quadrupled, and I was able to read almost any text and see all sorts of divine significance in it. And that week or that month I had to take an examination in John Stuart Mill. And instead of writing about his ideas I got completely hung up on his experience of reading – was it Wordsworth? Apparently the thing that got him back was an experience of nature that he received keyed off by reading Wordsworth, on 'sense sublime' or something. That's a very good description, that sense sublime of something far more deeply interfused, whose dwelling is the light of setting suns, and the round ocean, and the ... the *living* air, did he say? The living air – see just that hand again – *and* in the heart of man. So I think this experience is characteristic of all high poetry. I mean that's the way I began seeing poetry as the communication of the particular experience – not just any experience but *this* experience.

INTERVIEWER: Have you had anything like this experience again?

GINSBERG: Yeah. I'm not finished with this period. Then, in my room, I didn't know what to do. But I wanted to bring it up, so I began experimenting with it, without Blake. And I think it was one day in my kitchen – I had an old-fashioned kitchen with a sink with a tub in it with a board over the top – I started moving around and sort of shaking with

my body and dancing up and down on the floor and saying,
'Dance! dance! dance! dance! dance! spirit! spirit! spirit! dance!'
and suddenly I felt like Faust, calling up the devil. And
then it started coming over me, this big ... creepy feeling.
cryptozoid or monozoidal, so I got all scared and quit.

Then, I was walking around Columbia and I went in the
Columbia bookstore and was reading Blake again, leafing
over a book of Blake, I think it was 'The Human Abstract':
'Pity would be no more. . . .' And suddenly it came over me
in the bookstore again, and I was in the eternal place *once
more,* and I looked around at everybody's faces, and I saw
all these wild animals! Because there was a bookstore clerk
there who I hadn't paid much attention to, he was just a
familiar fixture in the bookstore scene and everybody went
in the bookstore every day like me, because downstairs there
was a café and upstairs there were all these clerks that we
were all familiar with – this guy had a very *long* face, you
know some people look like giraffes. So he looked kind of
giraffish. He had a kind of a long face with a long nose. I
don't know what kind of sex life he had, but he must have
had something. But anyway, I looked in his face and I
suddenly saw like a great tormented soul – and he had just
been somebody whom I'd regarded as perhaps a not particularly beautiful or sexy character, or lovely face, but you
know someone familiar, and perhaps a pleading cousin in
the universe. But all of a sudden I realized that *he* knew
also, just like I knew. And that everybody in the bookstore
knew, and that they were all hiding it! They all had the
consciousness, it was like a great *un*conscious that was running between all of us that everybody *was* completely conscious, but that the fixed expressions that people have, the
habitual expressions, the manners, the mode of talk, are
all masks hiding this consciousness. Because almost at that
moment it seemed that it would be too terrible if we communicated to each other on a level of total consciousness and
awareness each of the other – like it would be too terrible,
it would be the end of the bookstore, it would be the end
of civ – ... not civilization, but in other words the position
that everybody was in was *ridiculous,* everybody running

around peddling books to each other. Here in the universe! Passing money over the counter, wrapping books in bags and guarding the door, you know, stealing books, and the people sitting up and making accountings on the upper floor there, and people worrying about their exams walking through the bookstore, and all the millions of thoughts the people had – you know, that I'm worrying about – whether they're going to get laid or whether anybody loves them, about their mothers dying of cancer or, you know, the complete death awareness that everybody has continuously with them all the time – all of a sudden revealed to me at once in the faces of the people, and they all looked like horrible grotesque masks, grotesque because *hiding* the knowledge from each other. Having a habitual conduct and forms to prescribe, forms to fulfil. Roles to play. But the main insight I had at that time was that everybody knew. Everybody knew completely everything. Knew completely everything in the terms which I was talking about.

INTERVIEWER: Do you still think they know?

GINSBERG: I'm more sure of it now. Sure. All you have to do is try and make somebody. You realize that they knew all along you were trying to make them. But until that moment you never break through to communication on the subject.

INTERVIEWER: Why not?

GINSBERG: Well, fear of rejection. The twisted faces of all those people, the faces were twisted by rejection. And hatred of self, finally. The internalization of that rejection. And finally disbelief in that shining self. Disbelief in that infinite self. Partly because the particular ... partly because the *awareness* that we all carry is too often painful, because the experience of rejection and lack-love and cold war – I mean the whole cold war is the imposition of a vast mental barrier on everybody, a vast antinatural psyche. A hardening, a shutting off of the perception of desire and tenderness which everybody *knows* and which is the very structure of ... the atom! Structure of the human body and organism. That desire built in. Blocked. 'Where the Youth pined away with desire,/ And the pale Virgin shrouded in snow.' Or as

Blake says, 'On every face I see, I meet/ Marks of weakness, marks of woe.' So what I was thinking in the bookstore was the marks of weakness, marks of woe. Which you can just look around and look at anybody's face right next to you now always – you can see it in the way the mouth is pursed, you can see it in the way the eyes blink, you can see it in the way the gaze is fixed down at the matches. It's the self-consciousness which is a substitute for communication with the outside. This consciousness pushed back into the self and thinking of how it will hold its face and eyes and hands in order to make a mask to hide the flow that is going on. Which it's aware of, which everybody is aware of really! So let's say, shyness. Fear. Fear of like total feeling, really, total being is what it is.

So the problem then was, having attained realization, how to safely manifest it and communicate it. Of course there was the old Zen thing, when the sixth patriarch handed down the little symbolic oddments and ornaments and books and bowls, stained bowls too ... when the *fifth* patriarch handed them down to the sixth patriarch he told him to hide them and don't tell anybody you're patriarch because it's dangerous, they'll kill you. So there was that immediate danger. It's taken me all these years to manifest it and work it out in a way that's materially communicable to people. Without scaring them or me. Also movements of history and breaking down the civilization. To break down everybody's masks and roles sufficiently so that everybody has to face the universe *and* the possibility of the sick rose coming true and the atom bomb. So it was an immediate messianic thing. Which seems to be becoming more and more justified. And more and more reasonable in terms of the existence that we're living.

So. Next time it happened was about a week later walking along in the evening on a circular path around what's now I guess the garden or field in the middle of Columbia University, by the library. I started invoking the spirit, consciously trying to get another depth perception of cosmos. And suddenly it began occurring again, like a sort of break-through again, but this time – this was the last time in that period – it was the same depth of consciousness or the same cosmical awareness but suddenly it was not blissful at all but it was *frightening*. Some like real serpent-fear entering the sky. The sky was not a blue hand anymore but like a hand of death coming down on me – some really scary presence, it was almost as if I saw God again except God was the devil. The consciousness itself was *so* vast, much more vast than any idea of it I'd had or any experience I'd had, that it was not even human any more – and was in a sense a threat, because I was going to die into that in-human ultimately. I don't know *what* the score was there – I was too cowardly to pursue it. To attend and experience completely the Gates of Wrath – there's a poem of Blake's that deals with that, 'To find a Western Path/ Right through the Gates of Wrath.' But I didn't urge my way there, I shut it all off. And got scared, and thought, I've gone too far.

INTERVIEWER: Was your use of drugs an extension of this experience?

GINSBERG: Well, since I took a vow that this was the area of, that this was my existence that I was placed into, drugs were obviously a technique for experimenting with consciousness, to get different areas and different levels and different similarities and different reverberations of the same vision. Marijuana has some of it in it, that awe, the cosmic awe that you get sometimes on pot. There are certain moments under laughing gas and ether that the conscious-ness does intersect with something similar – for me – to my Blake visions. The gas drugs were apparently interesting too to the Lake Poets, because there were a lot of experi-ments done with Sir Humphry Davy in his Pneumatic In-stitute. I think Coleridge and Southey and other people used to go, and De Quincy. But serious people. I think there hasn't been very much written about that period. *What went on* in the Humphry Davy household on Saturday mid-night when Coleridge arrived by foot, through the forest, by the lakes? Then there are certain states you get into with opium, and heroin, of almost disembodied awareness, looking down back at the earth from a place after you're dead. Well, it's not the same, but it's an interesting state, and a useful one. It's a normal state also, I mean it's a holy state of some sort. At times. Then, mainly, of course, with the hallucinogens, you get some states of consciousness which subjectively seem to be cosmic-ecstatic, or cosmic-demonic. Our version of expanded consciousness is as much as *un*conscious information – awareness comes up to the surface. Lysergic acid, peyote, mescaline, sylocidin, Aya-huasca. But I can't stand them any more, because something happened to me with them very similar to the Blake visions. After about thirty times, thirty-five times, I began getting monster vibrations again. So I couldn't go any further. I may later on again, if I feel more reassurance.*

However, I did get a lot out of them, mainly like emotional understanding, understanding the female principle in

---

* Between occasion of interview with Thomas Clark June '65 and publication May '66 more reassurance came. I tried small doses of LSD twice in secluded tree and ocean cliff haven at Big Sur. No monster vibration, no snake universe hallucinations. Many tiny jewelled violet flowers along the path of a living brook that looked like Blake's illustration for a canal in grassy Eden: huge Pacific watery shore, Orlovsky dancing naked like Shiva long-haired before giant green waves, titanic cliffs that Words-worth mentioned in his own Sublime, great yellow sun veiled with mist hanging over the plant's oceanic horizon. No harm. President Johnson that day went into the Valley of Shadow operating room because of his gall bladder & Berkeley's Vietnam Day Committee was preparing anxious manifestos for our march towards Oakland police and Hell's Angels. Realizing that more vile words from me would send out physical vibrations into the atmosphere that might curse poor Johnson's flesh and further unbalance his soul, I knelt on the sand surrounded by masses of green bulb-headed Kelp vegetable-snake undersea beings washed up by last night's tempest, and prayed for the President's tranquil health. Since there has been so much legislative misconception of the LSD boon I regret that my unedited ambivalence in Thomas Clark's tape transcript interview was published wanting this footnote.

Your obedient servant
Allen Ginsberg, *aetat* 40
June 2, 1966

a way – women, more sense of the softness and more desire for women. Desire for children also.

INTERVIEWER: Anything interesting about the actual experience, say with hallucinogens?

GINSBERG: What I do get is, say if I was in an apartment high on mescaline, I felt as if the apartment and myself were not merely on East Fifth Street but were in the middle of all space time. If I close my eyes on hallucinogens, I get a vision of great scaly dragons in outer space, they're winding slowly and eating their own tails. Sometimes my skin and all the room seem sparkling with scales, and it's all made out of serpent stuff. And as if the whole illusion of life were made of reptile dream.

Mandala also. I use the mandala in an LSD poem. The associations I've had during times that I was high are usually referred to or built in some image or other to one of the other poems written on drugs. Or after drugs – like 'Magic Psalm' on lysergic acid. Or mescaline. There's a long passage about a mandala in the LSD poem. There is a good situation since I was high and I was looking at a mandala – before I got high I asked the doctor that was giving it to me at Stanford to prepare me to set of mandalas to look at, to borrow some from Professor Spiegelberg who was an expert. So we had some Sikkimese elephant mandalas there. I simply describe those in the poem – what they look like while I was high.

So – summing up then – drugs were useful for exploring perception, sense perception, and exploring different possibilities and modes of consciousness, and exploring the different versions of *petites sensations*, and useful then for composing, sometimes, while under the influence. Part II of 'Howl' was written under the influence of peyote, composed during peyote vision. In San Francisco – 'Moloch'. 'Kaddish' was written with amphetamine injections. An injection of amphetamine plus a little bit of morphine, plus some Dexedrine later on to keep me going, because it was all in one long sitting. From a Saturday morn to a Sunday night. The amphetamine gives a peculiar metaphysical tinge to things, also. Space-outs. It doesn't interfere too much there because I wasn't habituated to it, I was just taking it that one weekend. It didn't interfere too much with the emotional charge that comes through.

INTERVIEWER: Was there any relation to this in your trip to Asia?

GINSBERG: Well, the Asian experience kind of got me out of the corner. I painted myself in with drugs. That corner being an inhuman corner in the sense that I figured I was expanding my consciousness and I had to go through with it but at the same time I was confronting this serpent monster, so I was getting in a real terrible situation. It finally would get so if I'd take the drugs I'd start vomiting. But I felt that I was duly bound and obliged for the sake of consciousness expansion, and this insight, and breaking down my identity, and seeking more contact with primate sensation, nature, to continue. So when I went to India, all the way through India, I was babbling about that to all the holy men I could find. I wanted to find out if they had any suggestions. And they all did, and they were all good ones. First one I saw was Martin Buber, who was interested. In Jerusalem, Peter and I went in to see him – we called him up and made a date and had a long conversation. He had a beautiful white beard and was friendly; his nature was slightly austere but benevolent. Peter asked him what kind of visions he'd had and he described some he'd had in bed when he was younger. But he said he was *not* any longer interested in visions like that. The kind of visions he came up with were more like spiritualistic table rappings. Ghosts coming into the room through his window, rather than big beautiful seraphic Blake angels hitting him on the head. I was thinking like loss of identity and confrontation with nonhuman universe as the main problem, and in a sense whether or not man had to evolve and change, and perhaps become nonhuman too. Melt into the universe, let us say – to put it awkwardly and inaccurately. Buber said that he was interested in man-to-man relationships, human-to-human – that he thought it was a human universe that we were destined to inhabit. And so therefore human relationships rather than relations between the human and the nonhuman. Which was what I was thinking that I had to go into. And he said, 'Mark my word, young man, in two years you will realize that I was right.' He was right – in two years I marked his words. Two years is sixty-three – I saw him in sixty-one. I don't know if he said two years – but he said 'in years to come'. This was like a real terrific classical wise man's 'Mark my words, young man, in several years you will realize that what I said was true!' Exclamation point.

Then there was Swami Shivananda, in Rishikish in India. He said, 'Your own heart is your guru.' Which I thought was very sweet, and very reassuring. That is the sweetness of it I felt – in my heart. And suddenly realized it was the heart that I was seeking. In other words it wasn't consciousness, it wasn't *petites sensations*, sensation defined as expansion of mental consciousness to include more data – as I was pursuing that line of thought, pursuing Burroughs's cutup thing – the area that I was seeking was heart rather than mind. In other words, in mind, through mind or imagination – this is where I get confused with Blake now – in mind one can construct all sorts of universes, one can construct model universes in dream and imagination, and with lysergic acid you can enter into alternative universes and with the speed of light; and with nitrous oxide you can experience several million universes in rapid succession. You can experience a whole gamut of possibilities of universes, including the final possibility that there is none. And then you go unconscious – which is exactly what happens with gas when you go unconscious. You see that the universe is going to disappear with your consciousness, that it was all dependent on your consciousness.

Anyway, a whole series of India holy men pointed back to the body – getting *in* the body rather than getting out of the human form. But living in and inhabiting the human form. Which then goes back to Blake again, the human form divine. Is this clear? In other words, the psychic problem that I had found myself in was that for various reasons it had seemed to me at one time or another that the best thing to do was to drop dead. Or not be afraid of death but go into death. Go into the nonhuman, go into the cosmic, so to speak; that God was death, and if I wanted to attain God I had to die. Which *may* still be true. So I thought that what I was put up to was to therefore break out of my body, if I wanted to attain complete consciousness.

So now the next step was that the gurus one after another said, Live in the body: this is the form that you're born for. That's too long a narration to go into. Too many holy men and too many different conversations and they all have a little *key* thing going. But it all winds up in the train in Japan, then a year later, the poem 'The Change', where all of a sudden I renounce drugs, I don't renounce drugs but I suddenly didn't want to be *dominated* by that nonhuman any more, or even be dominated by the moral obligation to enlarge my consciousness any more. Or do anything any more except *be* my heart – which just desired to be and be alive now. I had a very strange ecstatic experience then and there, once I had sort of gotten that burden off my back, because I was suddenly free to love myself again, and therefore love the people around me, in the form that they already were. And love myself in my own form as I am. And look around at the other people and so it was *again* the same thing like in the bookstore. Except this time I was completely in my body and had no more mysterious obligations. And nothing more to fulfil, except to be willing to die where I am dying, whenever that be. And be willing to live as a human in this form now. So I started weeping, it was such a happy moment. Fortunately I was able to write then, too, 'So that I do live I will die' – rather than be cosmic consciousness, immortality, Ancient of Days, perpetual consciousness existing forever.

Then when I got to Vancouver, Olson was saying 'I am one with my skin.' It *seemed* to me at the time when I got back to Vancouver that everybody had been precipitated back into their bodies at the same time. It seemed that's what Creeley had *been* talking about all along. The *place* – the terminology he used, the *place* we are. Meaning this place, here. And trying to like be real in the real place ... to be aware of the place where he is. Because I'd always thought that that meant that he was cutting off from divine imagination. But what that meant for him was that this place would be everything that one would refer to as divine, if one were really here. So that Vancouver seems a very odd moment, at least for me – because I came back in a sense completely bankrupt. My energies of the last ... oh, 1948 to 1963, all completely washed up. On the train in Kyoto having renounced Blake, renounced visions – renounced *Blake*! – too. There was a cycle that began with the Blake vision which ended on the train in Kyoto when I realized that to attain the depth of consciousness that I was seeking when I was talking about the Blake vision, that in order to attain it I had to cut myself off from the Blake vision and renounce it. Otherwise I'd be hung up on a memory of an experience. Which is not the actual awareness of now, now. In order to get back to now, in order to get back to the total awareness of now and contact, sense perception contact with what was going on around me, or direct vision of the moment, now I'd have to give up this continual churning thought process of yearning back to a visionary state. It's all very complicated. And idiotic.

INTERVIEWER: I think you said earlier that 'Howl' being a lyric poem, and 'Kaddish' basically a narrative, that you now have a sense of wanting to do an epic. Do you have a plan like this?

GINSBERG: Yeah, but it's just ... ideas, that I've been carrying around for a long time. One thing which I'd like to do sooner or later is write a long poem which is a narrative and description of all the visions I've ever had, sort of like the *Vita Nuova*. And travels, now. And another idea I had was to write a big long poem about everybody I ever fucked or slept with. Like sex ... a love poem. A long love poem, involving all the innumerable lays of a lifetime. The epic is not that, though. The epic would be a poem including history, as it's defined. So that would be one about present-day politics, using the methods of the Blake *French Revolution*. I got a lot written. Narrative was 'Kaddish'. Epic – there has to be totally different organization, it might be simple free association on political themes – in fact I think an epic poem including history, at this stage. I've got a lot of it written, but it would have to be Burroughs' sort of epic – in other words, it would have to be *dis*sociated thought stream which includes politics and history. I don't think you could do it in narrative form, I mean what would you be narrating, the history of the Korean War or something?

INTERVIEWER: Something like Pound's epic?

GINSBERG: No, because Pound seems to me to be over a course of years fabricating out of his reading and out of the museum of literature; whereas the thing would be to take all of contemporary history, newspaper headlines and all the pop art of Stalinism and Hitler and Johnson and Kennedy and Viet Nam and Congo and Lumumba and the South and Sacco and Vanzetti – whatever floated into one's personal field of consciousness and contact. And then to compose like a basket – like weave a basket, basketweaving out of those materials. Since obviously nobody has any idea where it's all going or how it's going to end unless you have some vision to deal with. It would have to be done by a process of association, I guess.

INTERVIEWER: What's happening in poetry now?

GINSBERG: I don't know yet. Despite all confusion to the contrary, now that time's passed, I think the best poet in the United States is Kerouac still. Given twenty years to settle through. The main reason is that he's the most free and the most spontaneous. Has the greatest range of association and imagery in his poetry. Also in 'Mexico City Blues' the sublime as subject matter. And in other words the greatest facility at what might be called projective verse, if you want to give it a name. I think that he's stupidly underrated by almost everybody except for a few people who are aware how beautiful his composition is – like Snyder or Creeley or people who have a taste for his tongue, for his line. But it takes one to know one.

INTERVIEWER: You don't mean Kerouac's prose?

GINSBERG: No, I'm talking about just a pure poet. The verse poetry, the 'Mexico City Blues' and a lot of other manuscripts I've seen. In addition he has the one sign of being a great poet, which is he's the only one in the United

States who knows how to write haikus. The only one who's written any good haikus. And everybody's been writing haikus. There are all these *dreary* haikus written by people who think for weeks trying to write a haiku, and finally come up with some dull little thing or something. Whereas Kerouac thinks in haikus, every time he writes anything – talks that way and thinks that way. So it's just natural for him. It's something Snyder noticed. Snyder has to labour for years in a Zen monastery to produce one haiku about shitting off a log! And actually does get one or two good ones. Snyder was always astounded by Kerouac's facility ... at noticing winter flies dying of old age in his medicine chest. Medicine cabinet. 'In my medicine cabinet/the winter flies/died of old age.' He's never published them actually – he's published them on a record, with Zoot Sims and Al Cohn, it's a very beautiful collection of them. Those are, as far as I can see, the only real American haikus.

So the haiku is the most difficult test. He's the only *master* of the haiku. Aside from a longer style. Of course, the distinctions between prose and poetry are broken down anyway. So much that I was saying like a long page of oceanic Kerouac is sometimes as sublime as epic line. It's there that also I think he went further into the existential thing of writing conceived of as an irreversible action or statement, that's unrevisable and unchangeable once it's made. I remember I was thinking, yesterday in fact, there was a time that I was absolutely astounded because Kerouac told me that in the future literature would consist of what people actually wrote rather than what they tried to deceive other people into thinking they wrote, when they revised it later on. And I saw opening up this whole universe where people wouldn't be able to lie any more! They wouldn't be able to *correct* themselves any longer. They wouldn't be able to hide what they said. And he was willing to go all the way into that, the first pilgrim into that new-found land.

INTERVIEWER: What about other poets?

GINSBERG: I think Corso has a great inventive genius. And also amongst the greatest *shrewdness* – like Keats or something. I like Lamantia's nervous wildness. Almost anything he writes I find interesting – for one thing he's always registering the forward march of the soul, in exploration; spiritual exploration is always there. And also chronologically following his work is always exciting. Whalen and Snyder are both very wise and very reliable. Whalen I don't *understand* so well. I did, though, earlier – but I have to sit down and study his work, again. Sometimes he seems sloppy – but then later on it always seems right.

McClure has tremendous energy, and seems like some sort of a ... seraph is not the word ... not herald either but a ... not demon either. Seraph I guess it is. He's always moving – see when I came around to, say, getting in my skin, there I found McClure sitting around talking about being a mammal! So I sudden realized he was way ahead of me. And Weiners ... I always *weep* with him. Luminous, luminous. They're all old poets, everybody knows about those poets. Burroughs is a poet too, really. In the sense that a page of his prose is as *dense* with imagery as anything in St.-John Perse or Rimbaud, now. And it has also great repeated rhythms. Recurrent, recurrent rhythms, even rhyme occasionally! What else ... Creeley's very stable, solid. I get more and more to like certain poems of his that I didn't understand at first. Like 'The Door', which completely baffled me because I didn't understand that he was talking about the same heterosexual problem that I was worried about. Olson, since he said, 'I feel one with my skin.' First thing of Olson's that I liked was 'The Death of Europe' and then some of his later Maximus material is nice. And Dorn has a kind of long, *real* spare, manly, political thing – but his great quality inside also is tenderness – 'Oh the graves not yet cut.' I also like that whole line of what's happening with Ashbery and O'Hara and Koch, the area that they're going for, too. Ashbery – I was listening to him read 'The Skaters', and it sounded as inventive and exquisite, in all its parts, as 'The Rape of the Lock'.

INTERVIEWER: Do you feel you're in command when you're writing?

GINSBERG: Sometimes I feel in command when I'm writing. When I'm writing. When I'm in the heat of some

truthful tears, yes. Then, complete command. Other times
– most of the time not. Just diddling away, woodcarving,
getting a pretty shape; like most of my poetry. There's only
a few times when I reach a state of complete command.
Probably a piece of 'Howl', a piece of 'Kaddish', and a piece
of 'The Change'. And one or two moments of other poems.

INTERVIEWER: By 'command' do you mean a sense of
the whole poem as it's going, rather than parts?

GINSBERG: No – a sense of being self-prophetic master
of the universe.

Thomas Clark

HAROLD PINTER

Harold Pinter had recently moved into a five-storey 1820 Nash house facing Regent's Park in London. The view from the floor-through top floor where he has installed his office overlooks a duck pond and a long stretch of wooded parkland; his desk faces this view, and in late October 1966, when the interview took place, the changing leaves and the lazy London sun constantly distracted him as he thought over questions or began to give answers. He speaks in a deep, theatre-trained voice which comes rather surprisingly from him, and indeed is the most remarkable thing about him physically. When speaking he almost always tends to excessive qualification of any statement, as if coming to a final definition of things were obviously impossible. One gets the impression – as one does with many of the characters in his plays – of a man so deeply involved with what he's thinking that roughing it into speech is a painful necessity.

He was not working at any writing projects when the interview took place, and questions about his involuntary idleness (many questions came back to it without meaning to) were particularly uncomfortable for him. His own work is alternatively a source of mystery, amusement, joy, and anger to him; in looking it over he often discovered possibilities and ambiguities which he had not noticed or forgotten. One felt that if only he would rip out his telephone and hang black curtains across the wide windows he would be much happier, though he insists that the 'great boredom one has with oneself' is unrelated to his environment or his obligations.

When he wrote his first plays, in 1957, he was homeless, constantly on tour as an actor with a repertory stage company, playing all sorts of parts in obscure seaside resorts and provincial cities. His wife, the actress Vivien Merchant, toured with him, but when she became pregnant in 1958 it was necessary for them to find a home, and they took a

*basement room in London's shabby Notting Hill Gate
section, in a building where Mr Pinter worked as a caretaker to pay his rent. When their son was born they borrowed enough money to move to a less shabby district in
Chiswick, but both had to return to full-time acting when
Mr Pinter's first full-length play,* The Birthday Party, *was
a full scale flop in 1958. The production of* The Caretaker
*in 1960 produced enough money for a move to the middle-
class district of Kew, and then, thinking he could live on his
writings, Mr Pinter moved his family to a bow-fronted
Regency house in the south-coast seaside town of Worthing.
But the two-hour drive to London became imperative too
often, and so they moved once again, to a rented flat in
Kensington, until Mr Pinter's lucrative film scripts made it
possible for them to buy the Regent's Park house. Though
it is not yet completely renovated, the size and comfort of it
are impressive, as is Mr Pinter's office, with a separate room
nearby for his secretary and a small bar equally nearby for
the beer and Scotch which he drinks steadily during the
day, whether working or not. Bookshelves line one half the
area, and a velvet chaise longue faces the small rear garden.
On the walls are a series of Feliks Topolski sketches of London theatre scenes; a poster of the Montevideo production
of* El Cuidador; *a small financial balance sheet indicating
that his first West End production,* The Birthday Party,
*earned two hundred sixty pounds in its disastrous week's
run; a Picasso drawing; and his citation when he was named
to the Order of the British Empire last spring. 'The year
after the Beatles,' he emphasizes.*

INTERVIEWER: When did you start writing plays, and
why?

PINTER: My first play was *The Room*, written when I was
twenty-seven. A friend of mine called Henry Woolf was a
student in the drama department at Bristol University at
the time when it was the only drama department in the
country. He had the opportunity to direct a play, and as he
was my oldest friend he knew I'd been writing, and he knew
I had an idea for a play, though I hadn't written any of it

I was acting in rep at the time, and he told me he had to have the play the next week to meet his schedule. I said this was ridiculous, he might get it in six months. And then I wrote it in four days.

INTERVIEWER: Has writing always been so easy for you?

PINTER: Well, I had been writing for years, hundreds of poems and short pieces of prose. About a dozen had been published in little magazines. I wrote a novel as well; it's not good enough to be published really, and never has been. After I wrote *The Room*, which I didn't see performed for a few weeks, I started to work immediately on *The Birthday Party*.

INTERVIEWER: What led you to do that so quickly?

PINTER: It was the process of writing a play which had started me going. Then I went to see *The Room*, which was a remarkable experience. Since I'd never written a play before, I'd of course never seen one of mine performed, never had an audience sitting there. The only people who'd ever seen what I'd written had been a few friends and my wife. So to sit in the audience – well, I wanted to piss very badly throughout the whole thing, and at the end I dashed out behind the bicycle shed.

INTERVIEWER: What other effect did contact with an audience have on you?

PINTER: I was very encouraged by the response of that university audience, though no matter what the response had been I would have written *The Birthday Party*, I know that. Watching first nights, though I've seen quite a few by now, is never any better. It's a nerve-racking experience. It's not a question of whether the play goes well or badly. It's not the audience reaction, it's *my* reaction. I'm rather hostile towards audiences – I don't much care for large bodies of people collected together. Everyone knows that audiences vary enormously; it's a mistake to care too much about them. The thing one should be concerned with is whether the performance has expressed what one set out to express in writing the play. It sometimes does.

INTERVIEWER: Do you think that without the impetus

provided by your friend at Bristol you would have gotten down to writing plays?

PINTER: Yes, I think I was going to write *The Room*. I just wrote it a bit quicker under the circumstances; he just triggered something off. *The Birthday Party* had also been in my mind for a long time. It was sparked off from a very distinct situation in digs when I was on tour. In fact, the other day a friend of mine gave me a letter I wrote to him in nineteen-fifty-something, Christ knows when it was. This is what it says: 'I have filthy insane digs, a great bulging scrag of a woman with breasts rolling at her belly, an obscene household, cats, dogs, filth, tea strainers, mess, oh bullocks, talk, chat rubbish shit scratch dung poison, infantility, deficient order in the upper fretwork, fucking roll on.' Now the thing about this is that was *The Birthday Party* – I was in those digs, and this woman was Meg in the play, and there was a fellow staying there in Eastbourne, on the coast. The whole thing remained with me, and three years later I wrote the play.

INTERVIEWER: Why wasn't there a character representing you in the play?

PINTER: I had – I have – nothing to say about myself, directly. I wouldn't know where to begin. Particularly since I often look at myself in the mirror and say, 'Who the hell's that?'

INTERVIEWER: And you don't think being represented as a character on stage would help you find out?

PINTER: No.

INTERVIEWER: Have your plays usually been drawn from situations you've been in? *The Caretaker*, for example.

PINTER: I'd met a few, quite a few, tramps – you know, just in the normal course of events, and I think there was one particular one ... I didn't know him very well, he did most of the talking when I saw him. I bumped into him a few times, and about a year or so afterwards he sparked this thing off.

INTERVIEWER: Had it occurred to you to act in *The Room*?

PINTER: No, no – the acting was a separate activity

altogether. Though I wrote *The Room*, *The Birthday Party*, and *The Dumb Waiter* in 1957, I was acting all the time in a repertory company, doing all kinds of jobs, travelling to Bournemouth and Torquay and Birmingham. I finished *The Birthday Party* while I was touring in some kind of farce, I don't remember the name.

INTERVIEWER: As an actor, do you find yourself with a compelling sense of how roles in your plays should be performed?

PINTER: Quite often I have a compelling sense of how a role should be played. And I'm proved – equally as often – quite wrong.

INTERVIEWER: Do you see yourself in each role as you write? And does your acting help you as a playwright?

PINTER: I read them all aloud to myself while writing. But I don't see myself in each role – I couldn't play most of them. My acting doesn't impede my playwriting because of these limitations. For example, I'd like to write a play – I've frequently thought of this – entirely about women.

INTERVIEWER: Your wife, Vivien Merchant, frequently appears in your plays. Do you write parts for her?

PINTER: No. I've never written any part for any actor, and the same applies to my wife. I just think she's a very good actress and a very interesting actress to work with, and I want her in my plays.

INTERVIEWER: Acting was your profession when you first started to write plays?

PINTER: Oh, yes, it was all I ever did. I didn't go to university. I left school at sixteen – I was fed up and restless. The only thing that interested me at school was English language and literature, but I didn't have Latin and so couldn't go on to university. So I went to a few drama schools, not studying seriously; I was mostly in love at the time and tied up with that.

INTERVIEWER: Were the drama schools of any use to you as a playwright?

PINTER: None whatsoever. It was just living.

INTERVIEWER: Did you go to a lot of plays in your youth?

PINTER: No, very few. The only person I really liked to see was Donald Wolfit, in a Shakespeare company at the time. I admired him tremendously; his Lear is still the best I've ever seen. And then I was reading, for years, a great deal of modern literature, mostly novels.

INTERVIEWER: No playwrights – Brecht, Pirandello ...?

PINTER: Oh, certainly not, not for years. I read Hemingway, Dostoevski, Joyce, and Henry Miller at a very early age, and Kafka. I'd read Beckett's novels, too, but I'd never heard of Ionesco until after I'd written the first few plays.

INTERVIEWER: Do you think these writers had any influence on your writing?

PINTER: I've been influenced *personally* by everyone I've ever read – and I read all the time – but none of these writers particularly influenced my writing. Beckett and Kafka stayed with me the most – I think Beckett is the best prose writer living. My world is still bound up by other writers – that's one of the best things in it.

INTERVIEWER: Has music influenced your writing, do you think?

PINTER: I don't know how music can influence writing; but it has been very important for me, both jazz and classical music. I feel a sense of music continually in writing, which is a different matter from having been influenced by it. Boulez and Webern are now composers I listen to a great deal.

INTERVIEWER: Do you get impatient with the limitations of writing for the theatre?

PINTER: No. It's quite different; the theatre's much the most difficult kind of writing for me, the most naked kind, you're so entirely restricted. I've done some film work, but for some reason or other I haven't found it very easy to satisfy myself on an original idea for a film. *Tea Party*, which I did for television, is actually a film, cinematic, I wrote it like that. Television and films are simpler than the theatre – if you get tired of a scene you just drop it and go on to another one. (I'm exaggerating, of course.) What *is* so different about the stage is that you're just *there*, stuck

– there are your characters stuck on the stage, you've got to live with them and deal with them. I'm not a very inventive writer in the sense of using the technical devices other playwrights do – look at Brecht! I can't use the stage the way he does, I just haven't got that kind of imagination, so I find myself stuck with these characters who are either sitting or standing, and they've either got to walk out of a door, or come in through a door, and that's about all they can do.

INTERVIEWER: And talk.

PINTER: Or keep silent.

INTERVIEWER: After *The Room,* what effect did the production of your next plays have on your writing?

PINTER: *The Birthday Party* was put on at the Lyric, Hammersmith in London. It went on a little tour of Oxford and Cambridge first, and was very successful. When it came to London it was completely massacred by the critics – absolutely slaughtered. I've never really known why, nor am I particularly interested. It ran a week. I've framed the statement of the box-office takings: two hundred sixty pounds, including a first night of one hundred forty pounds and the Thursday matinee of two pounds, nine shillings – there were six people there. I was completely new to writing for the professional theatre, and it was rather a shock when it happened. But I went on writing – the B.B.C. were very helpful. I wrote *A Slight Ache* on commission from them. In 1960 *The Dumb Waiter* was produced, and then *The Caretaker.* The only really bad experience I've had was *The Birthday Party*; I was so green and gauche – not that I'm rosy and confident now, but comparatively ... Anyway, things like stage design. I didn't know how to cope, and I didn't know how to talk to the director.

INTERVIEWER: What was the effect of this adversity on you? How was it different from unfavourable criticism of your acting, which surely you'd had before?

PINTER: It was a great shock, and I was very depressed for about forty-eight hours. It was my wife, actually, who said just that to me: 'You've had bad notices before,' et cetera. There's no question but that her common sense and practical help got me over that depression, and I've never felt anything like that again.

INTERVIEWER: You've directed several of your plays. Will you continue to do so?

PINTER: No. I've come to think it's a mistake. I work much as I write, just moving from one thing to another to see what's going to happen next. One tries to get the thing ... *true*. But I rarely get it. I think I'm more useful as the author closely involved with a play: as a director I think I tend to inhibit the actors, because however objective I am about the text and try not to insist that *this is what's meant*, I think there is an obligation on the actors too heavy to bear.

INTERVIEWER: Since you are an actor, do actors in your plays ever approach you and ask you to change lines or aspects of their roles?

PINTER: Sometimes, quite rarely, lines are changed when we're working together. I don't at all believe in the anarchic theatre of so-called creative actors – the actors can do that in someone else's plays. Which wouldn't, however, at all affect their ability to play in mine.

INTERVIEWER: Which of your plays did you first direct?

PINTER: I co-directed *The Collection* with Peter Hall. And then I directed *The Lover* and *The Dwarfs* on the same bill at the Arts. *The Lover* didn't stand much of a chance because it was my decision, regretted by everyone – except me – to do *The Dwarfs*, which is apparently the most intractable, impossible piece of work. Apparently ninety-nine people out of a hundred feel it's a waste of time, and the audience hated it.

INTERVIEWER: It seems the densest of your plays in the sense that there's quite a bit of talk and very little action. Did this represent an experiment for you?

PINTER: No. The fact is that *The Dwarfs* came from my unpublished novel, which was written a long time ago. I took a great deal from it, particularly the kind of state of mind that the characters were in.

INTERVIEWER: So this circumstance of composition is not likely to be repeated?

PINTER: No. I should add that even though it is, as you say, more dense, it had great value, great interest for me. From my point of view, the general delirium and states of mind and reactions and relationships in the play – although terribly sparse – are clear to me. I know all the things that aren't said, and the way the characters actually look at each other, and what they mean by looking at each other. It's a play about betrayal and distrust. It does seem very confusing and obviously it can't be successful. But it was good for me to do.

INTERVIEWER: Is there more than one way to direct your plays successfully?

PINTER: Oh, yes, but always around the same central truth of the play – if that's distorted, then it's bad. The main difference in interpretation comes from the actors. The director can certainly be responsible for a disaster, too – the first performance of *The Caretaker* in Germany was heavy and posturized. There's no blueprint for any play, and several have been done entirely successfully without me helping in the production at all.

INTERVIEWER: When you are working on one, what is the key to a good writer–director relationship?

PINTER: What is absolutely essential is avoiding all defensiveness between author and director. It's a matter of mutual trust and openness. If that isn't there, it's just a waste of time.

INTERVIEWER: Peter Hall, who has directed many of your plays, says that they rely on precise verbal form and rhythm, and when you write 'pause' it means something other than 'silence', and three dots are different from a full stop. Is his sensitivity to this kind of writing responsible for your working well together?

PINTER: Yes, it is, very much so. I do pay great attention to those points you just mentioned. Hall once held a dot and pause rehearsal for the actors in *The Homecoming*. Although it sounds bloody pretentious, it was apparently very valuable.

INTERVIEWER: Do you outline plays before you start to write them?

PINTER: Not at all. I don't know what kind of characters my plays will have until they ... well, until they *are*. Until they indicate to me what they are. I don't conceptualize in any way. Once I've got the clues I follow them – that's my job, really, to follow the clues.

INTERVIEWER: What do you mean by clues? Can you remember how one of your plays developed in your mind – or was it a line-by-line progression?

PINTER: Of course I can't remember exactly how a given play developed in my mind. I think what happens is that I write in a very high state of excitement and frustration. I follow what I see on the paper in front of me – one sentence after another. That doesn't mean I don't have a dim, possible over-all idea – the image that starts off doesn't just engender what happens immediately, it engenders the possibility of an over-all happening, which carries me through. I've got an idea of what *might* happen – sometimes I'm absolutely right, but on many occasions I've been proved wrong by what does actually happen. Sometimes I'm going along and I find myself writing 'C. comes in' when I didn't know that he was going to come in; he *had* to come in at that point, that's all.

INTERVIEWER: In *The Homecoming*, Sam, a character who hasn't been very active for a while, suddenly cries out and collapses several minutes from the end of the play. Is this an example of what you mean? It seems abrupt.

PINTER: It suddenly seemed to me right. It just came. I knew he'd have to say something at one time in this section and this is what happened, that's what he said.

INTERVIEWER: Might characters therefore develop beyond your control of them, changing your idea – even if it's a vague idea – of what the play's about?

PINTER: I'm ultimately holding the ropes, so they never get too far away.

INTERVIEWER: Do you sense when you should bring down the curtain, or do you work the text consciously towards a moment you've already determined?

PINTER: It's pure instinct. The curtain comes down when the rhythm seems right – when the action calls for a finish. I'm very fond of curtain lines, of doing them properly.

INTERVIEWER: Do you feel your plays are therefore structurally successful? That you're able to communicate this instinct for rhythm to the play?

PINTER: No, not really, and that's my main concern, to get the structure right. I always write three drafts, but you have to leave it eventually. There comes a point when you say, That's it, I can't do anything more. The only play which gets remotely near to a structural entity which satisfies me is *The Homecoming*. *The Birthday Party* and *The Caretaker* have too much writing. I want to iron it down, eliminate things. Too many words irritate me sometimes, but I can't help them, they just seem to come out – out of the fellow's mouth. I don't really examine my works too much, but I'm aware that quite often in what I write, some fellow at some point says an awful lot.

INTERVIEWER: Most people would agree that the strength in your plays lies in just this verbal aspect, the patterns and force of character you can get from it. Do you get these words from people you've heard talking – do you eavesdrop?

PINTER: I spend *no* time listening in that sense. Occasionally I hear something, as we all do, walking about. But the words come as I'm writing the characters, not before.

INTERVIEWER: Why do you think the conversations in your plays are so effective?

PINTER: I don't know. I think possibly it's because people fall back on anything they can lay their hands on verbally to keep away from the danger of knowing, and of being known.

INTERVIEWER: What areas in writing plays give you the most trouble?

PINTER: They're all so inextricably interrelated I couldn't possibly judge.

INTERVIEWER: Several years ago, *Encounter* had an extensive series of quotations from people in the arts about the advisability of Britain's joining the Common Market. Your statement was the shortest anyone made: 'I have no interest in the matter and do not care what happens.' Does this sum up your feeling about politics, or current affairs?

PINTER: Not really. Though that's exactly what I feel about the Common Market – I just don't care a damn about the Common Market. But it isn't quite true to say that I'm in any way indifferent to current affairs. I'm in the normal state of being very confused – uncertain, irritated, and indignant in turns, sometimes indifferent. Generally, I try to get on with what I can do and leave it at that. I don't think I've got any kind of social function that's of any value, and politically there's no question of my getting involved because the issues are by no means simple – to be a politician you have to be able to present a simple picture even if you don't see things that way.

INTERVIEWER: Has it ever occurred to you to express political opinions through your characters?

PINTER: No. Ultimately, politics do bore me, though I recognize they are responsible for a good deal of suffering. I distrust ideological statements of any kind.

INTERVIEWER: But do you think that the picture of personal threat which is sometimes presented on your stage is troubling in a larger sense, a political sense, or doesn't this have any relevance?

PINTER: I don't feel myself threatened by *any* political body or activity at all. I like living in England. I don't care about political structures – they don't alarm me, but they cause a great deal of suffering to millions of people.

I'll tell you what I really think about politicians. The other night I watched some politicians on television talking about Viet Nam. I wanted very much to burst through the screen with a flame-thrower and burn their eyes out and their balls off and then inquire from them how they would assess this action from a political point of view.

INTERVIEWER: Would you ever use this anger in a politically oriented play?

PINTER: I have occasionally out of irritation thought about writing a play with a satirical point. I once did, actually, a play that no one knows about. A full-length play written after *The Caretaker*. Wrote the whole damn thing in three drafts. It was called *The Hothouse* and was about an institution in which patients were kept: all that was presented was the hierarchy, the people who ran the institution; one never knew what happened to the patients or what they were there for or who they were. It was heavily satirical, and it was quite useless. I never began to like any of the characters, they really didn't live at all. So I discarded the play at once. The characters were so purely cardboard. I was intentionally – for the only time, I think – trying to make a point, an explicit point, that these were nasty people and I disapproved of them. And therefore they didn't begin to live. Whereas in other plays of mine every single character, even a bastard like Goldberg in *The Birthday Party*, I care for.

INTERVIEWER: You often speak of your characters as living beings. Do they become so after you've written a play? While you're writing it?

PINTER: Both.

INTERVIEWER: As real as people you know?

PINTER: No, but different. I had a terrible dream, after I'd written *The Caretaker*, about the two brothers. My house burned down in the dream, and I tried to find out who was responsible. I was led through all sorts of alleys and cafés and eventually I arrived at an inner room somewhere and there were the two brothers from the play. And I said, So you burned down my house. They said, Don't be too worried about it, and I said, I've got everything in there, everything, you don't realize what you've done, and they said, It's all right, we'll compensate you for it, we'll look after you all right – the younger brother was talking – thereupon I wrote them out a cheque for fifty quid ... *I* gave *them* a cheque for fifty quid!

INTERVIEWER: Do you have a particular interest in psychology?

PINTER: No.

INTERVIEWER: None at all? Did you have some purpose in mind in writing the speech where the older brother describes his troubles in a mental hospital at the end of Act II in *The Caretaker*?

PINTER: Well, I had a purpose in the sense that Aston suddenly opened his mouth. My purpose was to let him go on talking until he was finished and then ... bring the curtain down. I had no axe to grind there. And the one thing that people have missed is that it isn't necessary to conclude that everything Aston says about his experiences in the mental hospital is true.

INTERVIEW: There's a sense of terror and a threat of violence in most of your plays. Do you see the world as an essentially violent place?

PINTER: The world *is* a pretty violent place, it's as simple as that, so any violence in the plays comes out quite naturally. It seems to me an essential and inevitable factor.

I think what you're talking about began in *The Dumb Waiter*, which from my point of view is a relatively simple piece of work. The violence is really only an expression of the question of dominance and subservience, which is possibly a repeated theme in my plays. I wrote a short story a long time ago called 'The Examination', and my ideas of violence carried on from there. That short story dealt very explicitly with two people in one room having a battle of an unspecified nature, in which the question was one of who was dominant at what point and how they were going to be dominant and what tools they would use to achieve dominance and how they would try to undermine the other person's dominance. A threat is constantly there: it's got to do with this question of being in the uppermost position, or attempting to be. That's something of what attracted me to do the screenplay of *The Servant*, which was someone else's story, you know. I wouldn't call this violence so much as a battle for positions, it's a very common, everyday thing.

INTERVIEWER: Do these ideas of everyday battles, or of violence, come from any experiences you've had yourself?

PINTER: Everyone encounters violence in some way or other. It so happens I did encounter it in quite an extreme form after the war, in the East End, when the Fascists were coming back to life in England. I got into quite a few fights down there. If you looked remotely like a Jew you might be in trouble. Also, I went to a Jewish club, by an old railway arch, and there were quite a lot of people often waiting with broken milk bottles in a particular alley we used to walk through. There were one or two ways of getting out of it – one was a purely physical way, of course, but you couldn't do anything about the milk bottles – *we* didn't have any milk bottles. The best way was to talk to them, you know, sort of 'Are you all right?' 'Yes, I'm all right.' 'Well, that's all right then, isn't it?' And all the time keep walking towards the lights of the main road.

Another thing: we were often taken for Communists. If you went by, or happened to be passing, a Fascist street meeting and looked in any way antagonistic – this was in Ridley Road market, near Dalston Junction – they'd interpret your very being, especially if you had books under your arms, as evidence of your being a Communist. There was a good deal of violence there, in those days.

INTERVIEWER: Did this lead you towards some kind of pacifism?

PINTER: I was fifteen when the war ended. There was never any question of my going when I was called up for military service three years later: I couldn't see any point in it at all. I refused to go. So I was taken in a police car to the medical examination. Then I had two tribunals and two trials. I could have gone to prison – I took my toothbrush to the trials – but it so happened that the magistrate was slightly sympathetic, so I was fined instead, thirty pounds in all. Perhaps I'll be called up again in the next war, but I won't go.

INTERVIEWER: Robert Brustein has said of modern drama, 'The rebel dramatist becomes an evangelist proselytizing for his faith.' Do you see yourself in that role?

PINTER: I don't know what he's talking about. I don't know for what faith I could possibly be proselytizing.

INTERVIEWER: The theatre is a very competitive business Are you, as a writer, conscious of competing against other playwrights?

PINTER: Good writing excites me, and makes life worth

living. I'm never conscious of any competition going on here.

INTERVIEWER: Do you read things written about you?

PINTER: Yes. Most of the time I don't know what they're talking about; I don't really read them all the way through. Or I read it and it goes – if you asked me what had been said, I would have very little idea. But there are exceptions, mainly nonprofessional critics.

INTERVIEWER: How much are you aware of an audience when you write?

PINTER: Not very much. But I'm aware that this is a public medium. I don't want to *bore* the audience, I want to keep them glued to what happens. So I try to write as *exactly* as possible. I would try to do that anyway, audience or no audience.

INTERVIEWER: There is a story – mentioned by Brustein in *The Theater of Revolt* – that Ionesco once left a performance of Genet's *The Blacks* because he felt he was being attacked, and the actors were enjoying it. Would you ever hope for a similar reaction in your audience? Would you react this way yourself?

PINTER: I've had that reaction – it's happened to me recently here in London, when I went to see *US*, the Royal Shakespeare Company's anti-Viet-Nam-war production. There was a kind of attack – I don't like being subjected to propaganda, and I detest soapboxes. I want to present things clearly in my own plays, and sometimes this does make an audience very uncomfortable, but there's no question about causing offence for its own sake.

INTERVIEWER: Do you therefore feel the play failed to achieve its purpose – inspiring opposition to the war?

PINTER: Certainly. The chasm between the reality of the war in Viet Nam and the image of what *US* presented on the stage was so enormous as to be quite preposterous. If it was meant to lecture or shock the audience I think it was most presumptuous. It's impossible to make a major theatrical statement about such a matter when television and the press have made everything so clear.

INTERVIEWER: Do you consciously make crisis situations

humorous? Often an audience at your plays finds its laughter turning against itself as it realizes what the situation in the play actually is.

PINTER: Yes, that's very true, yes. I'm rarely consciously writing humour, but sometimes I find myself laughing at some particular point which has suddenly struck me as being funny. I agree that more often than not the speech only *seems* to be funny – the man in question is actually fighting a battle for his life.

INTERVIEWER: There are sexual undertones in many of these crisis situations, aren't there? How do you see the use of sex in the theatre today?

PINTER: I do object to one thing to do with sex: this scheme afoot on the part of many 'liberal-minded' persons to open up obscene language to general commerce. It should be the dark secret language of the underworld. There are very few words – you shouldn't kill them by overuse. I have used such words once or twice in my plays, but I couldn't get them through the Lord Chamberlain. They're great, wonderful words, but must be used very sparingly. The pure publicity of freedom of language fatigues me, because it's a demonstration rather than something said.

INTERVIEWER: Do you think you've inspired any imitations? Have you ever seen anything in a film or theatre which struck you as, well, Pinteresque?

PINTER: That word! These damn words and that word 'Pinteresque' particularly – I don't know what they're bloody well talking about! I think it's a great burden for me to carry, and for other writers to carry. Oh, very occasionally I've thought listening to something, Hello, that rings a bell. But it goes no further than that. I really do think that writers write on ... just write, and I find it difficult to believe I'm any kind of influence on other writers. I've seen very little evidence of it, anyway; other people seem to see more evidence of it than I do.

INTERVIEWER: The critics?

PINTER: It's a great mistake to pay any attention to *them*. I think, you see, that this is an age of such over-blown publicity and overemphatic pinning down. I'm a very good example of a writer who can write, but I'm not as good as all that. I'm just a writer; and I think that I've been overblown tremendously because there's a dearth of really fine writing, and people tend to make too much of a meal. All you can do is try to write as well as you can.

INTERVIEWER: Do you think your plays will be performed fifty years from now? Is universality a quality you consciously strive for?

PINTER: I have no idea whether my plays will be performed in fifty years, and it's of no moment to me. I'm pleased when what I write makes sense in South America or Yugoslavia – it's gratifying. But I certainly don't strive for universality – I've got enough to strive for just writing a bloody play!

INTERVIEWER: Do you think the success you've known has changed your writing?

PINTER: No, but it did become more difficult. I think I've gone beyond something now. When I wrote the first three plays in 1957 I wrote them from the point of view of *writing* them; the whole world of putting on plays was quite remote – I knew they could never be done in the reps I was acting in, and the West End and London were somewhere on the other side of the moon. So I wrote these plays completely unself-consciously. There's no question that over the years it's become more difficult to preserve the kind of freedom that's essential to writing, but when I do write, it's there. For a while it became more difficult to avoid the searchlights and all that. And it took me five years to write a stage play, *The Homecoming*, after *The Caretaker*. I did a lot of things in the meantime, but writing a stage play, which is what I really wanted to do, I couldn't. Then I wrote *The Homecoming*, for good or bad, and I felt much better. But *now* I'm back in the same boat – I want to write a play, it buzzes all the time in me, and I can't put pen to paper. Something people don't realize is the great boredom one has with onself, and just to see those words come down again on paper, I think: Oh Christ, everything I do seems to be predictable, unsatisfactory, and hopeless. It keeps me awake. Distractions don't matter to me – if I had something to write I would write it. Don't ask me why I want to keep on with plays at all!

INTERVIEWER: Do you think you'd ever use freer techniques as a way of starting writing again?

PINTER: I can enjoy them in other people's plays – I thought the *Marat/Sade* was a damn good evening, and other very different plays like *The Caucasian Chalk Circle* I've also enjoyed. But I'd never use such stage techniques myself.

INTERVIEWER: Does this make you feel behind the times in any way?

PINTER: I *am* a very traditional playwright – for instance I insist on having a curtain in all my plays. I write curtain lines for that reason! And even when directors like Peter Hall or Claude Régy in Paris want to do away with them, I insist they stay. For me everything has to do with shape, structure, and over-all unity. All this jamboree in happenings and eight-hour movies is great fun for the people concerned, I'm sure.

INTERVIEWER: Shouldn't they be having fun?

PINTER: If they're all having fun I'm delighted, but count me out completely, I wouldn't stay more than five minutes. The trouble is I find it all so *noisy*, and I like quiet things. There seems to be such a jazz and jaggedness in so much modern art, and a great deal of it is inferior to its models: Joyce contains so much of Burroughs, for example, in his experimental techniques, though Burroughs is a fine writer on his own. This doesn't mean I don't regard myself as a contemporary writer: I mean, I'm *here*.

Lawrence M. Bensky

THE MODERN WRITER
AND HIS WORLD

G. S. Fraser

Yeats, Eliot, Auden, Larkin; Wells, Lawrence,
Greene, Murdoch; Shaw, Priestley, Osborne, Wesker;
Grierson, Richards, Leavis – many people have read
widely among the leading poets, novelists, dramatists,
and critics of the twentieth century, yet for the general
reader very few books have tried to relate all the
main movements and innovators since the 1880s
to the changing English scene.

The Modern Writer and His World is, in effect, the
only book to offer the intelligent non-specialist
reader both an analysis of the major writers (and
most of the minor ones) and also an overall awareness
of the total literary and social scene as something from
which the great, apparently isolated, figures cannot be
divorced.

After an introductory survey, 'The Background of
Ideas', the author deals in turn with poetry, the novel,
drama, and criticism. Here, from the opening pages
on the meaning of 'modernism' to the newly-added
chapter, 'Epilogue, 1970' (with its re-assessment of
Ford Madox Ford and comments on Marshall
McLuhan and the latest cultural trends), is the world
of the modern writer.

THE JOURNALS
Arnold Bennett

Financially and socially Arnold Bennett was successful
in a way few writers have been in this century: envy
characterized him as a kind of literary mogul,
provincial, swaggering and vulgar. Men who knew
him, however, found him essentially modest, simple,
and of exceptional integrity.

From 1896 (when he finished his first novel, *A Man
from the North*, at the age of twenty-nine) to the end
of his life in 1931 (when Baker Street was 'strawed' to
hush the traffic) he kept a diary. Here he recorded
what he had done, or seen, or been told, whether in
England, France, America or elsewhere, whether at
home, in hotels, aboard liners or yachts. His journals
are of interest not only for his impressions of well-
known writers and political figures, but also for their
record of an author's life, of books planned, words
written, pounds earned.

In this edition the *Florentine Journal* and a new journal
recently discovered at Keele University have been
added to the condensed text prepared for Penguins by
Frank Swinnerton. The whole provides a clear
self-portrait of a writer whose reputation is now poised
to surmount old prejudice.

Not for sale in the U.S.A.

THE DIARIES OF
FRANZ KAFKA 1910–23

Edited by Max Brod

Franz Kafka is the great enigma of early twentieth-century literature. Advocates of Impressionism, Existentialism, and even Christianity vie with each other in claiming him as an exemplar of their doctrines. He is seen as the successor of Dostoyevsky, the disciple of Kierkegaard, and the forerunner of Sartre. Yet beside the profound searching of his great 'trilogy of loneliness' – the words are those of Max Brod, his lifelong friend and editor of the Diaries – such controversy seems insignificant.

Kafka's diaries cover the period from 1910–23, the year before his death at the age of forty. They reveal to us the extraordinary inner world in which he lived. Here he describes, perhaps to relieve the pain which they caused him, his fear, isolation and frustration, his feelings of guilt and his sense of being an outcast. In between come quick glimpses of the real world, of the father he worshipped, and of the woman he could not bring himself to marry.

And throughout this personal journal Kafka the writer is experimenting, searching for his true mode of expression.

JOURNALS 1889–1949

André Gide

These *Journals* are André Gide's main testament to
posterity. In them he records his sixty years of full
and active life, as teacher, naturalist, musician, moral
philosopher, critic and novelist, and discusses the
problems he faced in his major works, *The Vatican
Cellars, Strait is the Gate,* and *The Immoralist.* As an
artist Gide was both politically and intellectually
committed on all the important public issues of his day,
and this is a record of his views, both impulsive and
carefully considered, on the Dreyfus Case, the 1914
War, the spread of fascism and communism, and finally
the Second World War. But above all, they reveal Gide's
own serious moral attitude towards his art, which in
the course of the *Journals* he transformed from talent
to literary genius. This edition of the *Journals* has
been translated, selected and edited by Justin O'Brien.